Unexpected Outcomes

**Pitt Series in Russian
and East European Studies**

Jonathan Harris, Editor

Unexpected Outcomes

Electoral Systems,
Political Parties,
and Representation
in Russia

ROBERT G. MOSER

University of Pittsburgh Press

Manufactured in the United States of America
Printed on acid-free paper
10 9 8 7 6 5 4 3 2 1

Design: Dariel Mayer

Library of Congress Cataloging-in-Publication Data

Moser, Robert G., 1966–
    Unexpected outcomes : electoral systems, political parties, and
representation in Russia / Robert G. Moser.
            p.   cm.   —   (Pitt series in Russian and East European studies)
Includes bibliographical references and index.
    ISBN 0-8229-5746-9   (pbk. : alk. paper)
    1. Elections—Russia (Federation)   2. Representative government
and representation—Russia (Federation)   3. Russia (Federation)—Politics
and government—1991–   I. Title.   II. Series in Russian and East European
studies.
    JN6699.A5   M67   2000
    324.6'3'0947—dc21   00-012590

Contents

List of Tables

Acknowledgments

I have enjoyed the help and support of numerous people during the research and writing of this book. I am deeply indebted to Mark Beissinger who directed my studies at the University of Wisconsin. Graham Wilson and Charles Franklin provided key insights and a comparative perspective in the early stages of the project. I also received crucial advice and encouragement from Timothy Colton, Brian Silver, and Thomas Remington. Joel Ostrow, Michael McFaul, Sarah Oates, Evelyn Davidheiser, Moshe Haspel, Yitzhak Brudny, and Frank Thames gave useful insights and valuable assistance throughout the project. I owe a personal and intellectual debt, too, to my colleagues at the University of Texas, particularly Zoltan Barany, James Fishkin, John Higley, and Robert Luskin. And Matthew Shugart and Norma Noonan offered invaluable comments and suggestions on the entire manuscript. I would also like to thank Eileen Kiley, the acquisitions editor at the University of Pittsburgh Press; her early enthusiasm and confidence in this project were instrumental to its publication.

I am grateful for the financial support of several institutions. The International Research and Exchanges Board (IREX) made possible three trips to Russia during the crucial elections of 1995, 1996, and 1999, at which time I collected much of the data for this project. The University of Texas gave me support for summer research and a semester free from teaching, in which to complete the writing of the manuscript.

Chapter 2 is based on my earlier work on the number of parties in Russia: "Electoral Systems and the Number of Parties in Post-Communist States," *World Politics,* Vol. 51, No. 3 (1999), pp. 359-384; "The Impact of Parliamentary Electoral Systems in Russia," *Post-Soviet Affairs,* Vol. 13, No. 3 (1997), pp. 284-302; and "The Impact of the Electoral System on Post-Communist Party Development: The Case of the 1993 Russian Parliamentary Elections," *Electoral Studies,* Vol. 14, No. 4 (1995), pp. 377-389. Chapter 6 is a revised version of my article, "The Electoral Effects of Presidentialism in Russia," published in *The Journal of Communist Studies and Transition Politics,* Vol. 14, Nos. 1/2 (1998), pp. 54-75 by Frank Cass Publishers, London. I thank the publishers for permission to reprint portions of these articles.

While in Russia, I received help and encouragement from countless Russians. I would like to thank the numerous scholars, journalists, and politicians who agreed to talk with me—usually in the middle of an incredibly hectic electoral campaign. I owe a particular debt of gratitude to Sergei Markov, Elena Kochkina, Boris Bagirov, and Elena Markelova, and the hospitality of Rima and Timor Menadzhiev made my stays in Yekaterinburg enjoyable.

I would also like to thank my parents, Paul and Kathy, brother Joe, and sister Lori for their encouragement and support. My greatest appreciation goes to my wife Linda and our two boys, Sam and Jake. I dedicate this book to them. Linda selflessly tolerated my long research trips to Russia and long nights and weekends of writing; her unwavering support sustained me through the long and often painful process of writing this book. Sam and Jake provided some necessary perspective on the truly important things.

Unexpected Outcomes

1
Introduction

On December 12, 1993, Russia held its first competitive parliamentary election as an independent state, three months after a violent confrontation between President Boris Yeltsin and the Congress of People's Deputies brought the young postcommunist regime to the brink of chaos. In the wake of emergency presidential rule, electoral rules were fashioned by politicians familiar with Western scholarship on electoral systems with the intent of encouraging party formation and benefiting reformist parties. They decided that a mixed electoral system combining proportional representation (PR) and single-member district (SMD) elections best met these objectives.[1] The election was expected to produce a resounding victory for reformist parties, particularly Russia's Choice, the electoral bloc headed by former prime minister Yegor Gaidar and populated by many of Yeltsin's government ministers and advisers. To the horror and dismay of the architects of the new system, Vladimir Zhirinovsky's nationalist Liberal Democratic Party of Russia (LDPR) won the PR half of Russia's first election, and the new legislature was fractionalized and contained an antireformist plurality.

Lost amid dire warnings of the end of democracy in Russia was the fact that the same party that won the most votes in the PR tier performed miserably in the other half of the election, winning only 5 of the 225 seats elected in SMDs. This portion was dominated by independent candidates, who formed their own parliamentary factions after the election, multiplying the number of parties in parliament rather than consolidating the party system as expected. The next parliamentary election, held in 1995, witnessed a continuation of this disjuncture in the performance of most parties between the PR and SMD tiers. Meanwhile, party proliferation in the electoral realm increased rather than subsided. The presidential election held six months later produced another surprise—the reelection of the reformist president after two parliamentary elections that witnessed increasingly impressive electoral victories for anti-reformist forces. This book asserts that a prominent factor in all of these outcomes was the relationship between electoral systems and political actors—candidates, parties, and voters.

Objectives

This book examines the effects of electoral systems on political parties and representation in postcommunist Russia. Russia's mixed electoral structure, which combines PR and SMD arrangements in a single election, is used as a laboratory for controlled comparison of the effects of different electoral systems by holding other factors, such as culture or socioeconomic development, constant. Through this controlled comparison, I will show that electoral rules have had a profound effect on democratization in Russia, influencing the fractionalization of the party system, ascriptive representation of women and minorities, and the distribution of power among opposing ideological camps. However, the impact of electoral systems has not followed comparative experience or the expectations of the scholarly literature.

Electoral institutions have mattered greatly in Russia but often in ways we would not expect. Thus, this book contributes to the growing literature on electoral engineering and the central debate over the ability and inability of elites to fashion preferred political outcomes through institutional design. By placing Russia in comparative experience I hope to shed some light on the ability to further democratization in postcommunist states by getting the institutions right.

More than four decades ago, Maurice Duverger proposed a set of hypotheses regarding the relationship between electoral systems and the number of parties operating in a country, which came to be known collectively as Duverger's Law. He argued that plurality elections, in which the candidate with the most votes wins office in an SMD, produced two-party systems and single-party majority governments, while PR systems, in which candidates run on party lists in multimember districts, created multiparty systems and coalition governments. These hypotheses would become the basis for one of the most longstanding scholarly debates in political science. Over forty years of conceptual refinement and empirical testing in a wide number of cases have left Duverger's hypotheses relatively intact, leading scholar Arend Lijphart to imply a universal impact of electoral systems: "First of all, PR and plurality advocates disagree not so much about the respective effects of the two electoral methods as about the weight to be attached to these effects. Both sides agree that PR yields greater proportionality and minority representation and that plurality promotes two-party systems and one-party executives. Partisans disagree on which of the results is preferable."[2]

However, it remains to be seen whether these hypotheses, based for the most part on the experience of Western democracies, will actually hold in new democracies, particularly in the very different social and political context of postcommunist states. Much of the debate concerning the role of electoral systems in the third wave of democratization has followed the pattern suggested by Lijphart, not questioning the presumed effects of proportional representation or plurality elections and instead debating their relative merits for democratizing states. Given the absence of well-institutionalized party systems in most new democracies, it is crucial to return to the question of the effects of electoral systems on new democracies, particularly those farthest removed from Western experience and thus least likely to mimic its political processes and outcomes.

The literature has not treated Duverger's Law as an ironclad sociological law having no exceptions. In his groundbreaking book, *Making Votes Count,* Gary Cox argues that certain preconditions need to be met before voters and candidates behave strategically in reaction to electoral system incentives. Voters need to be driven by short-term instrumental considerations and have adequate information regarding the relative support of competing candidates. Yet, in plurality elections these conditions are met consistently enough to produce a noticeable lack of real-world exceptions, such as Papua New Guinea, that regularly and significantly defy Duverger's Law.[3] Postcommunist states, particularly Soviet successor states, may present a whole new set of cases that fail to meet the necessary preconditions for strategic behavior and thus fail to follow Duverger's hypotheses. Through the examination of Russia's mixed electoral system, the current volume shows how electoral systems have very different consequences in a political context that lacks the requisites for strategic voting.

This study offers two important findings. First, Russia is an exception; electoral systems have not had the effects predicted in the literature. In fact, Russia runs counter to some of the most well established hypotheses in electoral studies. Contrary to comparative experience, plurality elections have not been a significantly more powerful constraint on the number of parties than PR elections; in some ways the plurality tier has allowed greater party proliferation. This fractionalization is different from that found in India or Canada, where the constraining effect of plurality elections is experienced at the district level in two-candidate races but is not projected to the national level in a two-party system. In Russia, plurality elections are multicandidate affairs, with an average of nearly a half dozen significant candidates vying for office. Electoral systems have similarly surprising effects on minority representation in Russia. For example, women have been elected in greater numbers in plurality elections than in PR elections, again running counter to the well-supported hypothesis that PR promotes greater women's representation.

Second, electoral systems have been a key factor in Russian electoral politics. Electoral arrangements have affected the very status of political parties as vehicles of mobilization. Electoral rules have also helped to determine which parties win and lose parliamentary representation and have influenced the ideological composition of the legislature. Electoral systems have had important effects on political outcomes in Russia but neither the effects anticipated by the literature nor, in most cases, the institutional designers themselves.

In explaining the exceptional effects of electoral systems in Russia, this book analyzes the relationship between institutions and the social and political context in which they operate. The conclusion is simple, yet surprisingly absent from much of the neo-institutionalist research: context matters. One aspect of Russia's political context that mitigates electoral system effects is analyzed here—the weak institutionalization of political parties. Without parties to structure the vote and monopolize candidate nominations, the constraining effects of plurality elections are lost. Indeed, in states with weakly institutionalized party systems, proportional representation that utilizes a legal threshold for representation may be a more effective constraint on party fractionalization by forcing elites and voters to think of parties. Only once elites are forced to form parties can the constraining effects of disproportionality take hold.

The electoral system is particularly worthwhile to study when examining the relationship between political institutions and their environments, because comparative analysis has provided such impressive evidence of consistent effects of electoral systems (particularly plurality systems) across countries with very different social contexts. Exceptions can highlight the structural conditions necessary for institutions to have their effects, reintegrating institutional and structural approaches to democratization that might be lost when empirical examples are restricted to cases sharing similar political and social conditions. In studying Russia's distinct experience with electoral systems, this study builds on work by Cox and Sartori that examines the limits of Duverger's Law and the preconditions necessary for strategic behavior in response to electoral system constraints.[4] I also draw heavily upon the work of Scott Mainwaring, who argues that the fundamental distinction between third-wave democracies and consolidated democracies is the weak institutionalization of the party system in the former. Indeed, this book can be seen as an empirical investigation of the implications of weak-party institutionalization for electoral system effects. Russia is an important empirical example that buttresses theories that imply electoral system effects typically found in established democracies may not hold in all contexts, particularly countries with weakly institutionalized party systems and poorly developed sources of political information.

Although this project is centrally concerned with the impact of the electoral system on the consolidation of Russian democracy, the Russian experience with electoral systems should be of interest to students of democratization in general. If the third wave of democratization is to consolidate its gains and extend to regions further removed from Western political experience, democratic institutions will have to survive in conditions more similar to Russia's than to other more propitious environments in the West. Russia may represent the future of democratization, for good or for ill; thus, it is not enough merely to acknowledge the fact that the political context in Russia mitigates the effects of electoral systems, producing very different outcomes from those found in more established democracies. Too often such acknowledgment leads to an exclusion of special cases from comparative analysis as exceptions. It is better to integrate the study of less developed democracies into comparative politics and develop hypotheses that describe and explain patterns of behavior found in these contexts. Through direct comparison with other postcommunist states as well as other consolidated and unconsolidated democracies, I introduce a research program in need of much more empirical study—investigating the relationship between party institutionalization and electoral system effects. In order to more properly understand the impact of electoral systems on democratization we need to ask ourselves: Where does Duverger's Law seem to hold, and where does it not? Where it does not hold, what effects can electoral systems be expected to have, and is this non-Duvergerian equilibrium a stable or temporary state?[5] This study is designed as a first step in this larger research agenda.

Russia's Mixed Electoral System

In 1993, Russia adopted a system that employs both PR and SMD electoral structures. Although still rare among electoral systems around the world, the mixed system is becoming increasingly popular. It has been adopted by many postcommunist states (for example, Hungary, Lithuania, Ukraine, Croatia, Georgia, Armenia, and Azerbaijan) as well as a number of consolidated democracies that have recently enacted electoral system reforms (for example, Italy, New Zealand, and Japan). Modeled after the German electoral system, the 450 deputies to Russia's lower house, the State Duma, are equally divided into two electoral arenas. Each voter casts two ballots, one for an individual candidate and one for a party. Half of the deputies are elected in 225 SMDs; these SMD contests are held under a plurality rule, in which the candidate with the most votes wins the seat regardless of whether he or she won a majority of the votes cast. The other half are elected in a party-list PR election in one nationwide electoral district. Not only do the two halves of the system differ in electoral formula, but more importantly they also differ dramatically in district magnitude, which has been shown to be the element of the electoral system most responsible for the level of disproportionality and the number of parties produced by an electoral system. Finally, unlike the German system, Russia's two electoral tiers are not linked in a system of compensatory seats in which the PR tier is designed to correct the disproportionality of the SMD tier. Rather, the two parts of Russia's electoral system are more like two separate elections occurring simultaneously for the same legislative body. Results for the two halves are calculated separately, and distribution of seats for the PR portion in no way affects the distribution of seats in the SMD portion, and vice versa.[6]

Classifying Mixed Electoral Systems

The best way to fully understand the mixed electoral system of Russia is to compare it with other such arrangements around the world. Countries can combine PR and SMD elections in a number of ways that have substantial effects on the relationship between the electoral rules and party systems. While all mixed electoral systems share the distinction of allowing voters to cast two votes in distinct PR and SMD tiers, four defining characteristics distinguish mixed systems from one another: whether the two tiers are linked in a system of compensatory seats, the electoral formula used in the SMD tier, the ratio of seats in each tier, and the district magnitude and legal threshold of the PR tier. Table 1.1 presents a description based on these characteristics of eight mixed electoral systems examined in this book for comparative purposes.

Linked Tiers

The most important question about a mixed electoral system is whether the two tiers are linked in an arrangement of compensatory seats. In mixed systems with linked tiers, the number of seats or votes won by a party in one tier is subtracted from its total in the other tier. Systems such as Germany's, which use the PR tier to compensate for disproportional effects of the SMD tier, should deter the constraining effect of the SMD half, in terms both of strategic voting and of mechanical effects in translating votes into seats. It is precisely this link between the two that has led scholars to describe mixed electoral systems following the German model as simply forms of proportional representation rather than as combinations of PR and SMD systems. A linked system typically prioritizes the PR tier over the SMD tier by giving the former control over the final distribution of seats in parliament. Linking the tiers also affects calculations of voters and elites, by making the vote in the PR tier more important than that in SMDs. In this arrangement, smaller parties can remain viable by targeting the PR vote in their campaigns.[7] Moreover, although strategic voting has occurred in Germany, voters in mixed linked systems have less incentive to defect from small parties to large parties, because the SMD vote has virtually no effect on the final distribution of legislative seats.

The effects of linked tiers depend greatly on how seats are allocated and the number of seats reserved for compensation. Germany and New Zealand each have the most comprehensive system of compensation. The result is a distribution of seats fully controlled by the vote in the PR tier. Italy's compensation is less direct: if a party wins an SMD seat, the number of votes received by the second-place candidate in the district is subtracted from the winning party's vote in the PR tier. It is also less comprehensive, because Italy's PR tier does not have enough seats to fully overcome the disproportional effects of the much

Table 1.1: Description of Eight Mixed Electoral Systems

Country	Linked tiers	SMD electoral formula	SMD: PR ratio	Average PR district magnitude	PR legal threshold (percent)
Germany	yes[b]	Plurality	248:248	248[a]	5
Italy	yes[c]	Plurality	475:155	155	4
New Zealand	yes[b]	Plurality	65:55	55	5
Japan	no	Plurality	300:200	18.18	3
Russia	no	Plurality	225:225	225	5
Hungary	yes[d]	Two-round Majority	176:210	7.60 (territorial) 58 (national)	4 (1990) 5 (1994)
Lithuania	no	Two-round Majority	71:70	70	5
Croatia	no[e]	Plurality	28:80	28	5

Sources: Gary W. Cox, *Making Votes Count* (Cambridge: Cambridge University Press, 1997) 287–88; Kenneth Benoit, "Votes and Seats: The Hungarian Electoral Law and the 1994 Parliamentary Elections," in *The 1994 Election to the Hungarian National Assembly: Analyses, Documents and Data,* ed. Gabor Toka (Berlin: Edition Sigma, 1999), 2–5.

a PR mandates are distributed in ten territorial districts, but parties have the option to pool their votes for state lists at the national level—making the average district magnitude a single 248-member national district rather than a number of state districts, with an average of 24.8 members per district.
b In Germany and New Zealand, seats won in the SMD tier are subtracted from the total of any PR seats attained.
c In Italy a compensation system, known as the *scorporo,* links the PR and SMD tiers; if a party wins an SMD seat, its PR vote total is diminished by the number of votes received by the second-place candidate in the district.
d In Hungary there are three levels; the SMD and territorial PR tier are not linked, but surplus votes (all votes not used to win seats in either of the lower tiers) are aggregated in a third national tier, which allocates a minimum of fifty-eight seats (plus any not distributed in the territorial PR tier) on the basis of these surplus votes.
e Croatia also has special seats for representation of ethnic minorities, which are not included here.

larger SMD tier. Therefore, incentives for strategic voting and entry and departure by elites in the SMD tier are greater in Italy than in Germany and New Zealand.

Hungary's is the most complicated case of linkage; a tertiary tier of compensatory seats, which stands above both the SMD and the territorial PR tiers, distributes a minimum of fifty-eight seats to parties, on the basis of surplus votes not used to win seats in either the SMD or territorial PR tier—provided that a party crosses a 5 percent legal threshold. This system does not give enough seats to make it fully proportional, but it does produce a powerful deterrent effect on strategic defection from smaller parties in the SMD tier. Since votes not used to win seats are pooled in a national-level competition for compensatory seats, voters have incentives to stick with their preferred party, no matter how small its candidate's chances in the district race. Minor parties have greater incentives to run candidates in SMDs, in order to collect surplus votes to be used for compensatory seats. Hungary's use of a dual-round majoritarian system in its SMD tier—in which any candidate with at least 15 percent of the vote is allowed in the second round—combined with its mixed system, offers very few incentives for smaller parties to consolidate in the first round of the SMD tier.

Russia belongs to another category of mixed systems that do not link their PR and SMD tiers, which includes Japan, Lithuania, and Croatia. Disproportionality and incentives for strategic voting increase significantly under these systems; voters and elites have a greater reason to behave strategically, because parties realize the benefit of every SMD seat won. Moreover, the disproportionality of these mixed systems should be greater; because mechanical effects of the SMD tier are felt in the final distribution of seats in the legislature and not overridden by the PR tier.

SMD/PR Ratio

The ratio of seats elected in the SMD and PR tiers is another crucial element of a mixed electoral system. The more seats devoted to the SMD tier, the greater the constraining effect. This is particularly true in unlinked systems; but even if the two tiers are linked, the number of parties will be influenced by the SMD tier—if it is significantly larger than the PR tier. Thus, Italy's system, which has roughly three times as many SMD seats as PR seats, has a significant constraining effect on the number of parties, even though linkage between the two allows the PR tier to directly counter the disproportionality of the SMD tier. The even distribution of SMD and PR seats in Russia, along with that country's unlinked character, allows for a significant influence of both the PR and SMD tiers on its legislature.

Electoral Formula

The electoral formulae can be different for each level of a mixed system. In fact, the PR tier can distribute seats according to a variety of different formulae that benefit different types of parties.[8] While these differences do influence the proportionality of the PR tier and the system as a whole, they are relatively small and come into play only in the translation of votes into seats (not voter behavior) and are conditioned greatly by the district magnitude of the PR tier. The available options for electoral formulae in the SMD tier are more circumscribed and more consequential; countries can either employ a plurality system, in which the candidate with the most votes wins the seat, or a majoritarian system, which requires a candidate to win a majority of votes in a district to win election. If no candidate wins a majority, then a second run-off election is held, usually between the two top vote getters in the first round. If two-round majority elections are used in a mixed electoral system, there is a greater number of parties produced than if plurality elections are used.

Duverger claimed that the two-round majority election "tends to produce multipartism tempered by alliances."[9] Parties proliferate in the first round, because minor candidates face a lower threshold to the run-off than they would to victory in a plurality race. Cox has argued that two-round majority elections actually follow the same $M + 1$ rule for district-level effects, in which M equals the number of candidates allowed in the second round.[10] Disproportionality remains high, and coalition-building between rounds produces bipolar competition between broad-based alliances of parties. In a mixed system, the PR tier further reinforces the incentive for party proliferation. Therefore, more parties should exist in a mixed system that uses a two-round majority election rather than a plurality election in its SMD tier, especially with the increased opportunities for representation in the parallel competition in the PR half of the election. Conversely, the use of plurality elections in the SMD tier of Russia's mixed system should be an additional constraint on party proliferation.

PR District Magnitude and Legal Threshold

Finally, district magnitude and the presence of a legal threshold in the PR tier influence how proportional a mixed system will be. Two of the eight cases examined here elect their PR deputies in meaningful territorial districts, while the others distribute their PR seats in one nationwide district. All the cases impose some type of minimum legal threshold to win seats in the legislature, ranging from 3 to 5 percent of the vote. As Lijphart has shown, legal thresholds and district magnitude work in the same way to constrain party proliferation by setting a vote threshold necessary to gain election.[11] Usually territorial districts have few enough representatives that their effective threshold is higher than the typical legal threshold imposed. For example, in Japan magnitudes in PR districts range from seven to thirty-three, making the necessary percentage to attain a seat in the smallest district much higher than the legal threshold of 3 percent. Russia's use of a single nationwide district in its PR tier gives no effective impediment against party proliferation, but its 5 percent barrier should promote party consolidation and keep small parties out of parliament.

Based on these four elements, one can establish a continuum of the strength of mixed electoral systems' potential constraining effect on the number of parties. These structures are strongest if they do not link the PR and SMD tiers, use a plurality rather than two-round majority system in their SMD tiers, contain a significant proportion of SMD seats relative to PR seats, and impose a significant legal threshold in their PR tiers. Of course, different systems have different combinations of these traits, requiring an assessment of the relative importance of each distinguishing feature. While no formal weighting process is conducted, I argue that the relative influence of the various elements discussed corresponds to the amount of control over the final distribution of seats given to the SMD tier. Thus, linkage and the SMD/PR ratio are deemed most important and the effective threshold of the PR tier least important.

The mixed systems of Japan and Russia are the strongest, because both are unlinked and use plurality in their SMD tiers, with Japan's system stronger than Russia's, due to its greater share of SMD seats and low district magnitudes in its PR tier. Two other countries with unlinked tiers, Lithuania and Croatia, have systems relatively weaker than Russia's. Lithuania's uses a two-round majority method, which cuts down on strategic behavior in the SMD tier, but this does not weaken the disproportionality of the SMD tier, which is fully felt because it has direct influence on the distribution of its half of legislative seats. Croatia's system, though, has a much smaller share of SMD seats than PR ones.

All of the mixed systems with linked tiers are considered weaker than their counterparts whose are unlinked. Hungary's is the strongest of the former; its proportion of compensatory seats is the smallest, even though its complicated arrangement of compensatory seats encourages party proliferation. Nevertheless, the system does not link its SMD and territorial PR tiers, and the number of compensatory seats is not large enough to overcome the mechanical effect of the SMD tier and relatively low district magnitudes of the territorial PR tier. Italy is considered the next strongest case; its system of compensation is similar to Hungary's structure of surplus votes, but its proportion of compensatory PR seats is larger (25 percent versus 16 percent of total seats). The German and New Zealand systems are the weakest; they give the SMD tier virtually no control over the final distribution of votes.

The Russian mixed electoral system possesses two characteristics that make it an especially good case for a controlled comparison of PR and SMD electoral systems. First, its tiers are unlinked. This offers two crucial advantages. The absence of compensatory seats allows one to examine the psychological effects of strategic voting in the plurality tier more accurately, because this tier is more consequential to the final distribution of seats in the legislature; voters and elites should be more attentive to the electoral dynamics of the SMD tier in this context than in a mixed system with compensatory seats. Moreover, unlinked tiers allow one also to examine the mechanical effects of disproportionality of both tiers, because each tier of Russia's mixed system determines half of the legislative seats, untainted by the other tier.

Second, the Russian system presents one of the starkest comparisons of different types of electoral systems imaginable. Both tiers elect equal numbers of deputies to the legislature: Russia's SMD tier is a plurality system, deemed the strongest electoral system available for constraining the number of parties, while other postcommunist cases use two-round majority elections in their SMD tiers. Conversely, Russia's PR tier has the highest district magnitude available—one nationwide district electing 225 deputies—rather than a set of territorial PR contests with much smaller district magnitudes, as in Japan, that raise the electoral threshold for smaller parties.

Russia's Emergent Party System

The bulk of this book concentrates on general aspects of the Russian party system and representation—the number of parties, the proportion of women and minorities elected, and the number of presidential candidates. One chapter is devoted to the fate of individual parties. Despite this concentration on the general over the specific, it is necessary to give some background of the parties animating Russia's emergent system to ground the information on the general aspects of the system in the concrete (and often fluid and messy) reality of Russian politics.

I focus on what has become known as the Second Russian Republic—the current period, which began in December 1993 when Russia's constitution was passed in a national referendum.[12] This is the most suitable period of postcommunist Russia's short history for the study of electoral systems, because it represents the first instance in which political parties were able to compete for political office relatively unfettered by official and unofficial restrictions on their activities.[13] Although the First Russian Republic also witnessed competitive elections in 1990 and 1991, parties did not play a significant role in structuring the vote. The constitutional ban on alternative political parties, the Soviet constitution's infamous Article 6, was not removed early enough to give alternative parties time to organize for the 1990 parliamentary elections, and mechanisms left over from that institutional setting meant that even in the absence of legal barriers to party activity nomination procedures were controlled by the Communist Party of the Soviet Union and related state organizations.[14] While the electoral system used in the 1990 election probably had an impact on political outcomes, including the development of nascent preparty organizations, the primary influence (and impediment) on party development was clearly the domination of the nomination process by the Communist Party of the Soviet Union (CPSU) and other state agencies. As M. Steven Fish argues, this initial liberalization was too premature and too partial to be as conducive to the development of a multiparty system as founding elections have been in other cases of democratization. Moreover, the fact that both the 1990 election to the Russian Congress of People's Deputies (RCPD) and the 1991 election to the Russian presidency were held while Russia was still officially part of the Soviet Union precludes either of these elections from being accurately conceived of as a "founding election."[15] Only with the elections in 1993 did political parties emerge as central agents of electoral mobilization.

This is not to say that Russia's nascent political parties emerged fully developed in 1993. Some scholars have been hesitant to declare the fluid organizations nominating candidates for election in Russia full-fledged parties. The term "proto-parties" has been commonly used to connote the organizational weaknesses of Russia's electoral associations, their lack of organizational and ideological coherence, their fluidity of elite membership, and their general lack of party identification within the population.[16] Following Mainwaring, I prefer to conceptualize these weaknesses as deficient institutionalization of Russia's party system rather than to define this nascent system as one composed of organizations that are something less than political parties.[17] Thus, I adopt Leon Epstein's minimalist definition of a political party as "any group, however loosely organized, seeking to elect governmental office-holders under a given label. Having a label (which may or may not be on the ballot) rather than an organization is the crucial defining element."[18] Some of the organizations that have contested elections in Russia call themselves political parties, others electoral blocs. I use these two terms interchangeably; the differences between the two types of electoral organizations in the Russian context in terms of internal cohesion and organizational longevity are viewed as differences of degree not kind.

Most important, parliamentary elections held under the Second Russian Republic were the first in which Russian electoral organizations performed the minimal functions of a political party—competing for office under a given label—in any systematic way, thanks in large part to the initiation of a PR party-list election for half of the seats to the State Duma. Moreover, unlike the electoral associations of previous elections, the nascent parties that won representation in the PR tier of the new system formed corresponding parliamentary factions that played a dominant role in the policymaking process of the newly established legislature.[19] Beginning in 1993, although chronically weak, the blocs emerging out of elections formed the basis for a multiparty system in Russia after more than three years of stagnant party development, following the initial experience with competitive elections in 1989 and 1990. Thus, this study examines the period in which Russian politics began the crucial transition from a battle between social movements to a contest between political parties.[20]

The system that has emerged since 1993 is a confusing array of literally dozens of parties. Adding to the confusion, Russian parties are constantly changing their names, personnel, and platforms—as well as experiencing dramatic changes of fortune at the ballot box. This fluid nature constitutes the system's status as a weakly institutionalized one, which will be discussed at length in the next chapter. Yet, despite this fluidity, one can also identify certain families of parties or ideological camps that offer some order to this chaotic picture and provide a shorthand for classifying individual parties in Russia. These ideological classifications are not perfect and can differ from one observer to the next; what follows is my classification for the major parties discussed in this book, along with basic information on party leaders, platforms, and electoral fortunes. I first discuss the parties that competed in the 1993 election and then the much larger group of parties that vied for seats in the State Duma in 1995. In the epilogue, I briefly describe the parties that competed in the 1999 election.

I divide the Russian ideological spectrum into four major categories: reformists, centrists, leftists, and nationalists. Reformists generally support the move to a free market (but not necessarily the policies followed by the Yeltsin government) and individual freedoms. Centrists occupy a vague middle ground; they support a market economy but place greater emphasis on state intervention in the market, support for industrial production, and protection of social welfare. Leftist parties have been the strongest critics of market reforms and until 1999 offered programs for substantial reversals of the privatization program and other reforms of the Yeltsin era. Nationalist parties concentrate on populist appeals concerning the need to reestablish domestic law and order and international prestige as a great power.

There are some problems classifying certain parties according to this scheme. The most notable case is the so-called party of power. Since 1993 there has been a pro-government party that has close ties to the executive branch and enjoys its financial and symbolic support. It is difficult to classify these parties according to ideology, as they have become increasingly nonideological. The success of the party of power relies instead on its connections to the executive branch and patronage. In 1993, the party of power was Russia's Choice, which gave voters a clear ideological position in favor of market reforms. But in 1995 Viktor Chernomyrdin, then prime minister, formed Our Home is Russia, a new party of power, which offered a more moderate economic and social program.[21] The latest party of power, Unity, tied to the enormously popular Prime Minister Vladimir Putin, declared that it had no clear ideological platform and rode the nationalist appeal of a popular war in Chechnya to a surprisingly good showing in 1999 (see epilogue). This may be an indication of a more general trend in Russian politics; there has been a convergence of party platforms, which has diluted the distinctions between ideological camps that marked the polarized nature of Russian politics during most of the Yeltsin era.[22]

The thirteen blocs contesting the 1993 election fit rather neatly into the four categories outlined above, considering what was to follow in subsequent elections. The reformist camp was made up of four blocs: Russia's Choice, Yabloko, the Party of Russian Unity and Accord (PRES), and the Russian Movement for Democratic Reform (RDDR). As already noted, Russia's Choice was the pro-government party of power. It was led by former prime minister Yegor Gaidar and was populated extensively by members of President Yeltsin's administrative apparatus. Russia's Choice defended the shock therapy policies undertaken by the Yeltsin government after the collapse of the Soviet Union and promised voters more economic reforms. Yabloko also firmly supported a free market. But its leader, economist Grigory Yavlinsky, strongly criticized the Yeltsin-Gaidar economic policies. The party carved out a niche as the democratic opposition and refused to take part in the governments appointed by Yeltsin throughout the 1990s. PRES was the other reformist party with a footing in the executive branch. Led by Deputy Prime Minister Sergei Shakhrai, this group claimed the mantle of the party of Russia's regions and defender of the interests of Russians living outside the center, Moscow. PRES also offered voters a more moderate program of market reform that included greater state investment and protectionism from international competition. Finally, RDDR was led by politicians prominent in the perestroika period, including former Moscow mayor Gavriil Popov, Gorbachev advisor Alexander Yakovlev, and Saint Petersburg mayor Anatolii Sobchak. Three of these four parties managed to overcome the 5 percent legal threshold and formed factions in the State Duma. However, only one, Yabloko, would survive to contest the 1999 parliamentary election with its name and top leadership largely intact. (One of Yabloko's top triumvirate, Yuri Boldyrev, did defect.) Russia's Choice has also competed in all three post-Soviet parliamentary elections, but under different names and changing leadership. PRES and RDDR did not survive as viable parties after the 1993 election.

Six blocs that participated in the 1993 election are classified as centrist, although all parties claimed that label at some point in the campaign. The Democratic Party of Russia (DPR), led by Nikolai Travkin, was one of only three that were founded more than a year before the election. The DPR had its roots in the democratic opposition to the Soviet Union. However, the party charted a centrist position, including advocacy of a mixed economy and curtailment of presidential powers, that took it outside the reformist camp. The Civic Union for Stability, Justice, and Progress, headed by Arkadii Volsky, was the party of economic managers of large state enterprises. Civic Union advocated a mixed economy and state support for industry. I also include in the centrist camp four parties that appealed to specific social constituencies or single-issue groups. The Women of Russia was by far the most successful of these and the only one to pass the 5 percent barrier to gain representation in the Duma. It was led by Alevtina Fedulova and Yekaterina Lakhova and was based on the Soviet-era Union of Russian Women. There were also parties appealing to the young (Future of Russia-New Names), veterans and the disabled (Dignity and Charity), and environmentalists (Constructive Ecological Movement of Russia—KEDR); none of these overcame the 5 percent hurdle. Not a single party classified as centrist in 1993 won five percent of the vote in 1995, although the Women of Russia came close. However, other more popular parties, including the party of power, began to occupy this ideological space—particularly in the latest election in 1999 (see epilogue).

There were two leftist parties in 1993. The Communist Party of the Russian

Federation (KPRF), led by Gennady Zyuganov, led this ideological camp. The main successor to the CPSU, the KPRF promised a return to a largely state-controlled economy. It appealed to those most harmed by the economic reforms of the 1990s, particularly elderly and rural voters. The Agrarian Party of Russia (APR) took a similar message to its target constituency in the countryside. Led by former state farm director Mikhail Lapshin, this party was based in the old Soviet collective farm structure; its major issue was opposition to the private ownership of land, which it argued would open the door to widespread foreign ownership and misuse of the Russian countryside. These two groups displayed the greatest cooperation during the electoral campaign and most similarities in their ideological platforms.[23]

The LDPR and its flamboyant nationalist leader, Vladimir Zhirinovsky, were the big stories of the 1993 election. It was the only party to occupy the nationalist part of the political spectrum, which it used to great effect to win the PR portion of the 1993 contest. Zhirinovsky played on the people's disillusionment with both the Communist past and postcommunist reforms, providing a populist message of greater social order at home and the reestablishment of superpower status abroad. With pro-Slavic rhetoric and strains of anti-Semitism, he appealed directly to ethnic Russians. His economic program was vague and more anti- than pro-market in 1993, and in 1995 his party dropped virtually all discussion of concrete economic proposals.[24] Support seemed to be based primarily on the charisma of Zhirinovsky himself and his ability to tap into widespread disillusionment with both the Communist left and the reformist right. Table 1.2 gives basic information regarding the thirteen parties of the 1993 parliamentary election.

The 1995 election witnessed a nearly three-fold increase in the number of parties, with 43 electoral blocs making it on the PR ballot, greatly increasing the redundancy within each ideological camp. This is ironic, given that President Yeltsin sponsored the formation of two political parties with the intention of establishing a two-party system from above.[25] In this brief overview I will introduce those parties that won at least one seat in the State Duma; I will explore the reasons behind this proliferation in chapter three.

The greatest redundancy occurred in the reformist camp, where the collapse of Russia's Choice as the party of power produced fallout that spawned no less than eight new parties.[26] The most direct successor was the Democratic Russia's Choice bloc, which broke with the Yeltsin government over the first war in Chechnya in 1994. Gaidar continued to lead this bloc with his message of the necessity of radical economic transformation. But voters were faced with a myriad of parties led by prominent reformers, all offering only slightly different versions of the same message. These groups included Forward Russia! (Boris Fedorov), Common Cause (Irina Khakamada), Party of Economic Freedom (Konstantin Borovoi), the Pamfilova-Gurov-Lysenko bloc (Ella Pamfilova and Vladimir Lysenko), and PRES (Sergei Shakhrai). The reformist constituency

Table 1.2: Parties in the 1993 State Duma Election

Party	Leader	Political orientation	Number of PR seats	Number of SMD seats
Russia's Choice	Y. Gaidar	Reformist	40	30
PRES	S. Shakhrai	Reformist	18	1
Yabloko	G. Yavlinsky	Reformist	20	3
RDDR	G. Popov	Reformist	0	4
Women of Russia	A. Fedulova Y. Lakhova	Centrist	21	2
DPR	N. Travkin	Centrist	14	1
Civic Union	A. Volsky	Centrist	0	1
Future of Russia–New Names	V. Lashchevsky	Centrist	0	1
KEDR	A. Panfilov	Centrist	0	0
Dignity and Charity	K. Frolov	Centrist	0	2
KPRF	G. Zyuganov	Leftist	32	16
APR	M. Lapshin	Leftist	21	12
LDPR	V. Zhirinovsky	Nationalist	59	5

Note: PRES = Party of Russian Unity and Accord, RDDR = Russian Movement for Democratic Reform, DPR = Democratic Party of Russia, KEDR = Ecological bloc, KPRF = Communist Party of the Russian Federation, APR = Agrarian Party of Russia, LDPR = Liberal Democratic Party of Russia

was further split by other parties with more distinctive messages but a similar support base. Yabloko continued to hold its role as the democratic opposition, advocating movement to a free market but severely criticizing the policies of the Yeltsin-Gaidar period. Finally, a new party of power, Our Home is Russia, led by then prime minister Viktor Chernomyrdin, offered a more moderate approach to market reform and more loyal support to Yeltsin. Although often classified as centrist, I prefer to classify Our Home is Russia as reformist, given that the Chernomyrdin government continued many of the macroeconomic policies introduced by the preceding Gaidar government.[27] The increased fractionalization of this camp had predictable results: only two parties from the reformist camp (Yabloko and Our Home is Russia) managed to win more than 5 percent of the PR vote. Democratic Russia's Choice won less than a third of the votes gained by Russia's Choice two years earlier.

While reformist parties lost a significant number of seats from 1993 to 1995, centrist groups saw their representation in the PR tier vanish completely. No party classified as centrist managed to cross the 5 percent barrier in 1995. The largest centrist party from 1993, Women of Russia, came closest with 4.5 percent of the PR vote. This part of the spectrum saw a number of important new entrants, including world renowned eye surgeon Svyatislav Fedorov's Worker's

Self-Government bloc and the Ivan Rybkin bloc, led by the speaker of the State Duma. A large number of special interest parties representing ethnic groups, children, pensioners, lawyers, and youth also occupied this space on the political spectrum.

The leftist camp was perhaps the most stable and consolidated part of the political spectrum. Not only did the KPRF retain its dominant position within this ideological space, but the more than two-fold increase in the Communist vote also made it the largest parliamentary party in Russia. The Agrarian party remained the second major leftist party. It failed to overcome the 5 percent legal threshold but managed to win twenty seats in SMD contests, more than any other party. Despite this stability, there were important new entrants. A more radical Communist party, Communists–Working Russia–For the Soviet Union led by Viktor Anpilov, narrowly missed the 5 percent cut-off. The Power to the People bloc, led by former Soviet prime minister Nikolai Ryzhkov and nationalist Sergei Baburin, tried to combine leftist and nationalist appeals.

Given the surprising success of the LDPR in 1993, a substantial increase in nationalist parties and appeals could be expected in 1995. While the LDPR remained the only nationalist party to gain representation in the PR tier, its support was cut in half partly due to increased competition from blocs led by prominent nationalist politicians. The most anticipated (and disappointing) new party in this camp was the Congress of Russian Communities (KRO) led by Yuri Skokov and popular former general Alexander Lebed. Former vice president Alexander Rutskoi also threw his hat in the ring, as the leader of the Derzhava bloc, as did Gen. Boris Gromov (My Fatherland bloc). Together there were a dozen nationalist parties competing in the same ideological space that the LDPR occupied alone in 1993.[28] Table 1.3 gives general background for parties gaining at least one seat in the State Duma in the 1995 parliamentary election. Changes in the contours of the party system in the 1999 election are discussed in the epilogue.

Plan of the Book

This volume implements a controlled comparison of Russia's mixed electoral system, examining the effects of PR and plurality elections on political parties and representation in that country. I use concepts and hypotheses found in the literature on electoral systems, covering the theories and hypotheses associated with several issues, among them the number of parties, women's representation, and minority representation. Throughout the analysis, to place the Russian experience in comparative context, I bring in comparative examples from other postcommunist countries and consolidated democracies.

Chapter 2 describes the methodological approach of controlled comparison used throughout the book. I examine the strengths and weaknesses of treating

Table 1.3: Major Parties in the 1995 State Duma Election

Party	Leader	Political orientation	Number of PR seats	Number of SMD seats
Our Home is Russia	V. Chernomyrdin	Reformist	45	10
Yabloko	G. Yavlinsky	Reformist	31	14
DVR	Y. Gaidar	Reformist	0	9
Forward Russia!	B. Fedorov	Reformist	0	3
P-G-L bloc	E. Pamfilova	Reformist	0	2
Common Cause	I. Khakamada	Reformist	0	1
PEF	K. Borovoi	Reformist	0	1
TF	E. Rossel	Reformist	0	1
PRES	S. Shakhrai	Reformist	0	1
Women of Russia	A. Fedulova Y. Lakhova	Centrist	0	3
Ivan Rybkin bloc	I. Rybkin	Centrist	0	3
Worker's Self-Government bloc	S. Fedorov	Centrist	0	1
Trade Unions and Industrialists bloc	V. Shcherbakov	Centrist	0	1
Govorukhin bloc	S. Govorukhin	Centrist	0	1
Bloc 89	P. Medvedev	Centrist	0	1
Independents bloc	V. Komchatov	Centrist	0	1
KPRF	G. Zyuganov	Leftist	99	58
APR	M. Lapshin	Leftist	0	20
Power to the People	N. Ryzhkov	Leftist	0	9
C-WR-FSU	V. Anpilov	Leftist	0	1
LDPR	V. Zhirinovsky	Nationalist	50	1
KRO	Y. Skokov	Nationalist	0	5
My Fatherland	B. Gromov	Nationalist	0	1

Note: DVR = Democratic Russia's Choice, P-G-L = Pamfilova-Gurov-Lysenko bloc, PEF = Party of Economic Freedom, TF = Transformation of the Fatherland, PRES = Party of Russian Unity and Accord, KPRF = Communist Party of the Russian Federation, APR = Agrarian Party of Russia, C-WR-FSU = Communists–Working Russia–For the Soviet Union; LDPR = Liberal Democratic Party of Russia; KRO = Congress of Russian Communities.

the PR and SMD tiers of a mixed electoral system as separate systems operating simultaneously in the same political context. I also discuss the weak institutionalization of political parties in Russia, which is the main explanatory factor used to account for the unexpected outcomes found in the PR and plurality tiers of Russia's mixed electoral system.

Chapter 3 considers the relationship between electoral systems and the number of parties emerging out of Russia's 1993 and 1995 parliamentary elections. I examine the extent to which PR and plurality elections in Russia have constrained party proliferation through a psychological effect on strategic behavior and through a mechanical effect during the translation of votes into seats. Russian experience runs counter to comparative experience and the expectations of the literature.

Chapter 4 looks at electoral systems and women's representation. I show that women actually have had greater success in SMD elections than in PR elections in Russia, which also runs counter to the conventional wisdom that PR is more conducive to women's representation than plurality elections. Chapter 5 studies the connection between electoral systems and minority representation. Non-Russian minorities have been well represented in the State Duma in numbers proportional to their share of the population. Moreover, the PR and SMD tiers elect non-Russians to office at equal levels; the difference between the two lies in the type of minority group elected.

Chapter 6 examines the 1996 presidential election. Unlike the experience of SMD parliamentary elections, the SMD election for president did constrain the number of candidates. This occurred despite the fact that a weaker two-round majoritarian electoral formula was used in the presidential election. President Yeltsin's reelection can be attributed to a significant extent to the concentration of the vote produced by the presidential election. Chapter 7 looks at the impact of electoral systems on political outcomes. PR and plurality elections had a significant effect on the status of political parties in the political system. Electoral systems are also shown to affect the success of individual parties and the ideological character of the State Duma.

In chapter 8 I draw some conclusions. I argue that, although Russia is unique in many ways when compared to consolidated democracies, its experience is very applicable to new democracies, especially other postcommunist states. Under conditions of weakly institutionalized parties, a mixed electoral system offers the greatest chance for democratic consolidation, because the two tiers produce complementary incentives for party development. The PR tier elevates weak parties to center stage and forces elites and voters to think in partisan terms, and the SMD tier forces parties to develop grass-roots organizations and a strong cadre of local candidates and activists, strengthening national integration.

An epilogue brings the analysis through the 1999 parliamentary elections. I found the same general patterns of party development continued in this election. Candidate proliferation remained in SMD elections and women won more seats in SMDs than in the PR tier.

2
Mixed Electoral Systems and the Study of Electoral System Effects

This book stems from the idea that mixed electoral systems provide a unique opportunity to study the effects of different systems. The simultaneous use of a PR and an SMD system in the same country provides a laboratory in which other potential factors affecting candidates and voters can be controlled for by holding them constant. As noted in the introduction, such an arrangement is not unique to Russia, although the Russian mixed system does possess certain characteristics that improve the comparison of its PR and SMD tiers.

In this chapter I discuss in greater detail the controlled comparison approach used throughout this book. I examine the logic behind it, its assumptions, and its strengths and weaknesses. Next, I address the issue of institutional origins and the problem of endogeneity. Since politicians write electoral laws, electoral systems are creations of the very actors they are assumed to influence. Thus, it could be argued that such a system's effects merely reflect and solidify political arrangements that were in existence when it was formed. I argue that in the Russian case the electoral system has had an influence over political outcomes independent of the forces that brought it into existence. Finally, I examine the concept of party institutionalization, which I posit as a major intervening variable that explains the unexpected effects of PR and plurality elections in Russia. I argue that the emergent Russian party system described in the introduction is weakly institutionalized and that, moreover, the character of Russian party underdevelopment has certain unique qualities that alter the effects of the electoral system .

Methodological Approach

The interaction between social context and institutions has received renewed attention in recent years. Much of the scholarship on this question has focused on institutional performance, sparked by Robert Putnam's study of Italian regional government, *Making Democracy Work,* which studied the causes of successful governance by holding institutions constant, explaining differing levels of effectiveness under identical institutions by focusing on the role of civic culture.[1] Such an approach often de-emphasizes the effect of institutions as an explanatory factor, yet the present study takes the opposite approach. Russia's PR and plurality tiers are treated as two separate electoral systems operating simultaneously under identical social conditions. Thus, where Putnam's work focused attention on social capital by holding institutions constant, here social context is held constant, and different outcomes observed between the two tiers are attributed to differences in institutional design.

Mixed electoral systems produce complications for categorization and analysis of effects. Most scholars have thought of these as a modified form of PR, designed to curb the potential for party proliferation.[2] Such a conception may approximate the results produced by mixed systems with linked tiers, as in the German practice, that interlock the two halves of the electoral system, prioritizing the PR tier. But this does not accurately capture the results of unlinked mixed systems, which Shugart has argued are actually softened forms of SMD systems. Since there is no mechanism to prioritize the PR tier over the SMD one, the former will not be able to compensate for the disproportionality of the latter.[3]

Mixed electoral systems also produce moderate levels of multipartism and disproportionality, as designers have intended. In practice, such results may be laudatory and a major reason why the arrangement has been replicated so widely in East Central Europe and Eurasia. However, mixed electoral systems add little to the dichotomous debate between PR and plurality when the latter two are examined as a single, undivided entity. Western scholarship has shown that plurality systems provide a powerful constraining effect on the number of parties. Taken at face value, the electoral systems of East Central Europe and Eurasia do not offer any cases on which to test this hypothesis. The high levels of party fractionalization usually found in these cases can be attributed to the combination of a multifarious political cleavage structure and a weak electoral system. Given that no postcommunist state exclusively employs the strongest system—plurality elections—one cannot test whether a plurality electoral system would have been able to curb the party proliferation found in postcommunist states.

On the other hand, mixed systems offer certain opportunities for examination of electoral systems as well. I argue that one can treat a mixed electoral system that employs separate votes for each tier exactly as it appears to be—a mixture of two distinct electoral arrangements operating side by side. Such a concept provides a unique opportunity to study the effects of separate SMD and PR tiers while holding constant other possible intervening variables, such as culture, social cleavages, and level of socioeconomic development. I use this approach to examine the different effects PR and plurality elections have had on the Russian party system, the representation of women and minorities, and the social and ideological composition of the legislature. I then compare these findings with the experience of other postcommunist states (using "pure" PR or majoritarian systems and mixed systems) as well as that of consolidated democracies that use mixed electoral systems.

This conceptualization follows the method of controlled comparison that studies "cases that differ with regard to the variables one wants to investigate, but similar with regard to all other important variables that may affect the dependent variables; these other important variables can then be treated as control variables."[4] Although they are a powerful methodological tool, cases similar in everything but certain independent variables are very hard to find. Putnam has used such cases effectively in studying the relationship between political institutions and social environment in Italy; so has Lijphart in examining changes in electoral systems over time within individual countries.[5] Lijphart argued that in such change, "many potentially important explanatory variables can be controlled in the sense that they can be assumed not to differ or to differ only marginally: the same country, the same political parties, the same voters, and so on."[6]

Mixed electoral systems contribute a significant dimension of comparability not found in Lijphart's study. All of Lijphart's cases of electoral reform involved changes in electoral systems within the same broad categories, mostly changes within the class of PR systems. Mixed systems provide the unique opportunity of using this method to compare the diametrically opposed categories of PR and plurality elections on which the debate over electoral systems has been based. Moreover, simultaneously studying the effects of different electoral systems is important with regard to unstable new democracies. Lijphart's argument that parties and voter attachments do not change or change only marginally from one election to another does not hold in an inchoate party system like Russia's, in which new parties emerge with every new election and parties that won the last election fade quickly.

This approach is not without precedent; others have treated the two parts of Germany's mixed electoral system separately in testing for strategic voting. Steven Fisher, Ekhard Jesse, Kathleen Bawn, and Gary Cox have all used Germany's design to show the existence of strategic voting.[7] Such studies consistently have found that large parties there received more votes in the plurality tier and fewer votes in the PR tier and vice versa for smaller parties, as the strategic voting hypothesis would predict. By showing that voters behave differently in the separate tiers of a mixed system, even a linked one that prioritizes the PR tier, such studies bolster the case for treating the tiers as separate cases, as long as a vote is cast in each tier.

This controlled comparison does possess potential problems, the most severe of which is cross-contamination between the two tiers. Unlike in cross-national analysis or Lijphart's cross-time analysis, the electoral systems being compared in this test are separated by neither time nor place; they form two halves of one system for the same legislative body in the same election. No matter how independently the two halves operate, the separation of mixed electoral systems into two systems for the purposes of comparison remains artificial. The PR and SMD tiers surely will influence one another to some extent. For example, small parties that run in the PR tier of the election have already assumed many of the entry costs of electoral competition and could be expected to run candidates in the SMDs as well, with little regard to payoffs in seats. Or, if one or two large parties dominate the single-member plurality races, there may be coattail effects that produce greater vote shares in the PR contest, consolidating the vote in the PR tier to a greater extent than would have occurred under a pure PR system. Erik S. Herron and Misa Nishikawa have provided empirical evidence for contamination effects in the Russian and Japanese cases. On the basis of this evidence, they argue that studies that compare the independent effects of PR and SMD tiers of mixed systems must control for such effects.[8]

While it is important to keep the danger of cross-contamination in mind, I argue that it does not ruin this experiment of controlled comparison. Incentives for strategic entry and withdrawal by elites in the SMD tier may be weakened because the costs and payoffs of competition are changed. However, strategic voting should remain intact, as shown in studies of Germany. Instrumentally rational voters will still have incentives to abandon small parties in the plurality tier in favor of large parties in the SMD tier, especially in Russia, where the latter level determines the composition of half of the legislature. Moreover, the mechanical effects of SMD elections should remain intact, producing greater disproportionality in favor of large parties than in the corresponding PR tier. Over time such mechanical effects should produce strategic behavior by parties punished in the translation of votes into seats in the SMD tier. Finally, contamination effects should be a concern generally in analyses of the number of parties, which is an important part of this book but not the only aspect of electoral system effects examined. Comparison of women's and minorities' representation should be negligibly affected by the contamination of parties' and voters' strategies between the two tiers.

Finally, by comparing Russia with other countries using mixed systems, I do incorporate an indirect check on the influence of cross-contamination. If cross-contamination does promote party proliferation in the SMD tiers, one should see this in all cases. However, unlike in Russia, SMD tiers in mixed systems of consolidated democracies constrain the number of candidates at the district level to a much greater extent than they do in the corresponding PR tier. It is difficult to believe that the proliferation found in Russia's SMD tier results from contamination effects that do not hold in other mixed systems.

Origins of the Russian Electoral System

This book concentrates on the effects of electoral systems in Russia. However, the origins of that system also deserve some attention. Political institutions are intermediary variables, both products of concerted political action and factors that influence political behavior. The purpose of the following short discussion of the origins of Russia's mixed electoral system is to legitimate my concentration on this as an independent variable influencing political actors. To warrant this concentration, I intend to show that the system did not simply institutionalize the preexisting distribution of power among political actors. The Russian electoral system is an excellent example of the autonomous effects of institutions, in the sense that its effects were largely unexpected and even ran counter to the interests of its originators. What's more, when those possessing the predominant share of political power (namely President Yeltsin and his allies) tried to change the system to better fit their interests, they failed in the face of strong opposition from political forces brought into being by the electoral system itself.

The study of institutional origins has sparked a debate about the direction of the causal relationship between institutions and political actors. Some scholars have asked whether institutions should be viewed as independent variables affecting political actors' behaviors when in reality they are products of those same actors' interests and strategies. In the literature, this assertion has become known as the endogeneity critique; the electoral system can be seen as endogenous to the character of the party system rather than an exogenous factor influencing it. The crux of this critique is that the distribution of power among parties determines the type of electoral system that is adopted. Thus, countries with a large number of significant parties adopt PR systems, while countries with two parties or a single dominant party are more apt to adopt more constraining SMD ones.[9] Similarly, scholars are beginning to examine the roots of presidentialism and parliamentarism, arguing that preexisting elite structures, party systems, social cleavages, and historical legacies influence constitutional choices.[10]

Taken to its extreme, the endogeneity critique denies an important role to institutions in political outcomes. If political actors can manipulate rules to serve their interests, then institutions are merely reflections of the interests of powerful actors rather than autonomous factors influencing their behavior. If latent or actual multiparty systems choose PR and two-party systems choose SMD, then electoral systems merely institutionalize the structures that created them in the first place and do not have an autonomous effect. But several considerations weaken this critique. First, the manipulation of institutions to further political interests validates the influence of institutions on political behavior and outcomes. As Cox argues, "The claim that parties tinker with the electoral mechanism in order to ensure their survival, or increase their vote totals, pre-supposes a belief on their part in electoral engineering."[11] Second, uncertainty and incomplete information of potential effects make institutional engineering a very imperfect science and lead to unexpected effects that can then be attributed to the institutions themselves.[12] Third, institutions have a certain resilience that sustains their original form against change and manipulation even when they cease serving the interests of the actors that originally created them.[13] These considerations are particularly important during political transitions, when uncertainty is high and volatile swings in public support can drastically change power relationships with little warning. Institutions such as strong presidencies or particular electoral systems designed to serve the dominant group of elites at the time of institutional creation may suddenly come under the control of very different forces through elections and be used for very different purposes. Or, as this book emphasizes, institutions may not have the effects their creators expect, but by the time this is apparent, they are very difficult to change. The Russian case demonstrates these considerations quite clearly.

Russia's mixed electoral system was introduced by executive decree in the wake of a profound constitutional crisis that ended in the violent disintegration of the existing institutional arrangements. A protracted battle between the executive and legislative branches for control within the system produced a stalemate. In September 1993, President Yeltsin took the extraconstitutional step of dissolving the legislature, the Congress of People's Deputies (CPD). Opposition deputies refused to abide by Yeltsin's decree and barricaded themselves in the White House (premises of the CPD). These deputies voted to impeach Yeltsin and named Vice President Alexander Rutskoi (who had defected to the anti-Yeltsin opposition) as president. After two weeks of living in constitutional limbo, the opposition led a rebellion in the streets, which Yeltsin defeated with military force. Emergency presidential rule was imposed, and elections for a new parliament were scheduled for December 1993. It was during this roughly three-month period of presidential rule that Yeltsin and a close circle of advisors crafted a new constitution and a new electoral system.

This political context is important for two reasons. First, the exclusiveness of the process provided President Yeltsin and his supporters with the means to construct an electoral system and constitution that would serve their interests. Unlike in Hungary, which adopted a mixed system in roundtable talks that included all major political parties, Russia's electoral designers did not have to compromise with members of the opposition. Second, the intense conflict between Yeltsin and the Communist/nationalist opposition provided huge incentives to craft electoral rules favorable to pro-Yeltsin reformist parties. Why did such an exclusive, conflict-ridden environment produce a mixed electoral system more typical of an inclusive process requiring compromise? After all, one strength of such arrangements is the coexistence of PR and SMD elements that can satisfy both small and large parties. The answer lies in three interrelated factors.

First and most important, uncertainty played a large role in the choice of a mixed system, whose designers clearly wanted to benefit pro-Yeltsin reformist forces but were split on how to achieve this goal. Some advisors favored SMD elections, because they envisioned a two-party configuration emerging, in which a proreform coalition of democrats and regional economic elites would command a winning plurality over a Communist-led bloc. Others cautioned against SMD elections, because the grassroots organization left over from the Soviet period gave Communists and their allies a decided advantage. They argued that a strong PR element would provide reformist parties with the best chance to capitalize on voters' continued anti-Communist sentiment. A mixed system combining both PR and SMD elections allowed designers to "hedge their bets" in the face of great uncertainty about the effects of different electoral systems.

Second, electoral engineers had a number of different goals, best met through a mixed system. Besides wanting to promote the fortunes of reformist parties, Yeltsin's team sought to encourage the development of political parties in general. Certain advisors, Viktor Sheinis in particular, correctly assumed Russia needed a significant PR element to promote the formation of parties.[14] By requiring elites to form electoral associations to gain access to the PR ballot and compelling voters to choose on the basis of partisan labels, parties were propelled to center stage in Russian electoral politics for the first time. An SMD element was desirable to retain the direct connection between voters and a particular candidate. An SMD election was also (wrongly) assumed to be a powerful force for party consolidation.

Finally, a mixed system was adopted partially by default, because Yeltsin was not that concerned about the electoral system. He was most determined to establish a constitutional arrangement that concentrated most powers in the presidency. After having weakened the legislature so that it posed much less of a threat than its disbanded predecessor, Yeltsin was not overly concerned with how that body was to be elected. Ironically, Yeltsin's advisors in charge of designing the electoral law ended up crafting a decree that was very close to a proposal advocated by the CPD prior to its dissolution. This was probably due in part to the fact that much of the work had been done by a reformist legislator in the CPD, Viktor Sheinis, who was brought in as an advisor on the decree.

In 1993 the mixed system produced results that were deemed not only unsatisfactory but also disastrous for its creators. Armed with greater knowledge of its effects gleaned from the 1993 results, President Yeltsin moved to change the system to better reflect his interests. He had an excellent opportunity to do so, since the electoral decree that established it went out of effect and needed to be replaced by a duly passed electoral law. Yeltsin proposed a law that would retain the basic character of a mixed system but increase the number of SMD seats at the expense of the PR tier. More SMD seats were not expected to substantially increase the fortunes of reformist parties such as Russia's Choice. It was clear that independents would dominate the elections in the SMDs; however, it quickly became clear that independent deputies were potential allies of executive power who were more susceptible than partisan deputies to presidential pressure and pragmatic exchanges of legislative support for pork barrel projects in the regions and personal perks. Partisan deputies, particularly those elected from PR party lists, were more subject than independents to party discipline and thus insulated from executive pressure. Thus, Yeltsin's attempt to change the electoral system was an attempt to undermine the very parties promoted through the introduction of a PR tier.

However, this attempt to change the electoral law failed, and the State Duma registered one of the most important legislative victories in its short history. The Duma was able to overcome resistance from both President Yeltsin and the Federation Council (upper house) and to secure an electoral law that retained the most important aspects of the original mixed system that had created the Duma, namely an equal number of seats for the PR and SMD tiers. In this battle, the State Duma managed to mobilize a large majority coalition around the status quo, a majority that was promoted by the electoral system itself. One could imagine that half of the deputies—those elected in SMDs—would support Yeltsin's moves to increase the seats in the SMD tier. However, the electoral system produced a significant number of partisan SMD deputies who were members of PR parties. These deputies voted with their PR compatriots, who supported the even split between the two tiers, thus creating a natural majority coalition to maintain the status quo.

The system was self-sustaining, as long as external forces did not intervene to force an institutional change. Of course, the more powerful executive branch was just such a potential force. President Yeltsin could have imposed such an alteration by forcing a stalemate through his veto power and then establishing the electoral rules by decree. However, he decided that such a step risked undermining the legitimacy of elections and fueling a growing reputation of high-handed authoritarian intervention in democratic processes.[15] Instead, he acceded to the will of the Duma. Of course, the much greater powers of the executive branch made this legislative victory for the State Duma easier to accept.

I do not mean to imply that the origins of Russia's electoral system are unimportant. Rather, I argue that electoral engineers were subject to sufficient uncertainty and to misinterpretation of the potential effects of different electoral arrangements and also that the electoral system did not merely solidify the distribution of power at the time of its inception. Indeed, the outcomes produced by the electoral system ran counter to the interests of its creators. The fact that the electoral structure has had such unexpected and detrimental effects for the most powerful actors and thus far has withstood attempts at significant change supports my underlying assumption that it has had an autonomous influence on political actors.

Russia's Weakly Institutionalized Party System

Descriptions of the Russian party system typically have emphasized its unstable character.[16] The newly formed parties of Russia's young democracy have been quite inchoate. Each election brings forth the birth of many new parties as well as the death of several parties that were leading actors in the previous campaign. Even if a bloc retains its name, its personnel and even top leadership often go through dramatic transformations, as the disgruntled defect and the ambitious join. This picture of fluidity has begun to be challenged by those who view the presence of several significant parties (Communist, Yabloko, and LDPR) in all three elections as evidence that a stable multiparty system has already begun to take shape in Russia.[17] While I do not discount signs of growing stability, I argue that Russia has a weakly institutionalized party system. Indeed, Russian parties possess a quality that makes them particularly underdeveloped, compared to those in other new democracies. Russian parties do not monopolize access to elected office in the SMD tier of its mixed system, allowing independents a dominant role. I attribute many of the effects of Russia's electoral systems to its weakly institutionalized party structure, particularly weak elite partisanship in the SMD tier. Given its centrality to my thesis, it is important to discuss at length the concept of party institutionalization and its application to the Russian case.

Russia is not alone in having a weakly institutionalized party system; these are rather endemic among countries that were part of the so-called third wave of democratization of the late twentieth century. Scott Mainwaring has argued that party institutionalization is the most important characteristic differentiating party systems in many new democracies from those in consolidated democracies.[18] Institutionalization refers to the process of routinizing and embedding organizations, patterns of behavior, and expectations. An organization or behavior is institutionalized when it is stable, expected, and adhered to by all major actors involved. According to Mainwaring, a party system is institutionalized when "actors develop expectations and behavior based on the premise that the fundamental contours and rules of party competition and behavior will prevail into the foreseeable future. In such a system, there is stability in who the main parties are and how they behave."[19]

Institutionalization does not imply rigidity nor does it assume a linear progression from weak to strong parties. Italy, Japan, and New Zealand have experienced dramatic changes in and general weakening of their relatively well institutionalized party systems.[20] Nor does the process imply universal progress across all arenas of party development or among all parties within a single country. Party systems may show signs of relatively high institutionalization in one aspect and low institutionalization in another. Or, as the Russian case powerfully demonstrates, some parties can be highly institutionalized, while others are extremely weak. Party institutionalization is a complex process that includes electoral, social, attitudinal, and organizational dimensions of party life. Mainwaring offers four dimensions on which one can judge the relative institutionalization of a country's party system.[21] I will address each of these and discuss how well Russia measures up against other third-wave democracies, and I will give special attention to the organizational dimension, which I believe differentiates Russia from many other new democracies.

First, party institutionalization produces electoral stability. Institutionalized party systems do not witness dramatic shifts in the electoral fortunes of major parties on a regular basis. Russia scores particularly low on this dimension;

Mainwaring found that the electoral volatility between Russia's first two parliamentary elections in 1993 and 1995 was the second highest among his sample of twenty-six countries, topped only by Peru's.[22] Russian electoral volatility was twice as high as the average for major Eastern European states and also much greater than the instability found in the Baltic states.[23] This volatility has affected all types of parties, big and small, from all points along the ideological spectrum. Russia's Choice, the largest reformist party of 1993, saw its share of the vote cut by more than 70 percent from 1993 to 1995. The ultranationalist LDPR, centrist Women of Russia, and leftist Agrarian Party each lost around half of its electorate, while the Communist Party nearly doubled its percentage of the vote from 1993 to 1995. On the other hand, there are some islands of stability in this sea of turmoil. The Communist Party has settled into a pattern of attracting approximately a quarter of the electorate; its 1999 vote share was almost identical to its 1995 portion. Yabloko has won a steady 6 to 8 percent of the vote in each of Russia's first three elections.

Second, party institutionalization requires strong links between parties and society. For Mainwaring, the degree to which parties are rooted in society is manifested in several different ways. Institutionalized parties are connected to organized interests. At first glance, Russian parties seem quite divorced from society. Most parties are small and unknown to the general public; they usually serve as vehicles for single ambitious politicians, rather than as organizations representing particular interest groups or strata of the population. However, the connection between Russian parties is much more complex and contestable. Despite vivid weaknesses, some major parties do have identifiable social constituencies, which can be seen in both the organizational connections with interest groups and party identification.

Several Russian parties show rather high levels of interaction with organized interests. The Agrarian Party had its roots in the old collective farm network and was formed by former collective farm managers to represent their interests. Women of Russia stemmed from the Soviet-era women's organization and has remained a major organization in the women's movement. The Communist Party has relatively well established social networks and organizations, especially among the elderly. The various parties of power have come from the state's bureaucratic structures; thus, parties' ties to interest organizations in Russia present a mixed picture. Most major parties have increasingly worked on establishing some sort of base in social and economic interests. Yet, given the increasing importance of money in campaigns, it remains to be seen whether many of the social structures supporting parties really provide much connection to broader social interests.

The level of party identification is also seen as an indicator of the degree parties are tied to society. Here, the picture in Russia is also mixed. Russian party identification is low by comparative standards. White, Rose, and McAllister argue that only around a quarter of Russian voters identify at least somewhat with a party.[24] However, other scholars have noted a significant increase in the level of Russian partisanship since Russia's initial election; Colton, for example, has found that nearly half of Russian citizens (49 percent) could be classified as partisans.[25] Party identification also varies greatly among parties with the Communist Party enjoying a much more committed and stable following than all other parties.[26] Indeed, I argue in chapter 7 that party identification has increased significantly in Russia since 1993, due in large part to the introduction of proportional representation.

Third, party institutionalization requires that parties be seen as legitimate institutions. Voters need to believe in parties or at least view them as necessary for democratic government. Citizens in most democracies view parties cynically, but disdain for them ranks particularly high in Russia. White, Rose, and McAllister found that only 2 percent of respondents moderately or strongly trusted parties, while 60 percent were moderately or strongly mistrustful. Moreover, 43 percent of respondents supported the dissolution of parliament and parties.[27] Mainwaring found a similar lack of support for parties in Latin American countries with weak parties like Brazil and Peru, while countries such as Uruguay with more established party systems showed much higher levels of popular legitimacy for parties.[28]

Fourth, in strongly institutionalized systems, party organizations possess a certain level of structure and significance. It is in this regard that Russian parties are least developed. The lack of organizational strength of Russian parties is manifest in several ways. Many small and some prominent parties in Russia are merely vehicles of a single leader, and should that leader leave the party, it would likely dissolve. The most obvious case of this is Vladimir Zhirinovsky's nationalist LDPR, which, despite a relatively extensive local organization, is completely reliant on the charismatic appeal of its leader for legislative representation. Moreover, elites defect and join parties at will, undermining cohesion and discipline. Party lists regularly see high turnover in even their highest slots, as well-known politicians jockey for the most favorable slots on competing party lists and parties compete with one another to land national politicians who can deliver the most votes. Candidates in the SMDs regularly shift partisan affiliations from one election to the next, as they adjust to the volatile swings in party support.

But the most important sign of organizational weakness of Russian parties is their failure to monopolize access to elected office. Of course, this is not a concern in the PR tier since, by definition, elites must form parties to contest for office. However, in the SMD tier Russian parties have not been able to establish themselves as the major vehicles, much less the only ones, for candidates wishing to contest a seat in the State Duma in an SMD. The proliferation of independent candidates differentiates Russia from most other new democracies, even those with otherwise weakly institutionalized party systems.[29] In Russia, officially nonpartisan candidates gained 48 percent of the vote in 1993 and 36 percent in 1995. Independents not only made up a large proportion of candidates competing for office; they also accounted for the largest proportion of the winners. Fifty-two percent of winners were independents in the 1993 Russian elections and 34 percent in 1995. Even in other postcommunist states, non-partisan candidates in SMD elections were marginalized. In Lithuania independents won only 3 percent of the vote. In Hungary, the vote for independent candidates dropped from 7 percent in 1990 to only 2 percent in 1994. In Lithuania and Hungary's 1990 election, independents made up only 6 and 3 percent of winners, respectively. There were no nonpartisan winning candidates in Hungary's 1994 election. No independents won election in Croatia in 1995. Only in Ukraine have independent candidates been as dominant in legislative elections; in fact, electoral system effects in that country have closely resembled those in Russia.[30]

The failure of Russian parties to monopolize access to elected office in the SMD tier and the corresponding proliferation of independents have had a direct influence on the electoral system. Given this condition, the plurality tier in Russia has not had a constraining effect on the number of competitors in a district. Instead, there has been candidate proliferation at the district level, which has in turn had a number of important implications for party development and representation in Russia. These implications are the subject of the remainder of this book.

Conclusion

In this chapter I have laid out my methodological approach, defended my concentration on electoral system effects, and discussed the nature of Russia's weakly institutionalized party system. Russia is not unique in its political system; many other third-wave democracies also experience the high electoral volatility, weak party identification, and weak party organizations found in Russia. But Russia is distinct in its level of independents who contest and win elections, which has important consequences for electoral system effects.

Over the next several chapters I will examine the effects of PR and plurality electoral systems, using the controlled comparison method outlined in this chapter. Their unexpected effects on the number of parties, women's representation, and ethnic representation will be attributed in various ways to the weak party system currently found in Russia. Given that weak party institutionalization is a common feature of third-wave democracies, the experience of the Russian case may have broader implications for many new democracies.

3
Electoral Systems and the Number of Parties in Russia

This chapter examines the effect of PR and plurality electoral systems on the number of parties in Russia. Beginning with Duverger, scholars have consistently shown SMD systems constrain the number of parties to a greater degree than PR systems do.[1] Such effects have important implications for the nature of party systems and the viability of emerging democratic regimes. PR systems are thought to be more representative, because they give greater access to government office for more social groups and may be seen as more legitimate because they facilitate greater correspondence between a party's proportion of the electoral vote and its share of seats in the legislature. Plurality systems are deemed less representative but provide greater government stability by producing two-party systems and single-party majority governments rather than the less stable multiparty coalitions associated with PR systems.[2]

Are the effects of electoral systems generalizable across all political contexts, however? Some scholars seem to think so. Arend Lijphart concluded his book on electoral systems in consolidated democracies with the following note: "When a first electoral system has to be chosen which will hopefully guide the new democracy's elections for a long time (or, in the case of a redemocratizing country, a new system that will hopefully work better than the old one), it is important to examine all of the options as well as their advantages and disadvantages. . . . Therefore, to the extent that this study of seventy electoral systems in twenty-seven democracies will have some practical utility, it may have more to offer to electoral engineers in the new democracies than in these twenty-seven old democracies."[3] Implicit in this statement is an assumption that the effects of electoral systems are more or less universal and will therefore hold in new democracies as well as old. However, it remains to be seen whether the hypotheses, based for the most part on the experience of Western democracies, will be borne out in new democracies, particularly in the very different social and political context of postcommunist states.

I will show that the Russian experience defies the expectations of Duverger's Law. The plurality tier of Russia's mixed electoral system has not produced two-party competition. This proliferation of parties exists at the national and district levels—a multitude of candidates compete for a single seat in each district. The 5 percent legal threshold in the PR tier also has had little effect on the number of parties contesting elections even though it has had a substantial mechanical effect, denying dozens of parties representation in the translation of votes into seats. Russian voters have shown no signs of strategic voting in Russia's first two elections, and Russian elites have not consolidated into larger electoral coalitions in response to electoral-system incentives. I will demonstrate that such proliferation differentiates Russia from consolidated democracies as well as from other postcommunist states in Eastern Europe. Moreover, I suggest that Russia's situation also differs from deviant cases found in the literature, such as the persistence of multiparty competition in India despite its longstanding plurality system or the continuation of such competition in Italy despite the recent introduction of a mixed electoral system that fills a majority of its seats in plurality elections. While plurality elections in India and Italy may produce multiple parties at the national level, they approximate two-candidate competitions at the district level, as Duverger's Law suggests.

Electoral Systems:
Key Elements and Effects

Electoral systems are differentiated by many characteristics, including ballot structure, electoral formula, district magnitude, electoral thresholds, and assembly size. I will concentrate on the three elements that have received the most attention in the electoral-systems literature: electoral formula, district magnitude, and legal threshold. Electoral formula is the method by which votes are translated into seats. There are an infinite number of possible electoral formulas, but in practice the vast majority can be grouped into four broad categories: plurality, two-round majoritarian, PR, and mixed. In plurality elections, the candidate who receives the most votes in an SMD wins, regardless of whether that total is a majority of votes cast. Two-round majoritarian elections are also held in SMDs but require the winner to receive a majority of votes cast. If no candidate wins a majority in the first round of elections, a second round run-off is held, usually between the top two vote-getters. PR formulae vary, but all involve contests between lists of candidates in multimember districts. The number of seats awarded to each list comes from the proportion of votes received in the district. Finally, mixed systems combine elements of PR and plurality or majoritarian elections by having voters cast two ballots in separate electoral tiers.[4]

District magnitude refers to the number of seats assigned each electoral district. A state can divide its territory into hundreds of electoral districts, each providing one representative to the legislature (SMDs); it can have territorial multimember districts with anywhere from two to several dozen representatives; or it can have a single, all-national electoral district that includes every representative. Although the debate over electoral systems commonly has been phrased as one between PR and plurality, that is, on the basis of electoral formula, district magnitude has been found to be the most powerful determinant of disproportionality and the number of parties.[5] The difference between plurality and PR systems is primarily that the former is held in SMDs while the latter is held in multimember districts. At low district magnitudes (five or fewer seats per district), even PR systems favor larger parties and marginalize smaller ones. In most consolidated democracies, it is only when district magnitudes reach twenty seats or more that small parties (those receiving 5 percent of the vote or less) have a reasonable hope of gaining representation in the legislature. Because of the vital importance of district magnitude, Taagepera and Shugart argue that electoral systems should be considered along a continuum of district magnitude rather than as a dichotomy between plurality and PR systems.[6]

A legal threshold for representation is also found in many PR systems. Legal thresholds establish an arbitrary percentage of the vote necessary to gain seats to the legislature. Russia uses a 5 percent legal threshold in the PR tier of its mixed system. These thresholds are designed to encourage party consolidation by denying smaller parties representation and therefore have effects similar to low district magnitudes.[7]

Scholars have concentrated on two major consequences of these three elements of electoral systems: the number of parties operating in the party system and the level of disproportionality between votes and seats. The former is self-explanatory, although its measurement is complicated. The latter is the difference between the proportion of votes a party receives in an election and the proportion of seats it gains in the legislature. The number of parties in a party system and the level of disproportionality between votes and seats have become the baseline measures of the relationship between electoral and party systems. But the operationalization of these two electoral outcomes is subject to debate. Surely, a system with ten parties of which two combine for 90 percent of the vote and the rest split the remaining 10 percent is actually less fractionalized than one with only four parties in which each receives 25 percent. In counting parties, some consideration of their size must be taken. I count the number of parties in the Russian system using the effective number of parties index created by Laakso and Taagepera, which has become the standard in the field.[8] This measure allows for the relative size of each party when counting parties. In this way, small, marginal parties are not given the same weight as large parties. Laakso and Taagepera's index can be calculated on the basis of votes (N_v) to measure the effective number of elective parties or on the basis of seats (N_s) to measure the effective number of parliamentary parties. A similar consideration must be given to measuring disproportionality between votes and seats. The disproportionality of the electoral system will be calculated according to the least-squared index of disproportionality that weights the vote-seat deviations by squaring them, giving larger deviations more importance.[9]

Duverger's Law and Its Limits

Duverger originally formulated his three laws of electoral system effects as follows: "(1) Proportional representation tends to lead to the formation of many independent parties . . . (2) the two-ballot majority system tends to lead to the formation of many parties that are allied with each other, . . . (3) the plurality rule tends to produce a two-party system."[10] It was the final proposition that Duverger claimed was "the closest to a sociological law."[11]

Subsequent studies have better specified the causal nature of these correlations both empirically and theoretically. District magnitude was found the decisive factor influencing disproportionality and multipartism: Low district magnitudes, particularly in SMDs, have a powerful constraining effect on the number of parties and produce high levels of disproportionality in the translation from votes to seats. High district magnitudes allow greater proliferation of parties and produce lower levels of disproportionality (but do not *cause* a multiplication of parties).[12] The constraining effect of electoral systems was found most directly at the district rather than national level.[13] Finally, the electoral system was found to interact with, not override, the cleavage structure in society.[14] The major modifications to Duverger's hypotheses arise from these findings.

Cox has contributed greatly to this debate by explicating the conditions under which strategic voting takes place. Using a rational choice model, he argues that strategic voting (and by implication, strategic entry and departure by elites) requires certain conditions regarding actors' motivations, preferences, time horizons, and the availability of accurate information. Thus, Cox has argued that even single-member plurality elections may fail to reduce the vote for minor parties if one or more of the following conditions arise: "(1) the presence of voters who are not short-term instrumentally rational; (2) lack of public information about voter preferences and vote intentions (hence about which candidates are likely to be 'out of the running'); (3) public belief that a particular candidate will win with certainty; or (4) the presence of many voters who care intensely about their first choice and are nearly indifferent between their second and lower choices." [15]

Even if conditions at the district level are favorable for the establishment of two-candidate races, the projection of this bipolarity to the national level is not assured. It depends on the ability of parties to unite prominent elites in single nationwide party organizations. If national parties do not form, the two candidates produced in plurality elections at the district level may belong to a multitude of different parties across the country. Cox cites institutional forces, most notably the direct election of a powerful national executive, as the primary factors promoting the nationalization of parties that is essential to the realization of Duverger's law at the national level.[16] This makes it crucial to examine electoral system effects with electoral data disaggregated at the district level. The presence of these preconditions for strategic behavior and projection of local bipartism to the national level are particularly questionable during initial elections in new democracies, especially in postcommunist states with little or no democratic tradition. The absence of previous electoral experience or of accurate polling information may deny voters and elites the information necessary to behave strategically.

Most important, the lack of well-established political parties undermines the ability of voters and elites to behave strategically. Parties serve as the primary mechanism to channel and aggregate public opinion, while electoral systems are a secondary mechanism, influencing the number of viable political parties.[17] If significant political parties do not exist, they can neither aggregate political elites into nationwide political organizations nor represent large segments of public opinion. In weak-party systems, the absence of party identification leaves voters with no cues on how to cast their votes—other than the personal characteristics of candidates and patronage. The transitory nature of organizations in the most unstable new democracies means that parties continually enter and exit the scene (usually in tandem with the political clout of their leaders), providing no continuity between electoral periods. Such conditions provide little opportunity for voters to cultivate lasting preferences for one group or another, leaving most uncommitted to any party. Under such conditions it is difficult to attribute the same party preferences to the majority of voters in unconsolidated democracies that we do to voters in consolidated democracies with institutionalized party systems. Without concrete party attachments, strategic voting as a process relating to a rank ordering of preferences seems very unlikely.

If one is restricted to the examination of consolidated democracies, the conditions necessary for strategic voting are usually approximated, and plurality systems constrain the number of parties to two as expected, at least at the district level. This is not the case for new democracies, particularly in the postcommunist world, where parties are not well developed and thus voters and elites cannot easily respond to incentives from electoral systems. It would be a mistake to assume that institutional effects found in established democracies would be replicated in the very different social context of new democracies.

Electoral Systems and the Number of Parties in Russia

As noted in chapter 2, I am treating the two tiers of Russia's mixed electoral system as separate systems, to show the different effects of proportional representation and plurality elections, controlling for other factors that may influence the number of parties by holding them constant. The PR half of Russia's mixed system was conducted in a single nationwide district and thus had a very high magnitude, similar to the most proportional PR systems of the world— such as Israel and the Netherlands. However, its relatively high legal threshold of 5 percent should have significantly constrained the number of parties and the proportionality of the system, making it similar to those Lijphart has called moderate PR, such as the ones found in Germany and Sweden.[18] If Russia follows the pattern of other democracies, one would expect this portion to produce more than two parties but not severe party proliferation. The plurality tier, conducted in 225 SMDs, should have produced greater disproportionality and two-party competition at least at the district level.

Table 3.1 reports the effective number of parties, the average effective number of candidates per district, and the level of disproportionality for the 1993 and 1995 parliamentary elections. These data show that PR and plurality elections did not have their expected effects on the number of parties in Russia's transitional elections: The plurality tier did not produce two-candidate races.

Table 3.1: Effects of the PR and Plurality Tiers of Russia's Mixed System

Election	Effective number of parties for system (both tiers)	Effective number of parties in PR tier	Effective number of parties in SMD tier	Least-squares index of disproportionality
1993	$N_v = 7.14$ $N_s = 8.16$[a]	$N_v = 7.58$ $N_s = 6.40$	$N_v = 5.48$[b] $N_s = 6.13$[a]	System = 4.60 PR = 4.94 SMD = 4.27
1995	$N_v = 10.00$ $N_s = 5.71$[a]	$N_v = 10.68$ $N_s = 3.32$	$N_v = 6.61$[b] $N_s = 5.00$[a]	System = 14.14 PR = 20.56 SMD = 11.09

Source: Foreign Broadcasting Information Service, *Report on Eurasia* (December 8, 1993): 1–57; Central Electoral Commission of the Russian Federation, "Rezul'taty golosovaniya na vyborakh v Gosudarstvennuyu Dumu po odnomandatnym izbiratel'nym okrugam," (Results of voting on elections to the State Duma in single-member voting districts), Unpublished report, Moscow: Central Election Commission, 1994; "Dannye protokolov No. 1 okruzhnykh izbiratel'nykh komissii o rezultatakh vyborov deputatov Gosudarstvennoy Dumy Federal'nogo Sobraniya Rossiiskoy Federatsii vtorogo sozyva po odnomandatnym izbiratel'nym okrugam" (Data of protocol No. 1 of district electoral commissions on the results of elections of deputies of the second State Duma of the Federal Assembly of the Russian Federation by single-mandate electoral district), *Rossiiskaya gazeta* (January 17, 1996); "Dannye protokolov No. 2 ob itogakh golosovaniya po federal'nomu izbiratel'nomu okrugu" (Data of protocol No. 2 on results of vote for federal electoral okrug), *Rossiiskaya gazeta* (January 24, 1996).

a Based on membership in parliamentary factions formed after the election.
b Average effective number of candidates per district.

Moreover, while multiparty competition was expected in the PR tier, there appeared to be no strategic reaction to the legal threshold.

PR and the Number of Parties

Party proliferation was endemic in PR elections in Russia, despite the legal threshold designed to deny representation to marginal parties. In 1993, thirteen electoral blocs managed to collect the 100,000 signatures necessary for inclusion on the ballot. In 1995, authorities doubled the signature requirement to 200,000, yet forty-three blocs were able to collect the necessary signatures required to get on the ballot. The biggest reason for the large increase in the number of parties has little to do with the electoral system, which did not change significantly. Rather, the nature and length of the electoral campaign produced the proliferation of parties in 1995. The 1993 election was called without notice and had a much shorter period for amassing the necessary petition signatures. Moreover, signature collection was hindered by the tense conditions following the constitutional crisis of October, in which President Yeltsin dissolved the legislature and then violently crushed an opposition uprising. Several parties were banned following these events, and likely some citizens felt uncomfortable giving their signatures and passport numbers under such conditions, particularly to opposition organizations. Quite simply, many aspiring parties and blocs did not have the time to establish the grassroots organization necessary to collect 100,000 signatures from across the country.[19]

In contrast, 1995 was a scheduled election. Electoral organizations had two years to build the organization necessary for overcoming the signature requirement. Moreover, in those two years private enterprise intervened as private signature-collection firms that would collect the necessary signatures for a price. In short, the 1995 campaign removed exogenous factors unique to the political context of Russia's founding election that curtailed the number of parties able to register in the PR tier. Given more time and a more open political environment, the number of parties exploded .

Nevertheless, the emergence of forty-three electoral blocs in 1995 represented a failure of elites to heed the constraints of the electoral system. Why did so many groups that clearly had no chance of overcoming the 5 percent legal threshold still spend the time and money to run in the PR tier? Some have argued that there was a lack of rational behavior among party leaders.[20] But I contend that the answer lies partly in conflicting incentives of the electoral system and partly in poor information. First, the PR contest offered parties more than just legislative seats. Being on the PR ballot entitled an electoral bloc to government financing as well as free television and radio airtime. Thus, a party with little or no chance of winning legislative representation might have entered the race to get its name and message out, largely at the government's expense. This free access to mass media produced an interesting dynamic between the PR and plurality elections. Clearly, some blocs associations existed primarily to promote the chances of their leaders in SMD races. Leaders of the Pamfilova–Gurov–Lysenko bloc, Common Cause, and the Party of Economic Freedom definitely owed their victories in the plurality election partly to the name recognition and exposure they received as leaders of PR blocs.[21]

Rather than a case of Russian elites acting irrationally, party proliferation in the PR tier seems in part to be one of hidden rationality caused by the many competing incentives of the mixed electoral system. This is analogous to George Tsebelis's concept of nested games, in which apparently irrational behavior of political actors results from the different and sometimes opposing enticements of the simultaneous multilayered political arenas that structure complex political behavior. In this case, an action deemed irrational from the perspective of one arena is actually rational when the incentives from all of the arenas are taken into account.[22]

Second, part of the explanation for party proliferation in 1995 was the uncertainty of the potential support parties would enjoy. In 1993, no one imagined that Vladimir Zhirinovsky would win the PR contest with 23 percent of the vote. Russian opinion polls, while continually improving, still produce conflicting and often inaccurate predictions. Thus, many parties using their own survey research or impressions of the electorate clung to the belief that they would be the exceptions, defy the odds, and overcome the 5 percent barrier.[23] Of course, there was also a strong element of personal ambition involved in the failure of parties to consolidate. Ambitious party leaders often did not want to give up leadership positions to rivals or surrender precious top spots on the party list for the sake of a political merger. But this ambition also has a rational basis in the strategic trade-off between a top spot on a marginal party's list that may not overcome the legal threshold and a marginal one on a major party's, which will overcome the threshold but may not get a large enough share of the vote to elect members in lower positions.[24]

The difference between the number of parties competing in 1993 and 1995 made for drastic disparities in the disproportionality produced by the 5 percent legal threshold. In the relatively less crowded field of 1993, the distribution of the vote was such that eight electoral blocs managed to overcome the threshold and a relatively small proportion of the popular vote (about 9 percent) was wasted on unsuccessful parties. Disproportionality for the PR tier in 1993 was 4.94, which was actually higher than the 1993 plurality election but much lower than that found in both the PR and plurality elections of 1995. In comparison to those in other countries, the 1993 Russian PR system produced an above-average amount of disproportionality for such a system with a legal threshold.[25] The disproportionality produced by the PR tier in 1995 was 20.56, greatly exceeding that of either tier in 1993 and was almost twice as high as that produced by the 1995 plurality election. By international standards, only India's plurality system has produced similar levels.[26]

Proportional representation has had conflicting effects in Russia; in the electoral realm, it allowed for the proliferation of parties both in 1993 and in 1995. The 5 percent legal threshold, designed to deter the proliferation of small parties, seemed to have no effect on the number of elective parties. In the transformation of votes into seats, the degree of party proliferation in the electoral realm conditioned the mechanical effect of the 5 percent legal threshold. In 1993, when party proliferation was high but not outrageous, the 5 percent barrier produced moderate levels of disproportionality and allowed party proliferation to be reflected in both the electoral arena and parliament. But when the number of electoral blocs competing in the PR party-list race exploded from thirteen to forty-three in 1995, the mechanical effects changed; many small parties received minuscule shares of the vote, producing an extremely high degree of disparity between votes and seats.

Plurality Elections and the Number of Parties

Russia's plurality elections afford the biggest surprise for electoral studies. The plurality system implemented by Russia to elect half of the deputies to the State Duma is considered the arrangement with the strongest constraining effect on the number of parties. Invariably, this has produced two large parties and a high incidence of parliamentary majorities even in social conditions of high pluralism; however, in Russia the plurality system did not have these effects.

I use the effective number of candidates per district in place of the effective number of electoral parties as the measure of party proliferation in the plurality tier. This measure counts the number of candidates competing in each district, taking into consideration the weight of each candidate's vote—using the same mathematical technique as the effective-number-of-parties index.[27] This measure taps into the core of Duverger's Law—plurality elections should produce two-candidate races at the district level—and also avoids the problem of how to classify independents. It shows how thoroughly fractionalized Russian politics is, even at the district level. The average effective number of candidates in SMDs for both 1993 and 1995 was dramatically higher than the theory predicts.

The plurality tier also did not produce the high level of disproportionality one might expect. Failures of strategic coordination in plurality systems typically penalize smaller parties and reward larger ones. This mechanical effect creates parliamentary majorities even when the vote distribution does not warrant it. Such was not the case in Russia's transitional elections; the level of disproportionality for the plurality tier in 1995 was half that of its PR counterpart.

In fact, the plurality election allowed for more representation to small parties than the PR election. Table 3.2 shows the vote and seat totals for parties in the

1995 SMD elections. If a 5 percent national legal threshold would have been applied to the plurality election in 1995, only four parties would have gained representation. But with only the effective threshold in each district as a barrier to representation, no less than twenty-three parties managed to win at least one seat in the legislature, resulting in a multiparty system arising out of a plurality election.

What accounts for these outcomes? One cannot attribute the proliferation

Table 3.2: Electoral Results of the 1995 SMD Tier

Electoral bloc	Percent of vote	Seat percent (number)	Vote/ Seat difference	Number of candi- dates	Average vote per candi- date	Winners' percen- tage of vote
KPRF	13.80	25.78 (58)	+11.98	129	65,162	67.14
APR	6.23	8.89 (20)	+2.66	80	47,422	61.44
LDPR	6.14	0.44 (1)	-5.70	165	22,674	2.34
Our Home is Russia	5.76	4.44 (10)	-1.32	99	35,445	23.51
Yabloko	3.56	6.22 (14)	+2.66	63	34,428	40.62
KRO	3.15	2.22 (5)	-0.93	87	22,074	29.61
DVR	3.01	4.00 (9)	-0.99	72	25,468	33.48
Power to the People	2.11	4.00 (9)	+1.89	39	32,907	67.15
C-WR-FSU	1.94	0.44 (1)	-1.50	59	20,018	2.37
Ivan Rybkin bloc	1.82	1.33 (3)	-0.49	62	17,836	16.42
Forward, Russia!	1.65	1.33 (3)	-0.32	61	16,490	18.77
Women of Russia	1.13	1.33 (3)	0.00	19	36,313	39.20
Trade Unions bloc	1.01	0.44 (1)	-0.57	39	15,753	11.86
Govorukhin bloc	0.79	0.44 (1)	-0.35	25	19,331	15.27
P-G-L	0.74	0.89 (2)	+0.15	31	14,521	26.02
Party of Workers Self-Government	0.72	0.44 (1)	-0.28	25	17,625	25.50
Independents bloc	0.61	0.44 (1)	-0.17	16	23,382	29.98
PRES	0.46	0.44 (1)	-0.02	20	13,915	31.27
My Fatherland	0.41	0.44 (1)	+0.03	16	15,537	38.16
PEF	0.33	0.44 (1)	+0.11	15	13,277	21.72
Bloc 89	0.29	0.44 (1)	+0.15	6	29,258	42.49
TF	0.28	0.44 (1)	+0.16	12	14,347	24.88
Common Cause	0.23	0.44 (1)	+0.21	6	23,505	70.08
Other	5.55	0.00 (0)	-5.55	320	10,562	0.00
Independents	38.15	34.22 (77)	-3.93	1099	21,843	n/a

Soures: Data presented in "Dannye protokolov No. 1," 1–6; and Central Election Commission document, 1995.

Note: DVR = Democratic Russia's Choice, C-WR-FSU = Communists–Working Russia–For the Soviet Union, P-G-L = Pamfilova-Gurov-Lysenko, PEF = Party of Economic Freedom, TF = Transformation of the Fatherland.

simply to a failure of national projection. Plurality elections did not produce two-party competition at the district level that was not manifested at the national level; the high effective number of candidates per district attests to that. Rather, I argue that the proliferation of candidates in the SMD tier was caused by the weakly institutionalized party system. The limitations of Russian parties in the SMD tier produced conditions that made strategic behavior by elites and voters difficult, if not impossible.[28] The lack of party identification meant that parties could not accurately estimate the level of support for themselves or their competitors, making strategic entry and exit difficult, and since voters did not know who was "out of the running," it was hard to defect from marginal candidates. This dynamic has a way of building on itself by changing expectations; if candidates and voters expect the vote to be distributed among a half dozen or more significant candidates, then any candidate who appeals to a significant minority in the district or has high name recognition has an incentive to enter the race. Voters also have less reason to defect from little-known candidates if the contest is fragmented enough to allow a candidate to win a seat with one-third of the popular vote or less.

While this explanation may account for the high number of parties in the electorate, it does not necessarily explain the relatively low level of disproportionality and the high number of parties that managed to win legislative seats. In fact, given the absence of strategic coordination, one might expect relatively high levels of disproportionality; minor parties should have been punished in the translation of votes into seats, and large parties should have been overrepresented. This was not necessarily the case in Russia. Some relatively large parties benefited from overrepresentation in the plurality tier while others were virtually denied representation in the SMD tier. A comparison of the Agrarian party and Zhirinovsky's LDPR is telling. The Agrarians benefited from the plurality tier, gaining 8 percent of the seats on 6 percent of the vote; However, the LDPR, which gained virtually the same vote share, was the only party to be seriously underrepresented, gaining less than 1 percent of the seats for its 6 percent of the vote (see Table 3.2). Moreover, rather than deterring the representation of small parties, the personalism endemic in the SMD elections allowed many small parties to choose one or two of their most prominent members. In chapter 7 I examine more fully how the PR and SMD tiers affected the electoral success of individual parties in very different ways.

The Cumulative Effect of Russia's Mixed System on the Number of Parties

What happened when these two different electoral systems were combined to elect the 450 members of the State Duma? Mixed electoral systems are designed to generate a moderate number of parties, as the PR tier compensates for the normally greater disproportionality of the SMD tier. But the dynamics of Russia's system produced much different results; when combined to elect the 450-member legislature, its two halves actually produced more fractionalization in the State Duma than would have occurred under a system strictly either PR or plurality (see Table 3.1). In 1993 this difference was quite stark. The effective number of legislative parties for the whole system (both tiers) was 8.16, which was substantially greater than the 6.40 effective number of legislative parties produced by the PR tier or the 6.13 effective number of legislative parties produced by the plurality tier. The difference between the system as a whole and the individual tiers was less significant, but still present, in 1995: 5.71 effective parties (both tiers), 3.32 (PR), and 5.00 (plurality).

How is it that the number of parliamentary factions produced by Russia's mixed electoral system was greater than either of its tiers taken separately? The answer lies in the system's institutional design and the differential success of parties in the two halves of the nation's election. Because Russia's mixed system was unlinked, the results of both tiers would be fully realized in the composition of the legislature, unlike the linked mixed systems in Germany or New Zealand, which prioritize the PR tier in the final distribution of seats in the legislature. This meant that each party could keep every seat it won in each tier.

The effects of an unlinked mixed system were exacerbated by the differential successes of parties in the two tiers. In 1995, except for the KPRF, no party enjoyed significant success in both tiers of the election. Thus, those parties that received substantial numbers of seats in the PR tier gained far fewer seats in the plurality elections. Other parties, such as the Agrarian, managed to survive in parliament on the basis of their successes in the plurality tier even though they failed to overcome the 5 percent threshold under PR. Moreover, independents from the plurality tier formed their own parliamentary factions rather than join a faction emerging out of the PR tier. Consequently, the parliamentary factions rising out of each looked very different from one another and when combined together in the same legislature created even greater fractionalization.

Russia in Comparative Perspective

How exceptional is the Russian experience? Several counterarguments could be made against highlighting the non-Duvergerian outcomes found in Russia's transitional elections. Perhaps the outcomes found in Russia are relics of its initial elections and tumultuous transition from Communism. This may be a temporary phenomenon that will evolve into a Duvergerian equilibrium over time as elites and voters adapt to institutional incentives. Furthermore, maybe cross-contamination between the two tiers of a mixed system produced the party proliferation found in Russia's plurality elections. The following section examines these arguments through a comparison of Russia's experience with PR and plurality electoral systems in other postcommunist states, with other new democracies, and with consolidated democracies that use mixed systems.

The Experience of Other Postcommunist States

Do other postcommunist states have similar encounters with electoral systems as Russia does? To answer this question, I will examine electoral systems in four postcommunist states. Two of these, Hungary and Lithuania, employ mixed systems of various combinations of PR and majoritarian elected seats. The two tiers will be analyzed individually as separate systems, following the controlled comparison method described above.[29] Two countries with single-tier electoral systems, Poland and Ukraine (Ukraine changed its electoral system to a mixed one after 1994.), will also be studied.[30] Table 3.3 gives a description of the systems analyzed in this section.

Table 3.4 shows the effects of PR and SMD systems in selected post-

Table 3.3: Electoral Systems in Five Postcommunist States

Country	Electoral system	PR tier	Plurality/ Majoritarian tier
Russia	Mixed	225 seats elected in one nationwide district with 5 percent legal threshold.	225 seats elected by plurality in SMDs.
Hungary	Mixed	152 seats elected in 20 multimember districts with 4 percent (1990) and 5 percent (1994) legal threshold. 58 compensatory seats elected in one nationwide district with same thresholds.	176 seats elected under two-round majoritarian rules in SMDs. Top three go to second round, as do any candidates with 15 percent or more of first-round vote.
Lithuania	Mixed	70 seats elected in one nationwide district with 4 percent (1992) and 5 percent (1996) legal threshold.	71 seats elected under two-round majoritarian rules in SMDs. Top two go to second round.
Poland	PR	391 seats elected in 37 multimember districts. 69 compensatory seats elected in one nationwide district. No legal threshold (1991), 5 percent (1993).	None
Ukraine	Majoritarian	None	450 seats elected under two-round majoritarian rules in SMDs. Top two go to second round.

Sources: Cox, *Making Votes Count,* 50–54; Bojcun, "The Ukrainian Parliamentary Elections"; "Polozhenie o vyborakh deputatov Gosudarstvennoy dumy v 1993 godu" (Provisions for elections of deputies of the State Duma in 1993), *Rossiiskie vesti,* October 12, 1993.

Table 3.4: Effects of PR and SMD Systems in Four Postcommunist States

Case	Effective number of parties in system (both tiers)	Effective number of parties in PR tier	Effective number of parties in SMD tier	Effective number of candidates in SMD tier	Least-squares index of disproportionality
Poland 1991	—	$N_v = 12.50$ $N_s = 10.87$	—	—	PR = 6.11
Poland 1993	—	$N_v = 9.80$ $N_s = 17.81$	—	—	PR = 17.81
Poland 1997	—	$N_v = 4.59$ $N_s = 2.95$	—	—	PR = 10.63
Lithuania 1996	$N_v = 7.87$ $N_s = 3.40$	$N_v = 7.94$ $N_s = 3.16$	$N_v = 7.75$ $N_s = 3.06$	5.59	System = 15.76 PR = 16.34 SMD = 20.37
Hungary 1990	$N_v = 7.00$ $N_s = 3.79$	$N_v = 6.71$ $N_s = 4.31$	$N_v = 7.14$ $N_s = 2.03$	5.97	System = 13.74 PR = 9.34 SMD = 31.88
Hungary 1994	$N_v = 5.75$ $N_s = 2.90$	$N_v = 5.49$ $N_s = 3.73$	$N_v = 6.17$ $N_s = 1.35$	5.64	System = 16.21 PR = 8.53 SMD = 40.89
Ukraine 1994	—	—	$N_v = 2.46$ $N_s = 4.15$	5.44	SMD = n/a

Sources: Poland: Frances Millard, "Poland," in *Political Parties of Eastern Europe, Russia and the Successor States,* ed. Bogdan Szajkowski (Essex: Longman Group, 1994): 313–42; Hungary: Kenneth Benoit, "Votes and Seats," *The 1990 Election to the Hungarian National Assembly: Analyses, Documents and Data* (Berlin: Edition Sigma, 1999). Dataset at http://data.fas.harvard.edu/staff/ken_benoit. Lithuania: Ole Norgaard, Lars Johannsen, and Anette Pedersen, "The Baltic Republics Estonia, Latvia and Lithuania: The Development of Multi-party Systems," in *Political Parties of Eastern Europe, Russia and the Successor States,* ed. Bogdan Szajkowski (Essex: Longman Group, 1994), 60; Lithuanian Seim, "Lietuvos Respublikos Seimo rinkimo '96." Dataset at http://rc.lrs.lt/rinkimai/seim96/, 1996.

Note: Due to the incongruence of the data for electoral and parliamentary parties a least-squares index of disproportionality for Ukraine was not computed.

communist states. The most striking characteristic of all the cases is the level of party fractionalization; while party proliferation is expected in PR elections, the number of significant parties operating in postcommunist states outstrips anything found in developed countries. The average effective number of elective parties for the cases studied here is 7.30, which is higher than in any consolidated democracy except Belgium and nearly twice the average for consolidated democracies using PR.[31] It is also higher than most new democracies, with the exception of Ecuador and Brazil, which each have an effective number of electoral parties of about ten.[32]

Clearly, the high number of parties in postcommunist states is due in part to fragmented and fluid cleavage structures. However, the high level of disproportionality produced by legal thresholds (which were used in every PR case but one) suggests an absence of strategic behavior in those cases with the highest level. The average level of disproportionality produced by seven PR systems was 10.90 (11.70 excluding Poland 1991, which had no legal threshold), more than twice that for PR systems in consolidated democracies and also higher than the average of majoritarian systems.[33]

According to Taagepera and Shugart's Law of Conservation of Disproportionality, the number of parties, and hence the level of disproportionality produced by a system, will be underestimated by the actual vote shares (as opposed to real voter preferences) because voters and elites make strategic decisions favoring larger parties before votes are translated into seats.[34] Thus, postcommunist parties and voters should have anticipated the disproportionality produced by the legal threshold imposed and gravitated toward larger parties capable of overcoming the threshold. Then there would have been fewer electoral parties, fewer votes would have been wasted on sure losers, and disproportionality would have been lower. As voters and elites learn the rules and adapt to the incentives of the system, this process should increase over time.

There is significant difference in the amount of learning that seemed to occur in these postcommunist cases. Poland offers the strongest evidence of adaptation to the incentives of a legal threshold and learning. It had the highest party proliferation among our cases in 1991, when there was no legal threshold, and it had very limited consolidation and very high disproportionality in 1993, when a 5 percent legal threshold was first introduced—suggesting an absence of strategic behavior. But in 1997 elites seemed to learn from the devastating effect the 5 percent legal threshold had on small parties in 1993 and consolidated into broad electoral blocs, cutting the effective number of electoral parties in half. As a consequence, the level of disproportionality dropped significantly, because there were fewer small parties subject to underrepresentation. A less dramatic decrease in the effective number of parties and disproportionality over time in Hungary also shows support for learning strategic behavior. Like Russia, however, Lithuania shows an opposite trend; in both countries the number of parties in the PR tier increased substantially from the first to the second election, exponentially raising disproportionality.

What accounts for this difference in learning of strategic behavior among our cases? Party fragmentation does not seem to be the culprit. Poland had the most fractionalized party system in its first election yet displayed the greatest amount of adaptation to electoral constraints over time. Hungary also has a relatively high degree of party fractionalization but low degrees of disproportionality. On the other hand, Lithuania had the lowest degree of party fragmentation in 1992 but almost doubled the number of significant electoral parties at the next election, despite an increase in the legal threshold from 4 to 5 percent.

I argue that the difference in learning is caused by the degree of party institutionalization. Hungary has the most stable party system in this sample; in its first two elections it was dominated by the same six major parties that consistently crossed the legal threshold and left little room for marginal parties. Poland's has been much more tumultuous; however, Tworzecki has argued that underneath its fluid surface, Polish society is split along several dominant divides and is evolving toward a cleavage structure (and ultimately a party system) that is similar to Western Europe's.[35]

The situation is different in countries of the former Soviet Union. With the exception of the Baltic republics, these countries had no significant experience with democratic governance or even independent statehood in the twentieth century. Politics is polarized, and political parties with identifiable social constituencies have been slower to emerge. In Russia the most developed parties have occupied the extreme ends of the political spectrum and have had a small minority of dedicated followers, leaving a broad and amorphous "center" that encompasses the majority of voters and is represented by a multitude of fluid, minor parties. To a lesser extent, the same is true of Lithuania, which saw the former Communist party return to power in 1992 with a majority of seats, only to be replaced by the Lithuanian Conservatives of the right at the next election, with minor parties of the center increasing over time. Under such conditions voters ignore the incentives to defect from marginal parties, because they have no clear preference for a major party representing either end of the political spectrum. Moreover, it is difficult to decide which parties are viable or "out of the running," as the largest group in most opinion polls are undecided.[36]

This is not to say that voters and elites in Soviet successor states will never respond to the incentives of legal thresholds; however, the likelihood of strategic behavior in these states is undermined by social conditions that retard the institutionalization of political parties. Thus, one may expect Lithuania to experience strategic behavior in response to electoral systems sooner than Russia or other former Soviet republics because there is a better environment for future party institutionalization there. This assessment is based on classifications of the potential for consolidation of party systems in postcommunist states. Kitschelt provides an index of the chances of program-based party formation for postcommunist states. Using Kitschelt's scale, Hungary and Poland have the highest scores at 5.5 and 5.0, respectively. The Baltic states are marginally lower at 3.5 to 5.0. Russia, Ukraine, and other Soviet republics have a much lower score of 0.5. Evans and Whitefield developed a similar classification of postcommunist states' potential for the development of stable party systems with East Central Europe (Poland, Hungary, and the Czech Republic) possessing the greatest potential for stable party development followed by the Baltic states with Russia, Ukraine, and other Soviet successor states having much lower chances for successful party development.[37]

The experience with SMD systems in other postcommunist states shows both similarities and differences with Russia. Like Russia, SMD elections in other postcommunist states did not produce the effective number of elective parties expected in the literature ($M + 1$, where M signifies the number of candidates winning election).[38] For Lithuania and Ukraine the expectation would be three significant candidates per district since the run-off is between the two top vote getters, an expectation neither comes close to approximating. Hungary allows into the second round the top three finishers plus any candidate with 15 percent of the vote. Thus, only in that country could the high number of candidates be attributed to a permissive electoral system. This is true especially because Hungary has a third national tier of compensatory seats that employs votes not used to win seats from both the SMD tier and the territorial PR tier. This provides even more incentive for party proliferation—a vote for a candidate with no chance of getting to the next round is still not wasted because it can be used for compensatory seats in the national tier.

But, unlike Russia, both Hungary and Lithuania experienced high levels of disproportionality and great reductions of the number of parties in the translation of votes into seats in their SMD tiers. In these cases the effective number of parliamentary parties was less than half the effective number of elective parties. Moreover, the level of disproportionality in SMD elections in Lithuania and Hungary was extremely high, with values equal to or higher than Russia's very disproportional PR election in 1995, in which half of the votes were wasted on parties that did not overcome the 5 percent legal threshold. Within each individual country comparisons further support the increased reductive force of SMD elections in these cases. In Lithuania and Hungary, the effective numbers of parliamentary parties were lower and the levels of disproportionality were higher in the SMD elections than in their corresponding PR tier, just as the literature would lead one to expect.

The Hungarian experience is particularly striking. Although that country's effective number of electoral parties was quite similar in the PR and majoritarian tiers in the 1990 and 1994 elections, the effective number of parliamentary parties produced in the SMDs was less than half of that in the PR tier. Indeed, the impressive victories of the Hungarian Democratic Forum (MDF) in 1990 and the Hungarian Socialist Party (MSZP) in 1994 were driven in large part by seats won in SMDs. The MDF won 67 percent of the 176 SMD seats on 24 percent of the first-round vote in 1990, whereas the MSZP won 86 percent of those seats on 31 percent of the first-round vote.[39]

Disproportionality in Ukraine was more like the Russian experience. The effective number of parties reaching parliament (4.15) show none of the dramatic mechanical effect found in the other cases. Moreover, this measure probably underestimates the amount of party fractionalization produced by Ukraine's two-round majoritarian system, because independents made up the largest "bloc" of representatives entering parliament (40 percent) and can hardly be considered a cohesive group—although they were treated as a single entity in computing the effective number of parliamentary parties measure.[40]

What distinguishes Ukraine and Russia from the other postcommunist states is the level of party institutionalization. As noted in chapter 2, in Russia and

Ukraine parties failed to control access to elected office. In Ukraine, 61 percent of the first-round vote in the 1994 election went to independent candidates.[41] This even exceeded the Russian experience, in which nonpartisan candidates gained 48 percent of the vote in 1993 and 36 percent in 1995. Lithuania and Hungary had very few independent candidates. Therefore, unlike Hungary and Lithuania, Russia and Ukraine did not have large parties that benefited from the disproportionality of SMD elections. Instead, SMDs produced a proliferation of nonpartisan candidates. Once in parliament, the mass of independent candidates did not act as a unified group but splintered further: some joined parties they eschewed during the campaign, others formed new parliamentary factions unrelated to electoral associations fielding candidates in the campaign, and others became atomized members of parliament without any consistent affiliation with a larger group. Consequently, once in parliament, deputies elected from SMDs in Russia and Ukraine dispersed themselves across a much larger number of parliamentary parties than in Hungary or Lithuania.

This comparison suggests that electoral systems in postcommunist states share some distinctive features found in Russia. In all such nations examined here, except Poland, electoral systems have not led to a significant level of strategic behavior by voters and elites. But, there are also some marked differences between East European and Baltic states, with more developed party systems, and Soviet successor states, with weakly institutionalized systems. In Hungary and Lithuania, party proliferation in SMDs led to extremely high levels of disproportionality, which constrained the number of parties entering parliament. In Russia and Ukraine, no such mechanical effect occurred.

The Experience of Other New Democracies

Is a lack of strategic coordination in SMDs peculiar to postcommunist states or common among initial elections in all new democracies? Perhaps the proliferation of electoral parties seen in postcommunist states is a normal condition of initial elections, which will subside as increased information and experience rewards viable parties and weeds out nonviable ones. If so, comparisons with other new democracies should show similar party proliferation in initial elections and contraction in the number of electoral parties over time. A historical comparison with older democracies that have had large numbers of competitive elections would be instructive. Two postwar democracies—(West) Germany, with its mixed electoral system employing both plurality elections and PR, and India, employing one of pure plurality—will be examined to shed some light on the degree of party proliferation in initial elections under plurality systems and each system's reductive properties over time.

Postwar Germany's early electoral history provides support for the idea that party proliferation may be a common phenomenon in initial elections but that over time reductive effects of the electoral system do take hold. Scholars have found evidence of strategic voting under plurality rules in the difference in vote totals for parties between the PR tier and the SMD tier. The two largest German parties, the Christian Democratic Union/Christian Social Union and the Social Democratic Union, generally have gained more votes in the SMDs than the PR race while smaller parties like the Free Democratic Party have lost votes suggesting that voters defect from small parties less likely to win in SMDs and gravitated toward parties with better chances for representation. While the discrepancy in the vote between the two tiers is not that significant, averaging a gain or loss of less than 2 percent for the three parties most affected (CDU/CSU, SPD, and FDP), it does a provide persuasive evidence of strategic voting under plurality rules even when the vote does not really influence the final distribution of seats among parties (because Germany's mixed system is linked and final seat distributions are decided exclusively by the PR tier).[42]

This was not always the case in Germany. The plurality tier did not produce a smaller number of electoral parties in the initial election held under the mixed system in 1953. In that election, the SMD tier produced more than three effective electoral parties (3.38), which was actually higher than the effective number of electoral parties in the corresponding PR tier that year (3.31). By the next election, the effective number of electoral parties produced in the SMDs had fallen to 2.75 and the SMD tier produced fewer effective electoral parties than the PR tier (2.78) as the literature would suggest.[43] This trend has grown over the years, reducing the chances for victory by marginal parties in the SMDs to virtually nothing and solidifying a two-party system in the SMD tier. Since 1961, when Germany's third election under the mixed system was held, no party other than the CDU/CSU or SPD has won an SMD seat. Thus, Germany provides a case of increased consolidation that began to take place in the second election. German voters and elites did not need much time to adjust to the incentives of the electoral system.

India provides an example of the opposite phenomenon—a persistent absence of strategic voting under a plurality system. Party proliferation has remained high in India despite the fact that this consistently produced very high disproportionality, severely penalizing marginal groups. As a consequence, until the late 1980s India experienced a dominant party system in which the Congress Party maintained a majority of seats on the basis of a minority of votes, whereas the opposition was fragmented. Unlike Germany, India shows no evidence of consolidation over time as a result of learning. In the latter country's first two elections, the effective number of electoral parties stood at 4.21 despite the fact that the high disproportionality of the plurality system narrowed that down to fewer than two effective parliamentary parties (1.79). Although one would expect voters and elites to adjust to the severe disincentives against small parties, the high level of party fractionalization did not subside over several decades of repeated democratic elections. In the six elections from 1962 to 1984, India actually experienced an increase in the average effective number of electoral parties (4.31) even though the electoral system's mechanical effect repeatedly reduced the number of effective parties entering parliament to two (2.27).[44]

By the end of the 1980s the mechanical effect of India's plurality electoral system even failed as the Congress Party lost power and the manufactured majorities Congress enjoyed for decades gave way to coalition governments. In 1996, thirty parties were represented in parliament with an effective number of parliamentary parties measure of 5.88. The 1998 parliamentary elections produced a similar outcome, with 5.29 effective parliamentary parties, strikingly similar to the fractionalization produced by Russia's SMD elections.[45]

The above calculations for Indian elections are taken from national-level data and are thus not a completely accurate test of Duverger's Law, which posits only that plurality elections produce bipartism at the district level. Indeed, at the district level Indian plurality elections produced two- to three-person contests for each seat, providing support for Duverger's Law in this country. The real source of India's multipartism is the lack of nationally competitive parties that can project the district-level bipartism produced by plurality elections to the national level.[46] Such a condition buttresses Sartori's claim that plurality elections do not produce two parties in unstructured party systems but do still have a district-level effect.[47] This is much different from the proliferation of candidates found at the district level in plurality elections in Russia.

These two examples show that party proliferation may occur in initial elections using a plurality system. Germany's situation illustrates a case of learning that produced strategic voting beginning in the second election, but the Indian experience shows that the passage of time and repeated elections alone are not

Table 3.5: Effective Number of Parties/Candidates and Disproportionality for Consolidated Democracies with Mixed Systems

Country/ Election	Effective number of parties for system (both tiers)	Effective number of parties for PR tier	Effective number of parties for SMD tier	Effective number of candidates for SMD tier	Least-squares disproportionality for system and each tier
Italy/1996	$N_v = 7.35$ $N_s = 6.02$	$N_v = 7.14$ $N_s = n/a$	$N_v = 7.35$ $N_s = 5.56$	2.43	System = 5.18 PR = n/a SMD = 8.13
New Zealand/ 1996	$N_v = 4.25$ $N_s = 3.76$	$N_v = 4.39$ $N_s = n/a$	$N_v = 4.10$ $N_s = 2.62$	3.29	System = 3.42 PR = n/a SMD = 13.19
Japan/1996	$N_v = 4.10$ $N_s = 2.93$	$N_v = 4.27$ $N_s = 3.83$	$N_v = 3.86$ $N_s = 2.36$	2.95	System = 10.80 PR = 3.19 SMD = 15.95

Sources: Italy: Elections website, http://www.pds.it/elez96/Dati 96. New Zealand: Elections website, http://www.election.govt.nz. Japan: *Seiji handobokku* (A Handbook of Politics), No. 33, (Tokyo: Seiji Koho Center, 1997).

sufficient conditions for plurality elections to promote a national two-party system if it is unstructured. While the Indian case suggests party proliferation in
plurality elections may be a phenomenon that can occur in many new democracies, this diversity exists at the national level rather than the district level and is
thus more accurately conceptualized as a problem of party nationalization. None
of the unconsolidated democracies studied here, except Ukraine, showed the
type of candidate proliferation at the district level displayed in Russia's plurality elections. This type of party fractionalization does not seem to be typical of
founding elections held under plurality rules.

Mixed Systems in Consolidated Democracies

Finally, it is also instructive to compare the Russian experience with those of
other mixed systems in consolidated democracies to determine the origins of
the non-Duvergerian outcome witnessed in Russia's SMD tier. Perhaps the existence of a PR tier influences behavior in the SMD tier undermining strategic
coordination. As noted in chapter 1, the mixed systems of Italy, New Zealand,
and Japan differ from Russia's in some important ways. The most important
difference is the linked system of compensatory seats that prioritizes the PR tier
over the plurality tier in Italy and New Zealand. This feature makes New
Zealand's one of the mixed systems weakest (along with Germany's) in constraining capability. Despite its use of compensatory seats, Italy's is a bit stronger because its plurality tier elects a much greater proportion of seats to the legislature than the PR tier, diluting the control of the PR tier despite its preferred
status. On the other hand, Japan's system is one of the strongest, because its
tiers are unlinked and its plurality tier elects more deputies than its PR tier.

Following the methodology of this book, the two tiers of the mixed systems
of these consolidated democracies are compared with one another to ascertain
the effect of PR and plurality elections in each country. Table 3.5 shows the
effective number of electoral and legislative parties and the level of disproportionality for each tier and the system as a whole for the three cases. The average
effective number of candidates per district in the plurality tier is also given. Several features of the relationship between electoral and party systems in these
consolidated democracies differentiate them from both Russia and other postcommunist states.

First, as a group these systems had lower levels of disproportionality, especially in their PR tiers. [48] Consequently, the average percentage of votes cast for
parties failing to gain representation in the PR tier for Italy, New Zealand, and
Japan was 6.4 percent, compared to 28.6 percent for the two elections in Russia
and 21.3 percent for the six PR elections in other postcommunist countries examined above.[49] Perhaps this means that the psychological effect of the legal
thresholds in these countries played a greater part in deterring smaller parties

from entering the PR race or deterring voters from casting their ballots in favor of marginal parties with little chance to gain representation.

Second, plurality elections in the mixed systems of Italy, Japan, and New Zealand constrained the number of candidates at the district level to a much greater extent than plurality elections in Russia or two-round majoritarian elections in Hungary, Lithuania, or Ukraine. This provides support for Duverger's Law at the district level in these countries, although the number of candidates per district was closer to three than two in New Zealand and Japan. This runs counter to the idea that contamination from the PR tier might undermine the constraining power of the SMD tier. In general, Duverger's Law holds up rather well among our three consolidated democracies. At the district level the effective number of candidates in the plurality tier in these countries was substantially lower than the effective number of parties in the PR tier, despite the centrifugal tendencies fostered by a PR tier operating simultaneously in these countries.

If there was any contamination from the PR tier, it occurred in the projection of the district-level results to the national level. While plurality elections did constrain the number of competitors to two or three at the district level, there was greater proliferation of electoral parties at the national level. This was found most significantly in Italy, where party proliferation in the plurality tier rivaled that in the PR tier but was present in the two other cases as well. Thus, there may be a contamination effect of the PR tier that encourages party proliferation at the national level in the SMD tier. The existence of a PR tier lowers the threshold of representation and sustains the viability of minor parties that would have little reason to exist in a pure SMD system. This exacerbates the problem of party aggregation, since those minor parties hoping to gain seats primarily in the PR tier also field plurality candidates and gain votes from core constituents. Therefore, one finds a greater effective number of electoral parties in the SMD tier than effective candidates in each district. Since the theory of electoral system effects is based at the district level, this contamination does not undermine the controlled comparison approach upon which this book is based.

Finally, while the existence of a PR tier encouraged greater party proliferation in the electoral arena (at the national level) only in Italy did this proliferation persist in the legislature. In New Zealand and Japan the mechanical effect of the SMD tier reduced the effective number of parties entering the legislature from this level by nearly half. The relatively high levels of disproportionality in the plurality tiers of these two countries demonstrate the mechanical effect of plurality elections wrought by a failure of party elites to aggregate into nationwide parties. But this was not the case in Italy, which provides an interesting alternative resolution to the collective action problem facing candidates from multiple parties in plurality elections. Rather than two large nationwide parties, plurality elections in Italy produced bipolar competition between two large electoral cartels of allied parties. To avoid splitting their common electoral constituencies, allied parties coordinated nomination efforts. But rather than cede complete autonomy to single hierarchical party organizations, parties retained their individual identities.[50] This produced a local bipolar effect that resulted in the smallest effective number of candidates per district in the study while producing the highest effective number of electoral and parliamentary parties and the lowest level of disproportionality. Given Italy's history of party fragmentation, such an arrangement may very well have emerged even in a pure plurality electoral system. But the existence of a linked arrangement of compensatory seats surely provided an additional incentive for a coalitional arrangement to coordinate nominations of separate parties as a substitute for the formation of large catch-all parties.

Conclusions

This chapter has sought to establish Russia as an exception to Duverger's Law. Russian voters and party elites have not heeded incentives encouraging strategic coordination provided by the PR tier's 5 percent legal threshold or the low district magnitude of the plurality tier. This may not be that surprising, given the novelty of democratic elections in Russia and the fluidity of Russia's nascent party system. Duverger's Law has always been more a tendency than an ironclad law, making for numerous exceptions even in consolidated democracies. However, the relationship between the number of parties and the electoral system in Russia bears some unique characteristics that differentiate Russia from other exceptions—these have important implications for party development in unconsolidated democracies.

Unlike India or Italy, which experience district-level bipartism not projected to the national level, Russia's plurality elections experienced multicandidate competition at the district level. Indeed, the average effective number of candidates per district (seven in 1995) could be classified as extreme fragmentation, rivaling the feeblest PR systems in the most heterogeneous societies. This is a characteristic shared by other postcommunist states; none of the SMD systems used in postcommunist Russia constrained the number of electoral parties to the extent anticipated by the literature.

This country is also distinguished by the level of disproportionality produced by its SMD elections and the number of parties gaining representation to parliament. Although there are numerous cases in which SMD elections produced multiple parties at the electoral stage, there are considerably fewer that allow a multiparty system to exist in parliament. Coordination failures usually produce high levels of disproportionality that reward large parties and punish small ones, constraining the effective number of parliamentary parties—despite the proliferation of electoral parties. Often the result is a dominant party system. In Russia, the proliferation of electoral candidates at the electoral stage was replicated in parliament in the SMD tier. This was not the case in other postcommunist states, like Hungary or Lithuania, where coordination failure in the SMD tier led to landslide victories for the largest party. The absence of a mechanical effect in Russia is likely to encourage future coordination failures, since small parties and independents are not punished for their lack of consolidation.

This was not the case in Russia's PR tier in 1995, where extreme party proliferation in the election led to great disproportionality in translating votes into seats and a large reduction of parties entering parliament. The strong mechanical effect of the 5 percent legal threshold could provide the necessary incentive for future party consolidation. As a consequence, given Russia's weakly institutionalized party system, the PR tier may provide a stronger constraint on the number of parties than the plurality tier. These outcomes were attributed to a lack of party institutionalization Russia and Ukraine—its closest counterpart in cross-national comparisons undertaken here—for example, were marked by weak and fluid party systems, in which political parties did not even control access to office in SMD elections. The proliferation of independent candidates produced fragmentation that defied both the psychological and mechanical effects of SMD elections found in most states.

These findings also have broad implications for the new institutionalism approach in political science. New institutionalism concentrates on the independent influence of institutions. Although acknowledging that political institutions themselves are created and thus dependent upon individual action or social context, both rational choice and historical institutionalists claim that, once established, institutions have an independent effect on behavior separate from and often contrary to their creators' intentions. The Russian case suggests that the effect of social context goes beyond the endogeneity problem; institutional effects of electoral systems are dependent on the social contexts in which they operate. The number of parties is an interactive effect of electoral systems and social cleavages, but this may not fully acknowledge the influence social context has on institutional effects. In Russia, the absence of an institutionalized party system dramatically changed the reductive effects of PR and plurality systems themselves.

4
Electoral Systems and Women's Representation in Russia

Representation takes several forms: Voters may feel represented by their elected officials if the latter proclaim similar policy preferences and ideological tendencies or if their representatives share their politically significant descriptive characteristics on the basis of race, ethnicity, gender, or religion. While these two forms of representation often overlap, they are distinct components of the concept of representation that enhance or hinder the symbolic legitimacy and concrete policy output of legislative bodies. Legislatures composed predominantly or exclusively of a dominant social group are deemed less representative by excluded groups. Such exclusion may lead to a number of detrimental reactions by disenfranchised groups, ranging from political apathy and disillusionment with the political system to popular mobilization for redressing grievances and even to demands for autonomy or secession. Moreover, a failure of the legislature to accurately reflect the social diversity of the population may result in the failure to address key issues that are particularly salient to excluded groups. For example, legislatures with greater proportions of women have been shown to enact more legislation friendly to children and families than legislatures more heavily dominated by men.[1] Arguably, a governing body made up exclusively of males of the dominant ethnic group will result not only in a less equitable polity but one that is also less effective and less concerned with the social welfare of the whole population.

The representation of women and minorities should be of particular concern in a period of regime transition like that of post-Soviet Russia. First, transitions are typically periods of greater popular mobilization. A failure to properly incorporate all groups of a polity may result in mobilization of excluded groups that may threaten the stability of an already fragile young regime. This is particularly true of multiethnic states like Russia, which may face demands of minority populations for autonomy or secession. Institutional mechanisms that enhance minority representation in national legislatures or increase minority autonomy through federative intergovernmental structures help central authorities deal with centripetal forces that may threaten the territorial integrity of the state.

If the population is demobilized, failure to properly represent all politically significant elements of society may not challenge the regime but will undermine democratic consolidation, freezing into place inequities and disenchantment that will be increasingly difficult to overcome.

Second, social transformations on the scale of Russia's transition away from state socialism produce massive social dislocation usually concentrated among the most disadvantaged elements of society, namely women, the elderly, and minorities. Indeed, Russia's economic transformation has been particularly hard on women, who make up more than 70 percent of the unemployed in Russia and have seen their relative earnings drop from 70 percent of men's wages during Soviet times to 40 percent in the postcommunist period.[2] With the collapse of the welfare state in post-Soviet Russia, women and other disadvantaged groups are in desperate need of state assistance and protection. The attraction of ascriptive representation lies in the assumption that legislators from a politically marginalized group are more likely to appreciate and address the grievances of that group.

The next two chapters will analyze the representation of women and non-Russian ethnic groups in the 1993 and 1995 parliamentary elections, concentrating on the effects of electoral systems on the proportion of women and minority representatives elected. As in previous chapters, Russia's system will be used as a laboratory to study the effects of PR and plurality electoral systems on women and minority representation, holding other socioeconomic and cultural factors constant.

Electoral Systems and Women's Representation

Much like the relationship between the number of parties and the electoral system, cross-national analyses have shown a consistent relationship between the type of electoral system and the proportion of women elected to the legislature. Countries employing proportional representation have averaged twice the share of women legislators as countries using SMD elections.[3] Cross-national multivariate analyses have shown the type of electoral system, specifically the difference between proportional representation and plurality elections, to be the single most important variable affecting women's legislative representation.[4] Moreover, since 1970 women's representation grew at a dramatically higher rate in countries with PR elections than in countries with SMD elections.[5]

Cross-national analyses showing the positive relationship between PR and higher rates of women's representation have been augmented by single-country studies in which both PR and SMD elections are used. In these cases a similar divergence was found in women's representation under different electoral systems. In Germany's mixed electoral system, more than twice as many women typically are elected from the PR tier than from the SMDs in the same election, and in Australia women are three times as likely to win seats in the upper house, which is elected in multimember districts under the alternative vote (AV) system, than the lower house, elected in SMDs.[6]

Although the evidence showing a significant role for electoral systems in women's representation in consolidated democracies is striking, Matland has found no similar relationship between PR and the election of women in less developed countries. He argues that there may be a minimum threshold of political development that needs to be surpassed before women can effectively organize and use institutions such as the electoral system to further their interests. Prior to reaching this threshold, factors that commonly affect women's representation in industrialized democracies do not have an effect in less developed nations.[7]

Postcommunist states present an interesting set of cases to test this relationship. Under Communist rule women achieved levels of literacy, education, and participation in the work force that rivaled or exceeded levels in the West. But since women reached this status under regimes that allowed virtually no independent political organization, they did not develop the level of organization that accompanied increased gender equality in the West nor did they experience the level of activity of women's groups during transitions from authoritarianism in developing countries of Latin America.[8] This combination of relatively low levels of political organization of women but high levels of literacy, education, and economic activity may interact in different and unexpected ways with institutional arrangements, rendering the relationship between women's representation and political institutions in postcommunist states different from consolidated democratic and other third-wave democracies. Of course, many social, economic, and cultural factors influence women's representation in legislatures, including the strength of the women's movement, cultural biases for or against female participation in politics, the nature of the party system, and the educational and social status of women.[9] An electoral system only structures the context in which candidates and voters operate; it cannot determine how individual actors handle the incentives and disincentives embedded in that context.

While the empirical relationship between PR and greater representation of women is well established, the reasons behind the relationship are less clear. A myriad of interrelated features of PR systems seems to be at the heart of its greater propensity to elect female legislators. Some scholars have argued that party list elections mute cultural biases against women by forcing voters to ally themselves with parties rather than individuals. The candidate-centered elections associated with SMD elections allow gender to be a much more influential factor in the voting decision, usually to the detriment of women's chances for election.[10] Other explanations have focused on district magnitude, arguing that just as multimember districts increase the number of parties by reducing the threshold necessary for gaining election, they also allow more women to be elected.[11] However, the empirical evidence on the relationship between district magnitude and women's representation is mixed.[12] Still other studies have focused on party behavior under proportional representation. By making candidate nominations a centralized leadership decision, parties are deemed more capable of responding to pressures for increased women's representation than they are by decentralized nomination procedures that may involve local resistance to such initiatives.[13] Moreover, parties under PR may run women to balance their tickets and thus appeal to a broader electorate, a phenomenon absent when a single candidate is the center of competition in any one district. Finally, high incumbency rates in SMD elections freeze gender inequalities in place, a problem that is more easily overcome in party-list PR systems, which experience greater turnover.[14]

Matland and Studlar have integrated these elements of PR elections into a contagion model to explain the higher representation of women in PR elections. They contend that increases are initiated by small parties committed to promoting women, which in turn are emulated by larger parties competing for similar constituencies, until the process reverberates along the whole ideological spectrum. Such a pattern is not exclusive to PR systems but is, however, more extensive and spread more quickly under PR for several reasons. First, the multiple parties often produced under these systems provide greater opportunities for the emergence of parties committed to women's issues. These are often small and thus might be shut out of two-candidate competition produced by plurality elections. Second, centralized control over nominations makes it easier for parties under PR systems to react to stimuli for increasing women's representation. Finally, electoral threats from parties promoting women are more serious in PR elections because of lower disproportionality between votes and seats. In SMDs, the priority is finishing first, so as to capture the seat; the margin of victory does not matter. Thus, in safe districts even substantial defections toward a third-party female candidate do not necessarily challenge the major parties. In PR systems with large district magnitudes, even small shifts in vote distribution may take away seats from major parties.[15]

Women and Political Power in the Soviet Period

Quotas kept the official representation of women in Soviet political organs relatively high. Women made up 33 percent of the Supreme Soviet in 1984. However, genuine political power rested with the Communist Party, and men occupied the vast majority of top decision-making posts. Women made up less than 30 percent of Communist Party members and only 4 percent of the Central Committee in 1988.[16] With the introduction of competitive elections, women were quickly excluded from significant representation in the new democratic organs of power. Women's representation in the Soviet Congress of People's Deputies elected in 1989 dropped to 16 percent, and even this figure inflated the level of women's representation that would occur under fully competitive elections. The 1989 election reserved one-third of the deputies for public organizations, which sustained the quota mentality of Soviet times. One organization, the Soviet Women's Committee, was granted seventy-five seats, all to be filled by women. This accounted for 21 percent of the women elected to the Soviet Congress of People's Deputies.[17]

In 1990, seats to all but two republican legislatures in the Soviet Union were subject to competitive elections in territorial districts with no seats reserved to the Communist Party or other social organizations. Elections to the Russian Congress of People's Deputies were two-round majoritarian contests held in SMDs. Subject to unfettered electoral competition in SMDs, women's representation dropped dramatically across the Soviet Union. In the Russian and Moldovan elections, a dismal 5 percent of deputies were women, whereas, in Kazakstan made up only 7 percent of the legislature.[18]

This dramatic drop in women's representation during democratization in the Soviet period has been attributed largely to cultural factors; biases and stereotypes placed great constraints on women who were expected to shoulder the double burden of a profession and daily domestic responsibilities. Public service was deemed inappropriate for women, who were seen as not having the time to serve in the legislature.[19] Survey research confirmed a bias against female candidates; a 1990 survey of Moscow voters, for example, showed that only a slight majority of voters (54 percent) claimed that gender was not important in their voting decision and that those who did factor in gender overwhelmingly preferred a male to a female candidate.[20]

Such cultural biases were reinforced by a disadvantageous social status created by decades of token promotion of women without corresponding political or economic power. Once competitive elections were introduced in 1990, women were in a poor position to contest for power. Tainted by the discredited practice of Soviet quotas, most female elites were also closely tied to organizations controlled by the declining Communist Party of the Soviet Union.[21] Lacking financial and organizational resources, they comprised a very small minority of candidates in the Russian SMD elections of 1990 (less than 8 percent) and an even smaller number of winners.

Women's Representation in 1993

The 1993 election represented a breakthrough for women's representation. Under Russia's new mixed electoral system, women's representation shot up to over 13 percent, from 5 percent in the old Russian Congress of People's Deputies, an increase clearly fueled by the PR tier of the new electoral system and more specifically by the Women of Russia bloc. Women of Russia's twenty-one deputies made up 35.6 percent of the women in the State Duma. Moreover, Women of Russia was clearly oriented toward the PR election. The group ran candidates in only seven SMDs, winning two of them. This outcome suggests that Russia was another example of how a PR electoral system promotes women's representation. However, the success of Women of Russia in 1993 masks other features of women's representation that run counter to the conventional wisdom that PR is more favorable to women's representation than are SMD elections. These features became much more evident in 1995, when Women of Russia failed to overcome the 5 percent legal threshold.

Table 4.1 shows the number of male and female candidates for all electoral blocs in 1993. In terms of nominations, in Russia PR appears more supportive of women than do plurality elections; parties from across the political spectrum ran more female candidates on their PR lists than in SMDs. Even if one eliminates the Women of Russia bloc, there were still more women nominated in the PR half of the 1993 election (128) than in the SMD tier (116). However, measured as a proportion of candidates nominated, the level of female nominations was much closer between the two tiers, because Russian parties generally nominated a lower number of candidates in SMDs.

When considering the proportion of women winning legislative seats, the picture becomes more ambiguous. The PR tier did elect more women to the State Duma than to the plurality tier but only on the strength of the Women of Russia

Table 4.1: Number of Women and Men Candidates Nominated and Elected in 1993

Party	Number of men elected	Number of women elected	Number of women nominated in PR tier	Number of women elected in PR tier	Number of women nominated in SMD tier	Number of women elected in SMD tier
Russia's Choice	60	4	17	2	10	2
KPRF	35	7	16	3	5	4
LDPR	59	5	9	5	4	0
Yabloko	25	3	23	2	8	1
Women of Russia	0	23	36	21	7	2
PRES	22	0	6	0	2	0
Agrarian Party	36	2	7	0	5	2
DPR	14	1	11	1	4	0
RDDR	5	0	13	0	6	0
Civic Union	7	0	6	0	1	0
KEDR	0	0	9	0	6	0
Future of Russia—New Names	1	0	7	0	1	0
Dignity and Charity	3	0	4	0	0	0
Independents	123	15	n/a	n/a	57	15
Total	390	60	164	34	116	26

bloc. If one removes that faction from the calculation, it appears that more women were actually elected in the SMDs than under PR. Of course, such a comparison is unfair—one of the main reasons PR is more conducive to women's representation is precisely that it encourages smaller parties, like the Women of Russia, to contest elections. But excluding the Women of Russia bloc does highlight the fact that PR did not necessarily promote women's representation in all Russian parties. Of the eight blocs that overcame the 5 percent threshold in the PR election, three (Women of Russia, LDPR, and DPR) elected more women deputies in the PR tier than in the SMD tier; two (KPRF and the Agrarian Party) elected more women in the SMD tier than under PR; one (Russia's Choice) elected an equal number of women from both; and one (PRES) elected no women at all.

This ambiguous relationship between electoral tier and parties' female contingents to the legislature is particularly striking given the fact that parties ran more women in the PR tier than in the SMD tier by a factor of nearly three to one. If one measures performance as the proportion of women nominated who won election, female candidates performed much better in the SMDs than in the PR contest. Women running in SMDs won 23 percent of the time, whereas women running in the PR race won 19.5 percent. Not counting the Women of Russia, women only won 10.2 percent of the time in the PR tier.

This higher success rate for SMD candidates can be seen in the female SMD candidates running for certain parties. Of the five women nominated by the Communist Party in the SMD tier, four won election; and two out of the five female candidates from the Agrarian Party won. None of the APR's seven female PR candidates made it into the State Duma. The only party with comparable success rates in the PR tier (other than the Women of Russia) was the LDPR, which elected five of the nine women on its party list. If nothing else, this shows that while more women were nominated in the PR tier, they often occupied lower positions on the PR lists, virtually destining them to lose. A comparison of ranking on the party lists shows that the average position for women was sixty-sixth. When Women of Russia (which nominated only women) is removed from the analysis, the average position falls to seventy-ninth. This low ranking was devastating to women's chances for election, since the party electing the most candidates to the State Duma from the PR race, Zhirinovsky's LDPR, sent only fifty-nine deputies from its list. Just 30 percent of the women nominated on party lists occupied a position of thirty or higher, which could be considered the cut-off of "electability" on a party list—given that parties sent an average of twenty-eight candidates from their PR party lists and only the top three PR blocs (LDPR, Russia's Choice, and KPRF) elected more than thirty deputies from the PR tier. When Women of Russia is excluded from the analysis, the percentage of women on a party list with a position of thirty or higher drops to 15 percent.

Thus, while the success of Women of Russia in the PR election fueled a great expansion of women's representation in 1993, the PR system did not consistently favor female candidates in other parties. Though more women were nominated in the PR tier than in the SMDs, these candidates often were toward the bottom of the party lists, where election was remote at best. Conversely, women showed surprising strength in the plurality elections in 1993, winning 12 percent of the seats, more than double the percentage won in the 1990 majoritarian election to the Russian Congress of People's Deputies.

Women's Representation in 1995

The breakthrough for women's representation in 1993 fueled by Women of Russia's surprising success should have produced a contagion effect at the 1995 next election, as parties adapted their electoral strategies. Contagion theory suggests that parties would emulate Women of Russia by nominating a greater proportion of women and that this adaptation should occur in the PR tier to a greater degree than in the SMDs.

Table 4.2 shows the number of female and male candidates and deputies for twelve major parties in the 1995 election. This proportion increased in both the

Table 4.2: Number of Women and Men Nominated and Elected in 1995

Party	Number of men elected	Number of women elected	Number of women nominated in PR tier	Number of women elected in PR tier	Number of women nominated in SMD tier	Number of women elected in SMD tier
KPRF	140	17	28	9	14	8
Our Home is Russia	50	5	33	3	21	2
Yabloko	39	6	24	2	9	4
LDPR	50	1	17	1	9	0
APR	20	0	19	0	10	0
Power to the People	7	2	55	0	9	2
Democratic Russia's Choice	9	0	23	0	11	0
Women of Russia	0	3	61	0	18	3
Forward, Russia!	3	0	16	0	10	0
PSG	1	0	23	0	2	0
KRO	5	0	16	0	5	0
C-WR-FSU	1	0	27	0	3	0
Others	12	2	n/a	0	74	2
Independents	67	10	n/a	n/a	90	10
Total	404	46	265	15	285	31

PR and SMD tiers; while in 1993 women comprised 9.4 percent of PR candidates, 11.3 percent made it onto party lists of twelve major parties in 1995. However, the proportion of female candidates in the SMDs rose even more dramatically—from 7.3 percent in 1993 to 11.1 percent in 1995. There was also other evidence of increased opportunities for representation of women. A party was more likely to place women as one of its top three candidates, a coveted position—since the top three candidates' names appear on the PR ballot beside the name of each party. While only three parties had women in this position in 1993, six of the twelve major parties in 1995 did so. Moreover, in 1995 all twelve major parties except the Agrarian Party included a woman on the "national" list, which comprised the first twelve candidates. Only eight of thirteen parties in 1993 included a woman in the top twelve positions of their party lists.

However, these advances in the status of women were more symbolic than substantive; those women who broke into the top echelons of lists were usually alone in their achievements. Of the eleven parties that placed women in one of the top twelve positions of their national lists, only Women of Russia, Our Home is Russia, and Yabloko placed more than one woman, and none of the twelve major parties except for Women of Russia placed more than two. As one moves down most party lists, it becomes evident that women comprised close to the same proportion of candidates in 1995 as they did in 1993 and remained excluded from regional list positions most likely to gain election. Power to the People was the only party other than Women of Russia that appeared to systematically nominate significant numbers of women, over 20 percent of its party list. The Communist Party and Yabloko, which nominated the most women in 1993, did not increase this number in 1995.[22]

The 1995 strategy of most parties was strategic placement of a very small number of women in the upper echelons of the party lists. This token representation was intended to capture women's support and cut into the vote for Women of Russia without significantly altering the general balance of male/female representation.[23] Such tactics are not uncommon in PR systems and suggest that open-list PR elections that allow voters rather than parties to decide the rank ordering of candidates may be more conducive to women's representation in Russia, as it is elsewhere, by allowing voters to counteract low placement of women on the PR list by the party hierarchy.[24]

Given that it was only perfunctory representation, the nominal increase of women on party lists did not translate into an appreciable rise in the proportion of women elected by parties in the PR tier of the 1995 election. The LDPR chose only one woman from its PR list, as opposed to five in 1993. Yabloko elected just two women—the same number as in 1993. Our Home is Russia elected only three, despite nominating thirty-three on its party list. This was only a small improvement over the pro-government party in 1993, Russia's Choice, which elected just two women.

The only exception to this trend was the Communist Party, which showed a dramatic increase from three women elected in 1993 to nine in 1995. Much of this may be attributed to the improved showing of the KPRF in the PR tier, which allowed candidates much further down on its party list to gain election. A similar phenomenon occurred in 1993, when, out of its fifty-nine PR mandates, the LDPR sent five women to the State Duma, despite having one of the lowest proportions of women on its PR list. Had the KPRF been able to send the same number of candidates from its PR list in 1993 as it was to in 1995, fourteen women would have been elected by the Communists in the 1993 PR election, 87.5 percent of the total women nominated on the list.

Women continued to perform relatively well as individual candidates in SMDs in 1995. Among partisan candidates, female nominees did as well as or better than their counterparts in the PR tier. The Communist Party elected eight women in the SMDs, just one less than their PR total. Yabloko elected four women in SMDs, as opposed to two on their PR lists. Our Home is Russia and LDPR matched their poor performances in the PR tier by electing even fewer women in the SMDs. As in 1993, women had a greater chance at victory in the SMDs, as measured by the percentage of nominees winning office. Women nominated by the Communist Party won more than half of the seats they contested in the SMDs, whereas Yabloko's female candidates won over 40 percent of the districts they challenged. The greater degree of partisanship in 1995 meant that a smaller number of women won as independents, and the much greater number of female candidates in the SMDs meant a dramatic drop in the performance of female independents.

In general, contrary to comparative experience, SMD elections were friendlier to women candidates than PR ones by a margin of more than two to one in 1995. Women's representation in the PR tier dropped from 15.1 percent in 1993 to 6.7 percent in 1995 while women's representation in the SMD tier rose from 11.6 percent to 13.8 percent. As Table 4.2 shows, in the absence of a women's party, female nominees of political parties running in SMDs consistently matched or outperformed women running on PR party lists.

Russia in Comparative Perspective

Is this relationship between electoral systems and women's representation unique to Russia or common among postcommunist states? Do women gain greater representation in the PR tier of mixed electoral systems in other states, or is the correlation between PR and increased women's representation somehow lost in these countries? To answer these questions, I have compared the proportion of women elected in the PR and SMD tiers of mixed systems in nine countries. The electoral system is deemed to have an effect on women's representation independent of other possible factors (which are held constant), if there is a statistically significant difference in the proportion of women elected in the two tiers. The set of cases include four postcommunist states (Russia, Hungary, Lithuania, and Ukraine), four advanced industrial democracies (Germany, Italy, New Zealand, and Japan), and one developing democracy in Latin America (Venezuela). Each of these states employed a mixed electoral system, in which voters cast two votes simultaneously—one for a party in a PR party-list race and one for a candidate in a SMD race. All elections in which there was sufficient information were included as separate cases; therefore, there are two cases for Russia (1993 and 1995) and Hungary (1990 and 1994).[25]

Table 4.3 shows the percentage of women and men elected in PR and SMD tiers for each country and chi-square tests for a relationship between gender (0 = woman, 1 = man) and electoral system (0 = SMD, 1 = PR).[26] In every case but one (Russia 1995), a greater percentage of women was elected in the PR tier than in the SMD tier. However, there was a stark difference in the effect of electoral systems on women's representation in consolidated and unconsolidated democracies. The difference between the two tiers in consolidated democracies was statistically and substantively significant in all cases. More than twice as many women were elected in PR tiers than in SMD tiers in consolidated democracies, while the difference between the two was not nearly as substantial for the other cases.

Chi-square tests revealed that in all the consolidated democracies one could reject the null hypothesis that the electoral system was unrelated to women's representation, whereas this null hypothesis could be rejected in only one case among postcommunist states, Hungary. Venezuela also showed no such systematic relationship.

Russia does appear to be an exception among all the cases examined here. While most postcommunist states showed no statistically significant relationship between electoral system and women's representation, only Russia's 1995 election produced a statistically significant *negative* relationship between PR and the proportion of women elected to parliament. The phenomenon of SMD elections producing higher levels of women's representation appears to be unique to the Russian experience. Yet these findings suggest that the dynamic generally works very differently in postcommunist states than it does in industrial democracies.

Further evidence is provided for a strong connection between PR and increased women's representation in advanced industrial democracies, corroborating findings from other cross-national studies. This is all the more striking because initial elections under a newly adopted mixed system were examined for three of the four consolidated democracies analyzed here (Italy, New Zealand, and Japan). The impact of PR elections on women's representation was felt immediately. There was no delay as elites and voters adapted to the system. Moreover, there were no differential effects of PR in more patrimonial cultures. Japan, which has the lowest proportion of women in the legislature of all nine

Table 4.3: Women's Representation
in Nine Countries with Mixed Systems

Country/Year	Total percent of women elected	Percent of women elected in PR tier	Percent of women elected in SMD tier	Difference between PR and SMD tiers (percent change)	Chi-square	Phi
Postcommunist States						
Russia/1993	13.7	15.1	11.6	+3.5 (30.2)	1.150	.0506
Russia/1995	10.1	6.7	13.8	-7.1 (106.0)	6.199	-1173**
Hungary/1990	7.3	10.5	3.4	+7.1 (208.8)	6.963	.1343**
Hungary/1994	11.10	13.3	8.5	+4.8 (56.5)	2.239	.0762*
Lithuania/1996	17.52	20.0	14.9	+5.1 (34.2)	0.610	.0667
Ukraine/1998	7.55	8.7	6.3	+2.4 (38.1)	0.931	.0468
Industrial Democracies						
Germany/1990	19.94	28.10	11.78	+16.3 (138.1)	26.386	.1997***
New Zealand/1996	30.00	47.27	15.38	+31.9 (207.1)	14.426	.3467***
Italy/1996	11.45	18.71	9.05	+9.6 (105.5)	9.126	.1205***
Japan/1996	4.80	8.50	2.33	+6.2 (269.6)	9.871	.1408***
Less Developed Countries						
Venezuela/1993	6.06	7.29	4.90	+2.39 (48.8)	0.496	.0501

Sources: Russia: *Federal'noe Sobranie* (Moscow: Panorama, 1994) and *Federal'noe Sobranie: Sovet Federatsii, Gosudarstvennaya Duma Spravochnik* (Moscow: Panorama, 1996). Hungary: Montgomery and Burnette, "Explaining the Puzzle of Women's Representation in the Hungarian National Assembly," Table 5. Lithuania: Parliamentary website, http://rclrs.lt. Germany: Eva Kolinsky, "Party Change and Women's Representation in Unified Germany," in *Gender and Party Politics* ed. Joni Lovenduski and Pippa Norris (London: Sage Publications, 1993), 113–146. New Zealand: Parliamentary website, www.parliament.govt.nz. Italy: Elections website, http://www.camera.it. Japan: Parliamentary website, http://www.shugiin.go.jp. Venezuela: "Directory of deputies," Servicio Autonomo de Informacion Legislativa (SAIL) Congreso de la Republica de Venezuela.

* p = .1, ** p = .01, *** p = .001

cases examined here, experienced a strong boost in women's representation in its PR tier vis-à-vis its SMD races.

But this effect is not shared in most postcommunist states. Of course, these are only tentative results, given the small number of cases examined. Perhaps over time the relationship between electoral systems and women's representation in postcommunist states will approach the consistent pattern found in consolidated democracies. However, the evidence from the transitional elections studied here suggests that women in postcommunist states and other less developed states should not necessarily expect to gain higher rates of representation under PR, at least in the initial stages of democratization.

Explaining Women's Representation in Russia

What can account for the negative correlation between PR and women's representation in Russia? Following Matland, one may conclude that, like less developed democracies in the Third World, postcommunist states have not achieved a level of political and socioeconomic development that has allowed women to organize to take advantage of institutional opportunities.[27] This would only partially coincide with the evidence presented here. Venezuela shares the distinction of having no statistically significant relationship between its PR tier and increased women's representation. But Hungary follows the trend of Western democracies, providing at least one exception to this dichotomy between consolidated and third-wave democracies.

Certain patterns in women's representation under PR and SMD systems in Russia and other postcommunist states suggest that these governments are unique in the type of political underdevelopment that retards a positive effect between PR and women's representation. Postcommunist states, Russia in particular, are unique; the absence of a positive relationship between PR and women's representation is as much due to the relative success of women in SMDs as it is due to relatively low levels of women's representation under PR. If one compares the average percentage of women elected in PR and SMD tiers in postcommunist states and in advanced industrial democracies, one finds that women in the former states do marginally better in SMD elections than do their counterparts in the West (9.75 percent versus 9.64 percent) but significantly worse in PR elections (12.38 percent versus 25.65 percent).[28] Thus, the paradox of electoral systems and women's representation in postcommunist states is dual in nature. Why have women in postcommunist states achieved representation that is relatively low in PR elections but relatively high in SMD races? I offer three possible explanations for this relationship.

First, the intervening effect of individual political parties may account for the proportion of women elected in PR and SMD tiers. If parties more favorable to women have greater success in SMD elections, this may account for the higher level of success for women in this tier. Second, party fragmentation may lower the proportion of women elected under PR and increase the proportion of them elected in SMDs. Distributing the vote among many competitors in PR elections may have hindered female representation by reducing party magnitude; if a high number of parties are elected under PR but each party only elects a small number of candidates from its list, then women's representation is undermined.[29] However, this same party fractionalization in SMD races may have lowered the effective threshold for representation, offering more opportunities for women. Finally, party leaders may consciously or unconsciously discriminate against women in Russia. Given that PR consolidates nomination decisions in the party leadership, this bias is particularly damaging in the PR tier. Conversely, parties lack control over access to elected office in the SMD tier, thus lifting this elite barrier on female nominations. Ambitious women can more easily run in SMDs by either cracking a party's local hierarchy or running as independents. The relatively high socioeconomic status of women in Russia and other postcommunist states, once they are nominated, may account for their greater success in SMD elections. Legacies of Communist policies may have produced a critical mass of well-educated, politically active women who are more competitive in the local milieu of SMD elections than on the national stage at which competition for the choice spots on PR party lists takes place.

The Impact of Individual Parties

Perhaps lower women's representation in PR elections in Russia is due to the intervening effect of individual political parties. Cross-national research has suggested that socialist and social democratic parties often elect more women, whereas the existence of strong right-wing parties usually is negatively correlated with the proportion of women elected to parliament.[30] If certain parties nominate more women than others, then differences in gender representation between PR and SMD tiers of a mixed system may be due to the relative success of these parties in a particular tier. The use of compensatory seats in linked mixed systems exacerbates the potential intervening effect of individual parties.

Montgomery and Burnette make this argument for Hungary, whose 1990 election is the only postcommunist case examined here that showed a strong positive relationship between PR and the election of women. However, by 1994 this influence diminished; although it remained positively correlated with the election of women, the effect of the PR tier was not statistically significant (p = .135). Montgomery and Burnette argue that this was due to the increased success of the Hungarian Socialist Workers' Party (MSZP) in the SMD tier, which accounted for each of the fifteen female representatives elected.[31] Since the votes won by the MSZP in the SMD tier were subtracted from its pool of votes in the tertiary PR tier, it did not receive nearly as many seats in the PR tier as it would have otherwise.[32] Therefore, more women were elected in the SMD tier vis-à-vis the PR tier in Hungary because of a change in the electoral fortunes of particular parties under each system, rather than a shift in the general relationship between electoral systems and women's representation. This thesis was bolstered by the fact that the populist Democratic Forum (MDF), which elected low numbers of women, experienced the exact opposite pattern of success in the PR and SMD tiers (SMD success and fewer PR mandates in 1990 and SMD failure and more PR mandates in 1994).

This argument does not work well in Russia, where, in fact, the opposite seems true. If one controls for the effects of party success, the positive relationship between the SMD system and women's representation is bolstered in Russia. Logistic regression was used to test the relative importance of the electoral system and party affiliation in Russia. The dependent variable was the gender of the representative (0 = male, 1 = female), and the independent variables were the electoral system (0 = SMD, 1 = PR) and dummy variables for all significant parties (parties that won five seats or more).[33] Logistic regression was run on the two Russian elections and those in the four other postcommunist cases studied here. Controlling for party with logistic regression made a meaningful difference in the behavior of the electoral system variable in only one case—Russia in 1993. In the other cases, where the electoral system was not statistically significant in explaining gender representation, it continued to lack statistical significance.[34] In Russia's 1995 election, the electoral system continued to be negatively correlated with women's representation (that is, women were more likely to be elected in the SMD rather than the PR tier) even when one controls for party.

Table 4.4 shows the results of the logistic regression analysis for the 1993 Russian election. After controlling for the impact of political parties, the electoral system variable became statistically significant and negatively correlated with the election of women. The logistic regression model was statistically significant at the $p < .001$ level and correctly predicted 92 percent of the observations. Perhaps more telling, the model correctly predicted 38 percent of the women elected—which was by far better than the null hypothesis that would predict all representatives to be male. This negative relationship between PR and women's representation matches the one found in Russia's second election in 1995, when, upon the failure of Women of Russia to overcome the 5 percent legal threshold in the PR tier, a substantially greater proportion of women were elected from the SMD tier of the system. The logistic regression analysis suggests that the same general tendency existed in 1993 but was masked by the success of Women of Russia in the PR tier.

Put another way, in 1993 the PR contribution to women's representation in Russia was the emergence of a women's party, not the general promotion of women on all party lists. When this party failed to overcome the legal threshold in 1995, PR no longer promoted female representation as well as SMD elections. This further supports the exceptional nature of the Russian case. Unlike in each other situation, women are elected in greater numbers in SMD than PR elections in Russia, unless there is a successful women's party.

Party Fragmentation and Women's Representation

The 5 percent threshold in the PR tier can be seen as the main culprit in denying women representation in the form of their own party. However, two developments remain to be explained: the relatively low number of women elected under PR from other parties and the relative success of Russian women in SMDs. Both of these developments are rooted in the fragmentation and weakness of

Table 4.4: Logistic Regression of Electoral System and Party Affiliation on Gender of Elected Representative in 1993 Russian Election

Variable	B	(standard error)	Odds ratio
Electoral System	-.9670**	(.4998)	.3802
APR	-.1452	(1.158)	.8648
DPR	.4596	(1.158)	1.583
KPRF	1.247**	(.5870)	3.479
LDPR	.6164	(.6873)	1.852
PRES	-6.246	(21.01)	.0019
RC	-.0031	(.6209)	.9969
WR	12.33	(20.71)	227227.00
YAB	.7576	(.7373)	2.133
Constant	-2.226	(.2718)	—

Notes: N = 450; -2 Log likelihood = 239.971; Goodness of fit = 404.891; Model Chi-Square = 113.436, Significance = .0000; Percent correctly predicted 91.78

** p = .05

Russia's nascent party structure and the distribution of resources necessary for electoral success in the different tiers of Russia's mixed electoral system.

As emphasized throughout this book, Russia's party system is chronically weak and fragmented. Literally dozens of small blocs competed in the 1995 election, most of which had no chance of winning the 5 percent of the vote necessary to gain seats in the PR half. In the SMDs a similar situation developed; rather than having two major parties emerge, as found in most democracies with SMD elections, Russia saw a proliferation of candidates contesting each district, most of whom ran as independents. This fragmentation had a dual effect on women's representation—potentially undermining women's representation in the PR tier and promoting women's representation in the SMDs.

Party fragmentation may have hurt women's representation in at least two significant ways in the 1995 PR election. First, the dozens of parties entering the PR contest fragmented the vote to a much greater extent than in 1993, keeping smaller parties like Women of Russia from overcoming the 5 percent threshold. In 1993, Women of Russia benefited from being one of only thirteen parties, occupying a key centrist ideological position and offering a unique appeal to an underrepresented but large voting constituency. When the number of parties more than tripled in 1995, Women of Russia faced greater competition. Though no other women's party directly competed with Women of Russia, other blocs headed by popular, well-known women may have siphoned off votes that went to Women of Russia in 1993. Ella Pamfilova and Irina Khakamada, both well-known members of the State Duma, headed electoral blocs of their own and in 1995 won election in SMDs.

Moreover, several other major parties included women among the three top positions on their lists. These parties ranged across the ideological spectrum, from reformists (Democratic Russia's Choice, Yabloko, and Forward, Russia!) to leftists (Communist Party and Power to the People).[35] As mentioned above, almost all of the major parties included women among the top twelve spots on their national lists. With the explosion in the number of electoral blocs appearing on the ballot in 1995 and the increased prominence of women on all party lists, voters backing blocs promoting women conceivably had many more options than they had had in 1993.

While this marked a symbolic advance for women, it may have contributed to a dispersion of Women of Russia's core constituency and to its failure to overcome the 5 percent barrier. The high-ranking women on other lists were often token females among a sea of males. The higher visibility of women among top spots on party lists did not translate into an increase in the general proportion of women candidates nor into generally better positions on party lists. Thus, when Women of Russia failed to reach the 5 percent threshold, women's representation plummeted. Fueled by a single women's party in 1993, women's PR representation would be severely undermined when that same party could not sustain enough of its following to gain any seats in the PR tier. The other female-led electoral blocs would serve only to siphon off votes from Women of Russia yet not significantly contribute any female representatives of their own in the PR tier, as most were victims of the legal threshold as well.

Besides undermining Women of Russia's electoral strength, party fragmentation also damaged women's representation by dispersing well-known elites across several different parties. While one cannot speak of a shortage of well-qualified female candidates, there is surely a limited number of women with the name recognition, professional experience, and political clout to command a high spot on a major party's list. Fragmentation of the female elite meant a dilution of women's influence within major parties. Some women who could have commanded a relatively high place on a major party list opted instead to lead their own bloc. For example, Ella Pamfilova was third on Russia's Choice's list in 1993 but chose to lead her own bloc, which failed to gain election in 1995. Irina Khakamada decided not to join Yabloko when she was not offered the number three spot on the list and likewise led her own bloc.[36] By not concentrating on a few major parties with good chances of overcoming the 5 percent barrier, some major female candidates may have given up electable positions on winning parties, which ultimately were filled by men.

Fragmentation potentially had the opposite effect in the SMD races. A primary obstacle to women's representation in SMDs is the high electoral threshold necessary for victory, usually a majority or near majority. The two major parties that usually dominate such elections take a risk in nominating any type of candidate that diverges from the accepted stereotype of a "typical" representative who is usually deemed male and of the ethnic, racial, and religious majority. In competitive districts in which the margins for victory are small, the risk of turning away even a small proportion of voters with a woman or minority candidate hinders major parties from nominating these types of candidates.[37]

In Russia, party fragmentation may have removed these obstacles in the SMDs; since these were not two-candidate races, the threshold for victory was much lower, increasing women's chances.[38] A female candidate did not have to win a majority or near majority to capture a seat; rather, the victorious candidate in Russia's SMDs averaged 31 percent of the district's vote in 1993 and only 29 percent in 1995.[39] This changed the calculus for parties nominating women and for ambitious women running as independents. Unlike in a two-candidate race where parties take a risk-averse strategy, which usually includes nominating a man, being a woman may have been an advantage that set one off from the dozen candidates who often crowded Russian SMDs. This hypothesis will be tested below in a quantitative analysis of female nomination and election in the 1995 SMD election.

Party Control Over Nominations

The simplest answer to the question of why there was low women's representation in the PR tier is that party leaders who controlled nominations in the closed lists were not committed to promoting women. Conversely, the lack of party control over access to office in the SMD tier lifted this constraint on female candidates. Dawn Nowacki, who has conducted research on Russian regional elections, found a negative relationship between partisanship and women's legislative representation, which further supports the idea that parties hinder women's representation.[40]

The failure of parties to monopolize access to office may have opened up greater opportunities for women in SMD elections, but it did not guarantee greater success. To take advantage of these opportunities, women still needed to marshal the resources necessary for conducting a winning campaign. They were at a great disadvantage in Russia because of its patriarchal power structure and cultural biases against women practicing politics. A look at the occupational backgrounds of successful female candidates shows that women who won election in the SMDs overcame these obstacles by matching their male counterparts in political experience and social standing.

Cross-national analysis shows that the key social factor increasing women's representation is sufficiently high social status. Rein Taagepera has likened parliamentary representation to a social pyramid in which election to the national legislature is the tip: "When parliament members are typically college-educated, economically active, and professionally trained, the groups that strive for more representation in the parliament would be advised to increase the basic selection pool in these respects. If nationwide politicians largely emerge through the intermediary stage of local politics, increased participation on that level also widens the base of the pyramid."[41] Wilma Rule has argued that the socioeconomic and political status of women explains almost as much of the deviation in women's representation as elements of the political system.[42]

Social status and political experience in particular seemed to be key factors in the election of women in SMDs in Russia. Table 4.5 shows the occupational background of male and female deputies elected in 1995. Similarities, rather than differences, stand out when comparing successful female and male candidates in the SMDs; for both women and men, previous experience in political office was a great benefit to gaining election to the State Duma. Quite predict-

Table 4.5: Occupational Background of Women and Men Deputies in 1995

Occupation	PR women (N = 14)	SMD women (N = 29)	PR men (N = 206)	SMD men (N = 192)
SMD incumbent	0 (0%)	9 (31%)	11 (5.3%)	67 (34.9%)
PR incumbent	4 (28.6)	4 (13.8)	48 (23.3)	19 (9.9)
Federation council	0 (0)	1 (3.4)	0 (0)	5 (2.6)
National executive branch	0 (0)	0 (0)	2 (1.0)	2 (1.0)
Regional head of administration	0 (0)	0 (0)	6 (2.9)	2 (1.0)
City/raion head of administration	0 (0)	1 (3.4)	3 (1.5)	4 (2.1)
Regional executive branch	0 (0)	1 (3.4)	6 (2.9)	5 (2.6)
Regional legislature	1 (7.1)	2 (6.9)	3 (1.5)	11 (5.7)
City/raion legislature	1 (7.1)	1 (3.4)	1 (0.5)	1 (0.5)
Legislative aide	1 (7.1)	2 (6.9)	15 (7.3)	3 (1.6)
Professional intelligentsia[a]	1 (7.1)	3 (10.3)	17 (8.3)	2 (1.0)
Academic/artist	4 (28.6)	1 (3.4)	26 (12.6)	6 (3.1)
Party activist	1 (7.1)	0 (0)	9 (4.4)	9 (4.7)
Social movement	0 (0)	1 (3.4)	8 (3.9)	5 (2.6)
Trade union	0 (0)	0 (0)	5 (2.4)	2 (1.0)
Agricultural manager	0 (0)	1 (3.4)	5 (2.4)	6 (3.1)
Industrial manager	0 (0)	1 (3.4)	11 (5.3)	19 (9.9)
Entrepreneur/ banker	0 (0)	0 (0)	19 (9.2)	13 (6.8)
Military	0 (0)	0 (0)	3 (1.5)	4 (2.1)
Other[b]	0 (0)	0 (0)	6 (2.9)	3 (1.6)

a Includes doctors, lawyers, procurators, economists, school teachers/administrators, and engineers.
b Includes workers and pensioners.

ably, incumbents made up the largest contingent of winning candidates; however, since incumbents numbered much less than half of the deputies for both men and women, incumbency was not the obstacle to legislative turnover that it is in established democracies with SMD elections such as the United States. Over half of both female and male deputies had some experience in national, regional, or local political office, with a greater proportion of women (65 percent) than men (59 percent) holding some type of executive or legislative office.

The greatest difference between women and men was the proportion of winning candidates from among the economic elite. In the SMDs, 20 percent of male winners were industrial managers, collective farm chairmen, entrepreneurs, or bankers, whereas only 7 percent of women winning seats in SMDs came from the economic elite of Russia. This is hardly surprising, given that women have made up the bulk of victims of Russia's economic reforms, while they were nearly absent among its success stories. Such patterns point to political service at the regional and local level as women's primary route to the State Duma in the SMDs.

Female and male PR deputies also had similar backgrounds; incumbents and regional politicians made up a smaller share of the PR contingent than did academics. Like the SMD deputies, the economic elite made up a significant portion of the men elected from PR party lists but was completely absent among women. A comparison across electoral systems shows that rules affected not only the number of women elected but also the type. Political experience was much more important in the SMD elections than in the PR. Incumbents made up the bulk of SMD female deputies (45 percent), but academics and artists equaled them in number among the PR female deputies, each accounting for roughly 29 percent of the total. Regional political experience was also more pervasive among women elected in the SMDs than those elected on a party list. This is not surprising, given that name recognition was so decisive to electoral success in the SMD and that a certain anonymity existed for members ranked lower than the top three candidates, who appeared on the ballot. The regional character of the SMD elections made political service, particularly at the regional level, the best route to gaining essential name recognition and a reputation as a politician interested in protecting her constituency's interests in Moscow.

A Quantitative Test of Female Candidature and Success

Logistic regression analysis was conducted to test the hypotheses that party fragmentation and the relatively high socioeconomic status of women help to account for higher levels of women's representation in Russia's SMD elections.[43] The two independent variables of greatest concern for the regression model were the number of candidates per district (NUMBER) and the occupational status of female and male candidates in each district (OCCUP). Other variables were introduced to control for contextual factors that may have influenced the election of women including a district's urbanization operationalized as the population of the largest city or town in the district (URBAN), level of education defined as the percent finishing some years of post-secondary education in the district (EDUC), the percent of Russians living in the district (RUSSIAN), and the political climate as measured by the percent voting for the following parties in the 1995 PR election: Communist and Agrarian parties (KPRFAPR); the nationalist Liberal Democratic Party of Russia (LDPR); reformist parties—Our Home is Russia, Yabloko, and Democratic Russia's Choice (REFORM); and the Women of Russia (WR).

Occupational status was operationalized according to a five-point scale that indicated social status that could be translated into political prominence ranging from very high (5) to very low (1).[44] Since this study is based on district-level rather than individual-level data, occupational status scores were aggregated for both men and women by electoral district, with each district being assigned the value of its most prominent male (MENOCCUP) and female (WOMENOC-CUP) candidates.[45] The presence or absence of a male incumbent candidate who won the district in 1993 (MENINCUM) was included as a possible substitute for MENOCCUP to test for a dampening effect of male incumbency on female nominees.

The equation's dependent variable was the gender of the SMD election winner, coded "0" for a district won by a man and "1" for a district won by a woman. The test was conducted on only the 153 districts that had at least one female candidate, since a woman could not possibly win if none ran. The regression tests the following two hypotheses gleaned from the previous discussion on potential explanations for women's success in SMD elections: 1) All else being equal, women are more likely to run in districts with a higher number of candidates because there will be a lower effective threshold for representation and 2) All else being equal, women are more likely to win in districts where they have high occupational status. Personal characteristics weigh heavily in plurality elections, which are won by the most prominent candidate.

Table 4.6 shows the results of the logistic regression. The number of candidates per district did not have a statistically significant relationship to the likelihood of a woman's winning election; this undermines the hypothesis that fragmentation of the vote reduces the threshold of representation, allowing more women to win election. While fragmentation may increase the number of women running for office, occupational status seems to be the dominant factor in their election. Both women's (WOMOCCUP) and men's (MENOCCUP) occupational statuses had a statistically significant relationship at the .01 level with women's electoral success. When the top female candidate was a prominent individual, she was more likely to win election, and when there was a prominent male candidate, the prospects for women dropped.

Table 4.6: Logistic Regression on Election of Women Candidates in SMDs in 1995

Variable	B	(standard error)	Odds ratio
WR	.4427*	(.1997)	1.557
REF	.0880	(.0773)	1.092
COMMAPR	.0631	(.0511)	1.065
LDPR	.1128	(.0934)	1.119
URBAN	2.50	(.0001)	1.000
RUSSIAN	-.0006	(.0156)	0.999
EDUC	.0827	(.0976)	1.086
NUMBER	.0584	(.0792)	1.060
WOMOCCUP	1.3475**	(.3072)	3.848
MENOCCUP	-1.5518**	(.4640)	0.212
Constant	-8.1461	(5.371)	—

Notes: -2 Log Likelihood: 104.030; Percent correctly predicted: 0: Male winners = 95.08%, 1: Female winners = 41.94%, Overall = 84.31%. Variables: (See Table 3.6) MENOCCUP = Occupational status of top male candidate in district; WOMOCCUP = Occupational status of top female candidate in district

* p = .05 (one-tailed test), ** p = . 01 (one-tailed test)

One other variable that emerged as statistically significant was the vote for Women of Russia. Perhaps this suggests that voters in some regions are more predisposed to women candidates and parties or that women's organizations are stronger in certain regions of the country. All other contextual variables—urbanization, education, percentage of Russians, and support for Communist, nationalist, or reformist parties—did not have statistically significant effects on women's representation in SMDs. The model explained women's electoral success correctly and predicted 84 percent of cases. More importantly, the model properly identified 42 percent of the women who won.

Conclusions

Although the electoral success of Women of Russia in 1993 was a classic success story of proportional representation encouraging the representation of an excluded group, the failure of Women of Russia to overcome the 5 percent barrier in 1995 represents the risks of such a strategy. Party fragmentation can split women's votes among several parties espousing women's issues or led by prominent women. Moreover, competing parties can appeal to female voters with token promotion of women into prominent positions on their party lists—without significantly increasing the number of women in winnable positions on their lists. This challenges contagion theory, suggesting that in some cases major parties can accommodate the pressures for increased women's representation coming from marginal parties through token promotion, which will not result in a significant increase in the number of female legislators. In such cases, increased women's representation relies predominantly on the electoral success of those marginal parties, rather than the ripple effect of their example. As the Russian case demonstrates, electoral success of women's parties can be an unstable basis on which to sustain significant representation.

Russia's mixed system has had both positive and negative consequences for women's representation in Russia. On the one hand, the relatively high rate of success for women in the SMDs shows that there is a critical mass of highly educated, politically active women capable of building a political career beginning at the local level. Thus, the electoral success of women in the SMDs can be reproduced through incumbency and continued career development of regional female politicians. However, the fate of women in the PR tier rests on the more tenuous foundation of the success of a single women's party until women establish themselves on major parties' PR lists. The low level of female candidates in electable positions on party lists suggests that parties might actually block women's representation. If the 5 percent threshold continues to claim Women of Russia as its victim, the lack of women in major Russian parties will continue to produce the paradox of greater success for women in SMD elections than in PR elections.

What implications does the Russian experience have for the representation of women in other postcommunist states? The pattern of Russian women's representation was not repeated in other such nations with mixed electoral systems. However, cross-national comparisons showed stark differences in the influence of electoral systems between consolidated democracies and postcommunist states. Western democracies showed consistent and dramatic improvements in women's representation under PR, whereas postcommunist states largely failed to show a statistically significant difference between the two tiers. This suggests that the social context and the opportunity structure for women within parties in postcommunist states interact with and influence institutional effects of electoral systems. Consequently, women in these states should not count on an institutional remedy, such as PR elections, to increase levels of parliamentary representation.

5
Electoral Systems
and Ethnic Heterogeneity
in Russia

The relationships between electoral systems and the representation of women and of ethnic minorities are similar in most respects except one: geographic concentration. While women are, understandably, evenly distributed across a country's territory, ethnic minorities are often geographically concentrated. This may enable an ethnic minority group to constitute a majority or plurality status in some electoral districts. Under such circumstances SMD elections may offer certain advantages by enabling an ethnic party to become one of the two major parties in its "home districts" or by pushing major parties to run minority candidates in these districts to attract the concentrated minority vote. Consequently, the ethnic character of electoral districts becomes a major factor influencing the likelihood of minority representation. In the United States in 1990, African American congresspersons were almost exclusively elected from districts with majority minority populations in which African Americans made up a plurality.[1] A similar situation existed for Hispanic congresspersons, leading some scholars to argue that a total combined minority population above 50 percent is a virtual precondition for minority candidate success in the United States.[2]

Despite the advantages of SMD elections for concentrated minority populations, multimember PRs are usually seen as preferable to SMD systems for the representation of ethnic minorities, for the same reasons larger district magnitudes enhance opportunities for women's representation—greater viability for smaller parties. Taagepera argues that ethnoracial minority parties are counterproductive in SMDs, although such a bloc may win the few seats where its ethnic group is concentrated, it will win too few seats to play a meaningful role in a governing coalition or as an opposition party in the two-party systems that usually emerge out of SMD systems. Such parties are much more viable under PR rules, which produce lower effective thresholds to representation and multiparty coalitions that could better incorporate smaller parties in support of minority interests in decision-making structures.[3]

This chapter will look at the representation of ethnic minorities in Russia, using the same controlled-comparison approach employed in previous chapters.

The effects of PR and plurality systems on minority representation will be studied through a comparison of Russia's PR and SMD tiers, holding other explanatory factors constant. This chapter will also look at ethnic heterogeneity as an independent variable, examining the effect ethnic heterogeneity and electoral systems have on the number of parties in Russia.

Ethnic Minorities in Russia

Relatively speaking, the Russian Federation emerged from the collapse of the Soviet Union as an ethnically homogenous state. Russians comprise a large majority in the Russian Federation, over 80 percent, while the remaining non-Russian population is composed of literally dozens of very small ethnic groups. Table 5.1 shows the ethnic breakdown of the Russian Federation, from 1989 census data.

No single ethnic minority accounts for even 4 percent of the population in the Russian Federation, and only three groups (Tatars, Ukrainians, and Chuvash) make up more than 1 percent. A pan-national identity uniting non-Russians around a religious identity such as Islam is complicated by the religious diver-

Table 5.1: Ethnic Composition of the Russian Federation

Ethnic group	Number	Percentage of total population	Percentage with Russian as primary language
Russian	119,865,900	81.53	100
Tatar	5,522,100	3.76	14
Ukrainian	4,362,900	2.97	57
Chuvash	1,773,600	1.21	22
Bashkir	1,345,300	0.92	10
Belorussian	1,206,200	0.82	63
Mordva	1,072,900	0.73	31
Chechen	899,000	0.61	1
German	842,300	0.57	58
Other[a]	n/a	6.88	n/a

Source: Chauncy Harris, "The New Russian Minorities: A Statistical Overview," *Post-Soviet Geography* 34, no. 1 (1993); NUPI website on ethnicity in Russia, http://www.nupi.no/cgi-win/Russland/etnisk.exe/total.

a Sixty other ethnic groups, constituting less than 0.5 percent of the population, were listed in the 1989 census.

sity of non-Russians. While Islam has been perceived as the major threat to Russian territorial integrity in the wake of the war in Chechnya, large groups among non-Russian minorities are Christian—including Ukrainians, Belorussians, Mordva, and Karelians.[4] Language also gives little chance to unify the diverse non-Russian ethnic groups. Moreover, as a result of the state's Russification efforts and the effects of modernization, 7.5 million non-Russians (about a quarter of the minority population) have shifted from their first language to Russian for most communications.[5] The use of Russian as one's primary language is a good indication of the degree of a non-Russian group's assimilation into Russian society and conversely its degree of attachment to a non-Russian identity. As Table 5.1 shows, groups without their own ethnically defined federal units (Ukrainians, Belorussians, Germans, Jews) have the highest proportion of Russian-speakers and are most assimilated into Russian culture, compared with those non-Russian minorities that have their own ethnic homelands. Such ethnic groups were also the most geographically dispersed minorities, making assimilation even more necessary and easily accomplished.

Despite the numerical superiority of Russians, demands for secession and increased political and economic autonomy from non-Russian groups have been the greatest threat to Russia's territorial integrity. Tens of thousands of civilians have been killed in the battle over the sovereignty of Chechnya, without a lasting settlement being reached. Yet Chechnya is just the most recent of a long list of challenges to central authority coming from the regions. All of the twenty-one non-Russian republics have declared sovereignty, and most have signed power-sharing agreements with Moscow. During the October 1993 constitutional crisis, all of the non-Russian republics except Sakha (Yakutia) defied Yeltsin's orders to disband local soviets.[6] In 1993, elections were not held in Chechnya, and a boycott of the vote called by the leadership of Tatarstan invalidated the December elections, because voter participation failed to reach 25 percent.[7] Thus, the nationalities question that was such a crucial factor in the demise of the Soviet Union has continued to pose problems in Russia and other Soviet successor states as they struggle to build new national identities.

The political power of non-Russian minorities can be attributed largely to their high level of geographic concentration and politicization. Geographic concentration avails an ethnic group of much greater opportunities to mobilize and capture state power, especially at the regional and local levels. The politicization of certain ethnic groups in a state has many causes, including the strength of a group's ethnic identity and solidarity, its historical experience, its economic and organizational resources, and its leadership. Although much depends on the endogenous characteristics of the ethnic group, its environment also plays a role. The state can politicize ethnic groups through preferential programs dispersed according to ethnicity or, in the former-Soviet and Russian cases, by designating certain federal units as ethnic homelands.

The Russian Federation has continued the Soviet practice of defining some

of its federal units along ethnic lines.[8] Russia is composed of eighty-nine subjects or regions that are divided into twenty-one republics, forty-nine oblasts,
six krais, two cities (Moscow and St. Petersburg), ten autonomous okrugs, and
one autonomous oblast (the Jewish Autonomous Oblast). Republics, autonomous okrugs, and the Jewish Autonomous Oblast constitute the thirty-two regions made up of ethnic homelands.

Chauncy Harris argues that the establishment of an ethnic homeland has
played a large part in creation of an ethnic identity in Russia. "Official recognition of an ethnic group and the establishment of rights for education, publications, and cultural institutions in an ethnic homeland have promoted language
retention; absence of such rights has discouraged it. Many smaller ethnic groups
without such recognition have disappeared; others are in the process of gradu-
ally vanishing as viable cultural entities. Even very large majorities without such
rights *within the Russian Federation* have high rates of shift by members of the
group to Russian as mother language: 91 percent of the Jews, 58 percent of the
Germans . . . 63 percent of the Ukrainians. . . . No large ethnic group with appropriate ethnic homelands has such a high percentage of its members who have
shifted to Russian as their mother language" (emphasis in the original).[9] Regional governments in ethnic homelands cultivate ethnic identity, which can lead
to assertiveness and mobilization even in authoritarian structures like that of the
Soviet Union. The very designation of ethnic federal units produces incentives
for the cultivation of an ethnic cadre of elites and mass mobilization tied to
ethnicity.[10] As will be shown below, the titular nationality does not constitute a
majority in most of the ethnic federal units, which makes the symbolic power of
an ethnic homeland the most important factor in the representation of minorities in national and regional legislatures.

Among ethnically defined regions, republics enjoy a preferred status because
they have their own executives and legislatures while the autonomous okrugs
and oblasts are subordinate to the oblast or krai in which they are located. Although the Russian constitution explicitly states that all subjects of the federation have equal status within it, republics are deemed to have greater autonomy
and are able to extract more resources from the center, as illustrated by consistently greater fiscal transfers to republics in the national budget.[11] In light of
this perceived preference for republics, Sverdlovsk oblast launched a failed attempt at unilaterally changing its federal status from oblast to republic.[12]

Geographic concentration is manifested in two ways: as the proportion of an
ethnic group living in its designated homeland and as the proportion of the
homeland's population constituted by its titular nationality, the ethnic group for
which the region is named. From these two indices of minority concentration
can be discerned some important patterns. First, nationalities with ethnic homelands are relatively concentrated in those homelands, whereas groups without
them, such as Ukrainians, Belorussians, and Germans, are dispersed more across
Russia.[13] An average of 66 percent of titular nationalities live in their desig-

nated homelands, but there are several important exceptions. The largest non-Russian minority population, the Tatars, is also one of the most dispersed—with only 32 percent living in Tatarstan. Just two percent of Jews live in the Jewish Autonomous Oblast, and only 29 percent of the more than one million Mordva live in Mordovia.[14]

More importantly for issues of election to the national legislature, titular nationalities do not usually constitute a majority in their ethnic homelands. Table 5.2 shows the ethnic composition of thirty ethnic homelands.[15] The titular nationality makes up a clear majority of the population in eight regions and constitutes a plurality in another two. Russians make up over 50 percent of the population in eighteen of thirty-one ethnic homelands and are a plurality in another two. In fourteen, the titular nationality makes up less than 25 percent of the population.[16] This has translated into twenty-four of forty-six electoral districts of SMDs for State Duma elections, from non-Russian regions having non-Russian majority populations. Only fifteen districts in non-Russian regions had Russian populations under 40 percent.[17] If, following the American experience, non-Russian majorities are a precondition for electing a minority candidate in Russia's SMD elections, one would expect few non-Russians to win seats in this tier, unless large numbers of Russian voters supported non-Russian candidates.

Prospects for minority representation in the PR half of Russia's mixed system were not any better. Electoral rules—such as requiring signatures for registration PR blocs to come from at least seven different regions of the country—hindered the emergence of ethnic-based parties. More important, the PR tier's 5 percent legal threshold should hinder any minority ethnic party from gaining election, since no single ethnic group constituted that percentage of the population. Indeed, Nur (a Muslim bloc) and the Interethnic Union, ethnically based electoral blocs contesting the 1995 PR contest, each received less than one percent of the PR vote. The fact that the minority population is dispersed among so many very small ethnic groups has also given few incentives for the incorporation of non-Russian elites in choice spots on major party lists to attract the ethnic vote.

Ethnic Minority Representation in PR and SMD Elections in Russia

Given the ethnic composition of Russia, one would expect both the PR and plurality tiers of Russia's mixed electoral system to underrepresent non-Russian ethnic groups. Yet this was not the case. Each tier elected a percentage of non-Russian deputies that was proportional to the minority population. Politicization of ethnic minorities in ethnic homelands, along with assimilation of certain non-Russian groups, most notably Ukrainians, seems to have circumvented institu-

Table 5.2: Ethnic Composition of Non-Russian Regions

Non-Russian Region	Ethnic Composition (in percent)
Adigei Republic	Adigei = 31, Russians = 60, Kazakhs = 6
Bashkortostan Republic	Bashkirs = 22, Russians = 39, Tatars = 28
Buryat Republic	Buryats = 24, Russians = 70, Ukrainians = 2
(Gorno-) Altai Republic	Altai = 31, Russians = 60, Kazakhs =: 6
Dagestan Republic	Avars = 28, Dargins = 16, Kumyks = 13, Lezghins = 11, Russians = 9, Laks 5
Kabardino-Balkar Republic	Kabards = 48 Balkars = 9, Russians = 32
Kalmyk Republic	Kalmyks = 45, Russians = 38, Dargins 4
Karachayevo-Cherkess Repub.	Karachai 31, Cherkess = 10, Abaza = 7, Russians = 42
Karelian Republic	Karelians = 10, Russians = 74, Belorussians = 7
Komi Republic	Komi = 23, Russians = 58, Ukrainians = 8
Mari-El Republic	Mari = 43, Russians = 48, Tatars = 6
Mordovin Republic	Mordva = 33, Russians = 61, Tatars = 5
Sakha (Yakutia) Republic	Yakuts = 33, Russians = 50, Ukrainians = 7
North Ossetian Republic	Ossetians = 53, Russians = 30, Ingush = 5
Tatarstan Republic	Tatars = 49, Russians = 43, Chuvash = 4
Tuva Republic	Tuvins = 64, Russians = 32
Udmurt Republic	Udmurts = 31, Russians = 59, Tatars = 7
Khakass Republic	Khakass = 11, Russians = 80, Ukrainians = 2
Chuvash Republic	Chuvash = 68, Russians = 27, Tatar = 3
Jewish AO	Jews = 4, Russians = 83, Ukrainians = 7
Aginsky-Buryatsky AO	Buryats = 55, Russians = 41
Komi-Permyatsky AO	Komi-Permyak = 60, Russians = 36
Koryatsky AO	Koryaks = 16, Russians = 62, Ukrainians = 7
Nenetsky AO	Nentsy = 12, Russians = 66, Komi = 10, Ukrainians = 8
Taimursky AO	Dolgans = 9, Nentsy = 4, Ukrainian = 3
Ust-Ordinsky Buryatsky AO	Buryats = 36, Russians = 57
Khanti-Mansiisky AO	Khanty = 1, Mansi = 1, Russians = 66, Ukrainians = 12, Tatars = 6
Chukotsky AO	Chuckchi = 7, Russians = 66, Ukrainians = 17
Evenkiiksy AO	Evenki = 14, Russians = 67, Ukrainians = 5
Yamalo-Nentsky AO	Nentsy = 4, Russians = 59, Ukrainians = 59, Tatars = 5

Sources: Harris, "The New Russian Minorities," NUPI website on ethnicity in Russia.

tional constraints to minority representation and allowed surprisingly high numbers of non-Russians to be elected to the State Duma.

Table 5.3 shows the ethnic representation of deputies elected in the PR and SMD tiers of the 1993 and 1995 parliamentary elections, along with the representation/population ratios in each election for every ethnic group with at least one deputy in 1993 or 1995.[18] Several striking patterns persist in the two elec-

Table 5.3: Ethnic Representation in PR and SMD Elections

Ethnicity	Number (percent) of deputies in 1993 PR election	Number (percent) of deputies in 1993 SMD election	Representation/ population ratio in 1993 elections	Number (percent) of deputies in 1995 PR election	Number (percent) of deputies in 1995 SMD election	Representation/ population ratio in 1995 elections
Russian	191 (84.5)	182 (81.3)	1.02	186 (84.2)	182 (81.3)	1.01
Tatar	2 (0.9)	2 (0.9)	0.24	5 (2.3)	4 (1.8)	0.54
Ukrainian	13 (5.8)	9 (4.0)	1.65	13 (5.9)	12 (5.4)	1.89
Jewish	5 (2.2)	2 (0.9)	4.32	2 (0.9)	1 (0.4)	1.81
Armenian	2 (0.9)	1 (0.4)	1.94	1 (0.5)	2 (0.9)	1.86
Chuvash	0 (0)	0 (0)	0	1 (0.5)	0 (0)	0.18
Bashkir	1 (0.4)	3 (1.3)	0.98	0 (0)	2 (0.9)	0.49
Belorussian	5 (2.2)	2 (0.9)	1.95	3 (1.4)	3 (1.3)	1.65
Mordvin	0 (0)	0 (0)	0	1 (0.5)	2 (0.9)	0.92
German	0 (0)	3 (1.3)	1.43	0 (0)	1 (0.4)	0.39
Buryat	0 (0)	2 (0.9)	1.43	1 (0.5)	2 (0.9)	2.39
Darghin	0 (0)	1 (0.4)	0.83	0 (0)	1 (0.4)	0.92
Ingush	0 (0)	0 (0)	0	1 (0.5)	1 (0.4)	3.00
Ossetian	0 (0)	2 (0.9)	1.48	3 (1.4)	1 (0.4)	3.33
Karbar	0 (0)	1 (0.4)	0.77	0 (0)	1 (0.4)	0.85
Mari	0 (0)	1 (0.4)	0.45	0 (0)	1 (0.4)	0.50
Yakut	0 (0)	1 (0.4)	0.77	0 (0)	1 (0.4)	0.85
Avarets	1 (0.4)	1 (0.4)	1.08	0 (0)	1 (0.4)	0.59
Korean	0 (0)	1 (0.4)	2.86	0 (0)	2 (0.9)	6.43
Komi-Permyak	0 (0)	1 (0.4)	2.00	0 (0)	1 (0.4)	2.20
Evenk	0 (0)	1 (0.4)	20.0	0 (0)	1 (0.4)	22.0
Lakets	0 (0)	0 (0)	0	1 (0.5)	0 (0)	3.14
Kumyk	0 (0)	0 (0)	0	1 (0.5)	0 (0)	1.16
Chukots	0 (0)	0 (0)	0	0 (0)	0 (0)	0
Khakassian	0 (0)	0 (0)	0	0 (0)	0 (0)	0
Balkar	0 (0)	0 (0)	0	1 (0.5)	0 (0)	4.4
Adigets	1 (0.4)	0 (0)	2.50	1 (0.5)	0 (0)	2.75
Altai	0 (0)	0 (0)	0	0 (0)	0 (0)	0
Karelian	0 (0)	0 (0)	0	0 (0)	0 (0)	0
Nenets	0 (0)	0 (0)	0	0 (0)	0 (0)	0
Karachai	0 (0)	1 (0.4)	2.0	0 (0)	0 (0)	0
Komi	1 (0.4)	1 (0.4)	1.74	0 (0)	0 (0)	0
Tuvin	0 (0)	1 (0.4)	1.43	0 (0)	1 (0.4)	0.92
Kazakh	0 (0)	0 (0)	0	0 (0)	0 (0)	0
Cherkes	1 (0.4)	0 (0)	6.67	0 (0)	0 (0)	0
Lacassian	1 (0.4)	0 (0)	2.86	0 (0)	0 (0)	0
Georgian	1 (0.4)	0 (0)	2.22	0 (0)	0 (0)	0
Udmurt	0 (0)	1 (0.4)	0.41	0 (0)	0 (0)	0
Kalmyk	0 (0)	1 (0.4)	1.82	0 (0)	0 (0)	0
Latvian	0 (0)	1 (0.4)	6.67	0 (0)	0 (0)	0
Koryak	0 (0)	1 (0.4)	20.0	0 (0)	1 (0.4)	22.0
Khanti	0 (0)	1 (0.4)	10.0	0 (0)	0 (0)	0
Greek	1 (0.4)	0 (0)	3.33	0 (0)	0 (0)	0

Sources: Pyataya Rossiiskaya Gosudarstvennaya Duma (Moscow: Izdanniya Gosudarstvennaya Duma, 1994); *Gosudarstvennaya Duma Federal'naya Sobraniya Rossiiskoi Federatsii, Vtorogo Sozyva* (Moscow: Izdanniya Gosudarstvennaya Duma, 1996).

tions. Neither the PR nor the SMD tier gave any advantage to the majority ethnic group, despite the benefits Russians possessed under each. Russians were elected to the legislature in almost identical numbers in both tiers and in nearly equal proportion to their population; by comparison, Anglo men and women make up approximately 80 percent of the population of the United States but over 91 percent of the U.S. Congress.[19]

While the electoral system made little difference in the election of Russians to the State Duma, it had a more significant impact on the election of non-Russians. Although non-Russians generally benefited in equal measure in both PR and SMD elections, the type of non-Russian ethnic group enjoying representation differed substantially, depending on the electoral system. Ethnic representation was more concentrated among the larger ethnic minorities in the PR election and more dispersed across smaller nationalities in the SMDs. In 1993, each of thirteen non-Russian minorities gained at least one representative in the PR election, while twenty-five ethnic groups each elected at least one representative from the SMDs. In 1995, the number of non-Russian groups represented in the PR and SMD tiers was fourteen and twenty-one.

As one might expect, those ethnic groups without a designated homeland fared better in the PR election than in the SMDs; this was particularly the case in 1993. Ukrainians, Jews, and Belorussians all gained most of their parliamentary representation in the PR tier. Moreover, these groups were generally more successful in the PR tier than were other minorities. In 1993, these three groups managed to elect twenty-three deputies in the PR election, 66 percent of the non-Russian deputies elected in the PR tier, but only thirteen deputies in SMDs, which accounted for 31 percent of non-Russian winners in that tier. A smaller disparity existed in 1995, with Ukrainians, Belorussians, and Jews winning a total of eighteen seats in the PR election (51 percent of non-Russian winners), compared with 16 seats in the SMDs (38 percent of non-Russian winners).

This may be due to the fact that these non-Russian groups are the most assimilated into Russian society.[20] In fact, integration in the dominant culture rather than mobilization around ethnic distinctiveness seems to be the key to electoral success for assimilated minorities in the SMD tier as well. Of the sixteen non-Russians elected in districts in Russian regions (oblasts and krais), 75 percent came from highly assimilated groups that did not have their own ethnic homelands.[21] More than half were Slavs (Ukrainians or Belorussians), and only two came from ethnic groups with their own republic.

The contribution of cultural assimilation for electoral success was most evident for Ukrainians, who achieved overrepresentation in both tiers of the mixed electoral system. Constituting less than 3 percent of the national population and lacking an ethnic homeland, Ukrainians should have been among the most disadvantaged groups in electoral competition. But assimilation into Russian society and the legacy of integration of Ukrainians into the political elite from the Soviet period have led to disproportional electoral success. Ukrainians have not

Table 5.4: Ethnic Representation in SMDs in 1995

Ethnicity	Percent elected in districts with non-Russian majorities	Percent elected in districts with Russian majorities	Percent elected in districts in non-Russian regions	Percent elected in districts in Russian regions	Percent elected in districts in non-Russian regions with Russian majorities
Russians	33.3	87.1	42.2	91.1	52.4
Non-Russians	66.7	12.9	57.8	8.9	47.6

Source: *Gosudarstvennaya Duma Federal'naya Sobraniya Rossiiskoi Federatsii, Vtorogo Sozyva* (Moscow: Izdanniya Gosudarstvennaya Duma, 1996).

only managed to capture a disproportionate number of PR seats through penetration of electoral blocs and parties but have also won almost as many seats in the SMDs, all but one in districts with large Russian majorities. As fellow Slavs, Ukrainians (along with Belorussians) most closely resemble Russians, making ethnicity a less dramatic signal to voters.[22] By contrast, only 27 percent (seven of twenty-six) of non-Russians elected in ethnic republics and autonomous okrugs were from highly assimilated groups and only 13 percent (two of sixteen) of non-Russians elected in minority majority districts came from highly assimilated groups.

Ethnic representation in republics and autonomous okrugs was driven by a combination of institutional and demographic factors. Table 5.4 shows the proportion of non-Russian and Russian representation in different types of districts. Not surprisingly, non-Russians were most successful in districts with non-Russian majorities. However, demographic composition may be less important for minority representation than the designation of ethnic-based federal units. A dramatic example of this is that non-Russians were elected nearly four times as often in Russian majority districts located in ethnic republics and autonomous okrugs than in Russian majority districts in general.

Despite the positive influence of ethnic federalism, not all minorities have benefited equally from the designation of an ethnic homeland. This is most evident in the experience of the largest non-Russian minority, the Tatars, the most underrepresented major ethnic group in Russia. The failure of Tatars to be elected in numbers proportional to their share of the population, even in SMDs in their own region, is particularly striking given that, besides Chechnya, Tatarstan has been one of the most nationalist regions in Russia. In 1993, the December parliamentary election was invalidated because a Tatar nationalist boycott kept participation well under the 25 percent required. Elections to the State Duma were held again in March 1994, but only after Tatarstan's president Mintimer Shamiev personally sponsored the election following the signing of a bilateral treaty between Tatarstan and Russia that established a preferred status for Tatarstan in the Russian Federation.[23] Moreover, ethnicity plays a strong role in shaping political attitudes in the republic, with the republic's population polarized between Tatars who support various degrees of autonomy and separatism and Russians who demand that Tatarstan remain a constituent part of Russia.[24] Consequently, political elites have been able to effectively use a tacit threat of secession to wrench favorable terms from Moscow regarding its federal status.

However, Tatars have not translated this potential for ethnic mobilization into parliamentary representation in the State Duma. In the March 1994 by-elections, of the five SMD races held in the republic, only one Tatar got elected. Another Tatar was elected in Bashkortostan, the other republic with a large Tatar minority, but this was in a district where Russians were the predominant group.[25] Only two Tatars were elected in the PR tier of the 1993 election. Tatar representation doubled in 1995 but remained well below the minority's proportion of the population. Within Tatarstan, Tatars captured two out of five SMD races. By comparison, neighboring Bashkortostan had four Bashkirs elected in its six SMD races in 1993. This is particularly striking because Bashkirs constitute a mere 22 percent of Bashkortostan's population, behind both Russians (39 percent) and Tatars (28 percent).[26]

A combination of ethnic distinctiveness and geographic dispersion of Tatars has worked against their electoral success in both halves of Russia's mixed system. Being part of a relatively small, distinct, and unassimilated minority makes Tatar candidates risky bets on PR party lists. In the SMD races, where ethnic mobilization may be an advantage, Tatars are hurt by geographic dispersion. Only 32 percent of Tatars living in the Russian Federation live in Tatarstan. Thus, Tatars get a comparatively small number of electoral districts in their homeland. Even if Tatars won all of the districts in Tatarstan these 5 seats still would not constitute a proportion of 225 SMD seats equal to the group's share of the population. This geographic dispersion has implications within Tatarstan, as well. Tatars make up only 48.5 percent of the population, whereas Russians account for 43 percent. They constitute a majority in only two of the five districts in the republic. Of course, as shown above, minority status has not stopped many other non-Russian groups from gaining representation in their own republics. So demographic composition of the republic cannot be the only explanation for the relatively low level of parliamentary representation for Tatars.

In a search for other factors to account for Tatar underrepresentation, one must not discount the role of ethnic identity and rhetoric. It is possible that the heightened nationalist activity in Tatarstan may actually have worked against parliamentary representation of Tatars, by mobilizing ethnic Russians and other groups against them. By contrast, groups like the Bashkirs have had to de-emphasize ethnicity, given their minority status in their own homeland. In the process, less secessionist groups may have made themselves more electable by not antagonizing other ethnic groups.[27]

The representation of minorities in Russia poses a number of interesting questions. Given the demographic context, minorities should not have been as well represented as they were in 1993 and 1995. Unlike in the American experience, minority majority districts do not seem a prerequisite for minority candidate success. Non-Russian minorities have benefited from ethnic-based federalism, achieving great electoral success even in Russian majority districts located in non-Russian federal units. Moreover, the most assimilated non-Russian groups, most notably Ukrainians, have been able to gain election in the PR tier and in SMDs located in Russian oblasts and krais. More research needs to be done to disentangle the interaction between ethnicity, electoral institutions, and representation. Other factors—in particular the influence of regional executive power structures (regional parties of power), which play such a major role in who wins regional elections—need to be examined to explain the representation of minorities.

Comparing Minority and Women's Representation

Why were ethnic minorities more successful in gaining representation to the State Duma than women were? The multitude of very small non-Russian ethnic groups offered negligible incentives for inclusion of minorities on the PR list of major parties. The 5 percent barrier virtually precluded the possibility of a non-Russian ethnic electoral bloc. From this perspective, women with their greater numbers and own viable electoral bloc should have had a distinct advantage in gaining representation. However, the exact opposite was the case. In 1993 thirty-five non-Russians won election in the PR tier, which was one more seat than women achieved in this tier, despite the fact that Women of Russia won over 8 percent of the PR vote. In 1995, with Women of Russia failing to overcome the 5 percent legal threshold, women's representation in the PR tier fell by more than half, to fourteen seats, while the number of non-Russians remained steady at thirty-five.

What can account for these differences? Although such a complex phenomenon as ascriptive representation has numerous causes, I would emphasize the greater integration non-Russians enjoy in elite power structures in Russia. Party machines control local politics in most regions. When this local party of power is controlled by the titular nationality, which is often the case even when such nationality is a minority, non-Russian elites have greater opportunities to penetrate regional party structures and achieve competitive spots on PR lists or run competitive campaigns in the SMDs. This greater integration in power structures is a direct legacy of nativization policies of the Communist period that left behind a non-Russian nomenklatura in the republics. Other non-Russian groups without their own republics, such as Ukrainians and Jews, also managed to find places among the nomenklatura and to use these positions to maintain influence in the postcommunist period. On the other hand, women have always been left out of the upper echelons of power during the Soviet period, despite making great gains in education and professional development. Left out of the power structure, women had to rely on their own political party to gain substantial representation. When this party became vulnerable to the 5 percent threshold of the PR tier women again found themselves locked out of power.

Ethnic Heterogeneity and the Number of Parties in Russia

Ethnic heterogeneity has not been seen only as a factor influencing minority representation; it is also studied for its effects on the number of parties or candidates competing in elections. Used as a proxy for social heterogeneity, scholars have found a strong and positive relationship between the number of ethnic groups and the degree of party fractionalization.[28] This work has given important empirical support for a long-held axiom in the study of parties and elections—that the number of parties is a product of both the electoral system and the number of social cleavages found in society.[29]

The literature has not come to a consensus on whether ethnic heterogeneity has an independent effect on the number of parties or candidates contesting elections. Cross-national studies have often focused on the interactive effect of ethnic heterogeneity and electoral structure on the number of parties. When isolated as the only independent variable ethnic heterogeneity was not statistically significant in the two major cross-national studies by Gary Cox and by Peter Ordeshook and Olga Shvetsova. Cox found the effective number of ethnic groups to be statistically significant only when controlling for district magnitude and other institutional variables.[30] Cox and Ordeshook and Shvetsova argue that ethnic heterogeneity is best conceptualized as influencing party fractionalization when incorporated in an interactive variable with district magnitude, meaning that the effective number of parties is a product of the interaction of these two forces rather than the individual or cumulative effect of each.[31] Cox explains the interactive effect as follows: "A polity will have many parties only if it *both* has many cleavages *and* has a permissive enough electoral system to allow political entrepreneurs to base separate parties on these cleavages. Or, to turn the formulation around, a polity can have few parties either because it has no need for many (few cleavages) or few opportunities to create many (a strong electoral system)" (emphasis in original).[32]

Studies at the district level have presented a somewhat different picture. For example, Jones found that racial heterogeneity had a very strong and statistically significant effect on the number of candidates competing in SMD two-round majoritarian elections to the Louisiana state legislature. This effect was found when racial heterogeneity was examined individually and in combination with other variables, such as incumbency. Since district magnitude was held constant, no additive or interaction effect with the electoral structure was analyzed.[33] Cox used the level of urbanization rather than ethnic heterogeneity as a proxy for social heterogeneity at the district level in Japan. He found that urbanness of a district and district magnitude were both positively related to the effective number of candidates running in a district and statistically significant.[34]

Russia's is an interesting test case for hypotheses concerning ethnic heterogeneity, electoral systems, and party and candidate proliferation. I have already shown that plurality elections have not produced the type of constraints on the number of candidates at the district level that the literature suggests. Is social heterogeneity driving this proliferation, or is something else? The mixed system again creates a controlled environment in which to test the impact of such factors as ethnic heterogeneity and urbanization on the number of entrants in electoral competition.

The impact of social heterogeneity and electoral systems on the number of parties or candidates will be examined through an OLS regression analysis of electoral results in the 1995 parliamentary election. Two sets of regression analyses were conducted, one using electoral results at the district level and the other, electoral results aggregated up to the regional level. For each set of models, the results for the PR and SMD tiers were pooled together. Although the PR tier was contested in one nationwide electoral district, this variable was reconstructed according to the proportion of the vote for PR parties in each of the 225 SMDs of the plurality tier. This creates a district-level measure of party fractionalization for the PR election that allows for direct comparison of district-level fractionalization in the two tiers of Russia's mixed system.[35] Only the 1995 election was used because a key variable, the percent of Russians in electoral districts, was only available for this election.

The dependent variable was the effective number of contestants competing in the designated region (electoral districts or regions). This was operationalized as the effective number of parties per electoral district or region in the PR tier and the effective number of candidates per district in the SMD tier. For the regional-level analysis, the effective number of candidates for the SMD tier was operationalized as the average effective number of candidates for all districts in a given region.[36] The two tiers were pooled together, yielding 444 cases for the models in Table 4.4 and 174 cases for the models in Table 4.5.[37]

I analyzed three independent variables. The electoral system (ESYSTEM) was operationalized as a dummy variable indicating the electoral system employed (0 = SMD, 1 = PR).[38] Two variables were used as proxies for social heterogeneity: urbanization and ethnic heterogeneity.[39] Urbanization (URBAN) was measured as the proportion of the district or region's population living in urban areas. Following conventional wisdom in the literature, more urban districts were assumed to be more socially diverse. Two different measures were used to operationalize social heterogeneity. The proportion of Russians in each district was used as the measure of ethnic heterogeneity: the higher the proportion the more homogenous a district was assumed to be. Data were not available on the proportion of other ethnic groups in electoral districts. However, these data were available for regions of the Russian Federation. Given this more complete information, the effective number of ethnic groups (ENETH), a weighted measure of ethnic heterogeneity based upon the proportion of all ethnic groups in a region, was used to mark ethnic heterogeneity at the regional level.[40] Each of these variables behaved in similar ways in their respective models, which suggests that they each capture the underlying influence of the level of ethnic heterogeneity.

Findings for the first set of regressions on district-level data are shown in Table 5.5. Three models are presented, each focusing on a different set of explanatory variables. Model 1 offers an institutionalist model that examines only the effect of the electoral system on the district-level number of parties or candidates. This model suggests that the type of system, plurality or PR, did have a significant effect on the number of competitors at the district level. Although plurality elections did not produce two-candidate contests, they did produce fewer contestants than PR elections, when reconfigured along SMD lines.

Model 2 offers a sociological model that examines only the effects of the two social variables, urbanization and ethnic heterogeneity. This model suggests that social context is also an important factor in the number of parties at the district level. Unlike cross-national studies (but similar to Jones's district-level study), my study finds that social heterogeneity has its own statistically significant effect on the number of parties. The most surprising result from Model 2 is the positive relationship between the percent of Russians living in a district and the effective number of contestants at the district level. A high percentage of Russians reflects greater ethnic homogeneity, and one would therefore expect it to be negatively correlated with the number of electoral contestants. However, in the Russian case the opposite seems true. In 1995, greater ethnic heterogeneity reduced rather than expanded political fractionalization. The urbanization variable did behave as expected; however, greater urbanization was correlated with more electoral candidates and parties. Since both variables were statistically significant, different aspects of social heterogeneity seemed to be creating cross-pressures on political fractionalization—urbanization producing greater fragmentation but ethnic heterogeneity producing greater consolidation.

Model 3 offers the fully specified model, combining the effects of the electoral system, urbanization, and ethnic heterogeneity. All three independent variables remain statistically significant and retain the direction and degree of their relationship with the effective number of parties/candidates. The amount of variance explained is approximately the sum of the two more specific models, suggesting a cumulative effect of the three factors.

Table 5.6 shows the same three models for data aggregated to the regional level. The biggest contribution of this set of analyses is the more accurate operationalization of ethnic heterogeneity in the effective-number-of-ethnic-groups measure. Since the district-level measure of ethnic heterogeneity produced a surprisingly negative correlation, it is important to test this finding again using a more accurate measure of ethnic diversity.

This test reflects the findings at the district level; ethnic homogeneity is negatively correlated with the number of electoral participants and remains statisti-

Table 5.5: Determinants of the Effective Number of Candidates/PR Parties per District, 1995

Independent variables	Coefficient estimates (standard error)					
	Model 1		Model 2		Model 3	
ESYSTEM	1.93	(.26)***	—		1.93	(.22)***
URBAN	—		0.05	(.006)***	0.05	(.006)***
RUSSIAN	—		0.04	(.007)***	0.04	(.006)***
Constant	7.28	(.18)***	2.09	(.58)***	1.14	(.55)***
Adjusted R^2 =	.11		.22		.33	
N =	444		444		444	

Notes:
Variables: ESYSTEM = Electoral System (0 = SMD, 1 = PR)
             URBAN = Percent Urban,
             RUSSIAN = Percent Russian

*** $p < .001$

Table 5.6: Determinants of the Effective Number of Candidates/PR Parties per Region, 1995

Independent variables	Coefficient estimates (standard error)					
	Model 1		Model 2		Model 3	
ESYSTEM	2.82	(.39)***	—		2.83	(.36)***
URBAN	—		0.04	(.014)**	0.04	(.012)***
ENETH	—		-1.19	(.58)*	-1.17	(.50)*
Constant	6.62	(.27)***	5.85	(1.48)***	5.35	(1.23)***
Adjusted R^2 =	.23		.09		.32	
N =	174		174		174	

Notes:
Variables: ESYSTEM = Electoral System (0 = SMD, 1= PR)
             URBAN = Percent Urban
             ENETH = Effective Number of Ethnic Groups

* $p < .05$, ** $p < .01$, *** $p < .001$

cally significant, although at a lower level of confidence. (The sign switches in this model—a higher effective number of ethnic groups index connotes greater ethnic heterogeneity, whereas a higher percentage of Russians in an electoral district suggests greater homogeneity.) The electoral system remains the single most powerful constraint on the number of electoral competitors and urbanization remains positively correlated with party fractionalization.

One can only speculate about the causes and implications of these counter-intuitive findings, since they result from a single election's data. More research is needed to see whether this pattern is found in other post-Soviet states and more time needs to pass to see if this is a stable pattern of Russian electoral behavior or a transitional phenomenon. My preliminary assessment is that ethnic heterogeneity has been associated with greater party consolidation in Russia because ethnic republics often are more tightly controlled by the regional political elite than are Russian regions. Regional parties of power dominate ethnic republics and constrain political competition (and sometimes repress it), producing fewer electoral competitors despite greater social diversity. Another potential explanation is that ethnic identity may offer a basis for group aggregation in the chaotic context of political and economic transition. This aggregating force may unite a large portion of the electorate in non-Russian areas in a way that is missing in predominantly Russian regions.

6
The Electoral Effects
of Presidentialism in Russia

Until this point, this book has dealt with the effects of electoral systems in parliamentary elections. But one of the most significant aspects of the postcommunist regime in Russia is its strong presidency. Russia's semi-presidential organization has had numerous significant effects on the character of the party system and its prospects for democratic consolidation.[1] Thus, the purpose of this chapter is to concentrate on the impact presidential elections have had on the number of parties and electoral outcomes.

As has been argued throughout this book, it is not immediately clear that electoral systems will have the same effects in unconsolidated democracies with weakly institutionalized party systems as they have in consolidated democracies. There was little evidence of strategic voting that would limit the number of parties in Russia's first two parliamentary elections. Thus, parties and candidates proliferated, despite institutional mechanisms designed to constrain the number of electoral choices. Does this extend to Russian presidential elections held under a two-round majoritarian system?

Electoral systems in presidential elections may have different effects in Russia than they do in parliamentary elections; as Richard Rose and Evgeny Tikhomirov argue, "The election of a president is the opposite of electing a parliament."[2] Unlike a parliamentary election, which diffuses votes among a relatively large number of representatives, a presidential election concentrates votes into a choice for a single individual to fill a single office (except in the case of collegial presidencies). This difference produces greater majoritarian tendencies in presidential systems; thus, presidential elections may narrow the options for voters and consolidate party systems to a greater extent than do parliamentary elections.[3]

But other scholars suggest that there is not a qualitative difference between presidential and parliamentary elections. Each has effects that emanate from its district magnitude and electoral formula. Presidential elections constrain the number of parties not because they are presidential but because presidential elections are conducted in a single, nationwide electoral district with a district magnitude of one.[4] Presidential elections may have a nationalizing effect on party formation, providing a single nationwide office that removes the problem of projection from the district level to the national level.[5] But SMD parliamentary elections should have similar constraining effects as presidential elections with the same electoral formula, at least at the district level. In the Russian case, this would mean that one should expect more candidate proliferation in presidential elections than SMD parliamentary elections, because the former is a two-round majoritarian system and the latter is a plurality election.[6]

Russia provides an interesting case for examining the impact of presidential elections on the number of parties, as it employs SMD elections in both parliamentary and presidential elections. Of course, this is not unique; after all, the United States has plurality elections for executive and legislative offices. But in Mark Jones's study of presidential systems in Latin America, no national electoral system appeared to use a pure SMD system to elect its legislature. Some countries used mixed systems, but, rather than examining the tiers separately as in this study, Jones calculated the effective magnitude of the whole system based on an average of the two tiers.[7] If Russian presidential elections provide a greater constraint on party fractionalization than the plurality tier of parliamentary elections, one must explain why the same district magnitude (and a weaker electoral formula) apparently produced the strategic voting that did not occur in plurality elections for parliament.

I will show that the two-round majoritarian presidential election in 1996 had a significant constraining effect on the number of candidates that two previous plurality elections in the SMD tier of Russia's parliamentary elections did not. The 1996 presidential election marked the first time in post-Soviet Russia's short electoral history that an electoral system produced strategic voting, which significantly constrained the number of candidates prior to and during the campaign. This discrepancy has important policy implications, given that presidential and parliamentary elections in Russia are held nonconcurrently, diminishing the effect that the presidential election has on party fractionalization in the legislature. Why the difference? I argue that crucial factors include the national character, greater information, and higher stakes of presidential elections. In the absence of an institutionalized party system, these characteristics supplied the necessary conditions for strategic voting that were not present in Russia's plurality elections for parliament.

This consolidation of the choices in the presidential election had important political implications. It played a vital role in Boris Yeltsin's reelection only six months after the Communist Party of the Russian Federation won an impressive victory in parliamentary elections. It was more beneficial for reformists than for Communists, because the former had been more fractionalized in parliamentary elections than the latter. In fact, as the only well-organized political party with a stable constituency in the country, the Communist Party enjoyed a significant advantage in parliamentary elections. While much of the reformist vote was squandered on parties that failed to overcome the 5-percent legal threshold, the socialist vote went primarily to the KPRF. Under such conditions, that party's 23 percent of the PR vote greatly outdistanced its rivals and was translated into 44 percent of the 225 PR seats in 1995. But when the field of competitors was narrowed in the presidential election, the more fractionalized reformist camp naturally gained a greater windfall of votes, resulting in a Yeltsin victory. The implicit assumption of such an analysis is that voting patterns for broad ideological camps (reformists, socialists, nationalists) did not change much from 1995 to 1996; what did, however, were the rules of the game that structured the vote choice and translated the vote into political power.

This chapter will give empirical support for two assertions: first, the Russian presidential system produced a greater constraint on the number of candidates than parliamentary plurality elections; and second, this consolidation played major role in the reelection of Boris Yeltsin in 1996. I will do this through an analysis of voting results for the 1993 and 1995 parliamentary elections and the 1996 presidential election disaggregated to the district level of the SMD tier of parliamentary elections.[8] And I will use references to individual-level survey research as a complementary check on this analysis.[9]

Presidentialism and Party Development

One major theme of the democratization literature has been the relative merits of presidential and parliamentary constitutional arrangements in fostering democratic consolidation. While most scholars have argued that parliamentary systems are more supportive of democratic development, a growing minority has come to the defense of presidential or at least semi-presidential systems that combine a separately elected president and prime minister subject to parliamentary confidence.[10] The debate over constitutional systems has revolved around broadly systemic differences between presidential and parliamentary systems. Critics of presidentialism regard it as rigid, zero-sum, and prone to deadlock.[11] Defenders highlight the efficient representation provided by the stark choice of a directly elected executive and argue that the drawbacks of the system commonly cited operate predominantly when the president faces a contrarian legislative majority.[12] Such an occurrence can be minimized with institutional engineering, for example, employing presidential and parliamentary electoral systems that constrain the number of parties and concurrently holding presidential and parliamentary elections.[13]

Presidentialism has two competing effects on party formation. In regards to party performance in the state, directly elected presidents promote less cohesive parliamentary parties, whereas parliamentary regimes support much more disciplined factions within the legislature. This is because the separate electoral constituencies of executive and legislative power under presidential systems fail to provide incentives for cohesive legislative party discipline. Conversely, parliamentary systems, in which executive power emanates from and is contingent upon majority confidence, require disciplined parties and coalitions to form to keep the executive in power. Thus, in the governing sphere one can say that parliamentary systems produce more cohesive parties than presidential systems.[14] I will not explore this aspect of presidentialism in Russia here, however, leaving it for future research.

Instead, the focus of this chapter is on the electoral effects of presidentialism. In the electoral realm a directly elected executive often promotes the consolidation of smaller party formations into larger coalitions by providing the single political prize that is typically the center of political competition: the presidency. Consequently, depending on the type of electoral system used, parliamentary systems generally create greater fractionalization than do presidential systems.

The electoral effect of presidentialism has usually been studied in the context of scholarship on electoral systems in general. Since only a single individual can occupy the presidency, the district magnitude for a presidential race is necessarily one with the whole nation serving as the electoral district.[15] Thus, all of the psychological and mechanical effects of SMD elections discussed in chapter 3 are assumed to come into play. Voters will refrain from supporting marginal candidates out of fear of wasting their vote on a sure loser and will defect to more popular ones who are capable of winning even if they are not the voters' first choice. Similarly, smaller parties and marginal candidates may withdraw from competition and not expend their resources on a doomed campaign. Such groups are much better off joining in broader coalitions with like-minded parties. The fear of splitting the vote within a specific ideological camp's potential electorate and allowing victory to a candidate from the opposite end of the political spectrum further reinforces impulses for consolidation.

A majoritarian two-ballot presidential election as used in Russia has significant consequences for the number of presidential candidates and on the number of parties in the system generally, because it should provide incentives for party proliferation in the first round.[16] An individual party has little to lose and everything to gain by running a candidate in the preliminary first round; if its candidate has a good showing, it is either one of the finalists or it has some clout in establishing the second round coalitions. If a party's candidate does not perform well, it can still join one of the successful candidates' coalitions; however, because it retains a relatively low district magnitude, two-round majoritarian systems constrain the number of candidates to a greater extent than PR ones do.[17]

The mechanical effect of presidential elections is different from parliamentary elections in one respect: because only one individual can occupy the presidency, presidential elections are truly winner-take-all elections. Even when a presidential candidate wins a majority, presidential elections leave a huge proportion of the electorate unrepresented. Of course, the same is true for every parliamentary SMD race, but, since these are very numerous, a single party most probably will never capture all of the seats. Manufactured majorities in parliament allow for the existence of an opposition that provides some representation for the losing parties. Presidential elections usually produce winners with narrow majorities, manufactured majorities, or even negative majorities in which more voters than not rejected the winner (in plurality races) or chose him or her as the lesser of two evils (in two-round majoritarian races).[18] Thus, while parliamentary electoral systems may be more or less proportional in translating votes into seats, depending on district magnitude and electoral formula, they are always bound to produce lower levels of disproportionality than presidential elections, which offer nothing to losing parties.

The 1996 Presidential Election and the Number of Candidates

The constraining effect of the presidential election on the number of competitors can be seen by a comparison of the effective number of candidates produced in the first round of the 1996 presidential election with the two tiers of the 1993 and 1995 parliamentary elections. The effective-number-of-parties index (or effective number of candidates, for SMD elections) will be used again to weight electoral contenders by the share of the vote they received so that marginal contestants are not counted the same as major ones. The least-squares measure of disproportionality, which takes the same approach by weighting the difference between votes and seats so that marginal contestants have less influence on the measure than major ones, will also be used as a measure of electoral system effects.[19] Table 6.1 shows the effective number of parties or candidates and levels of disproportionality produced by Russia's parliamentary and presidential elections.

As discussed at length in chapter 2, parliamentary plurality elections have not produced the same results in Russia as in consolidated democracies around the world. This resulted in an average of more than six significant candidates competing in plurality district races across Russia. PR elections created even more fractionalization at the district level, but they also produced a greater mechanical effect in the translation of votes into seats, particularly in 1995.

By contrast, the first round of the 1996 presidential election produced an effective number of candidates that was approximately half the effective number of candidates in plurality elections. Although a bit high, at 3.89, the effective number of presidential candidates approximates the number of significant candidates expected in the literature. Following the $M + 1$ rule, one would expect

Table 6.1: Effects of Russian Parliamentary and Presidential Electoral Systems

Election	Effective number of elective parties or candidates	Effective number of parliamentary factions[a]	Least-squares index of disproportionality
1993 PR	7.58	6.40	4.94
1995 PR	10.68	3.32	20.56
1993 Plurality	5.48	5.79	4.27
1995 Plurality	6.61	6.21	11.09
1996 Presidential	3.89 (round 1)	n/a	64.72 (round 1)

Sources: "Rezul'taty golosovniya na vyborakh v Gosudarstvennuyu Dumu po odnomandatnym izbiratel'nym okrugam" (Moscow: Central Election Commission of the Russian Federation, unpublished manuscript); Timothy Colton, "Introduction: The 1993 Election and the New Russian Politics," in *Russia's Protodemocracy in Action: Perspectives on the Election of 1993,* ed. Timothy Colton and Jerry Hough (Washington, D.C.: Brookings Institution Press, 1998); "Dannye protokolov No. 1 okruzhnykh izbiratel'nykh komissii o rezultatakh vyborov deputatov Gosudarstvennoy Dumy Federal'nogo Sobraniya Rossiiskoy Federatsii vtorogo sozyva po odnomandatnym izbiratel'nym okrugam" (Data of protocol No. 1 of district electoral commissions on the results of elections of deputies of the second State Duma of the Federal Assembly of the Russian Federation by single-mandate electoral district), *Rossiiskaya gazeta* (January 17, 1996):1–16; "Dannye protokolov No. 2 ob itogakh golosovaniya po federal'nomu izbiratel'nomu okrugu" (Data of protocol No. 2 on results of vote for federal electoral okrug), *Rossiiskaya gazeta* (January 24, 1996).1–16; Tsentral'naya Izbiratel'naya Komissiya Rossiiskaya Federatsiya, *Vybory Prezidenta Rossiiskoi Federatsii 1996: Elektoral'naya Statistika* (Moscow: Izdatel'stvo "Ves' Mir," 1996), 198–279.

a Based on parliamentary factions formed immediately after the election.

three effective presidential candidates in the first-round election since district magnitude is two, because the top two finishers of the first round get to move on to a run-off for the presidency.

This consolidation of the first-round presidential vote was not due to a lack of choices on the ballot; there were originally eleven officially registered presidential candidates.[20] At the beginning of the campaign, most major candidates, including Communist Party leader Gennady Zyuganov, liberal economist Grigory Yavlinsky, and former general Alexander Lebed, all had approval ratings higher than did President Yeltsin, the eventual winner.

What accounts for the relatively low number of significant candidates in the first round of Russia's presidential election, when a theoretically stronger plurality system could not constrain the number of candidates in two previous parliamentary elections? I argue that presidential elections have special majoritarian effects independent of district magnitude and electoral formula, which account for the greater party consolidation found in the 1996 presidential election. First, the national character of the presidential election closed off options for small personal parties and even larger parties with regionally based support, such as the Agrarian Party. Thus, unlike parliamentary SMD elections, which only required plurality support in one of 225 districts to gain representation in the State Duma, a legitimate presidential candidate would have to be a national figure to have a chance of winning. This, quite naturally, made viability more challenging for candidates who entered the race.

Second, Russia's presidential elections raised the voting stakes to a new level. Under Russia's constitution, passed by referendum in 1993, the president holds the preponderance of power. Consequently, the choice of president was a monumental one, which could determine the character of the regime.[21] Given this added importance, voters were bound to choose more selectively and were less apt to support a marginal candidate to satisfy a narrow issue preference or to protest the system.

Finally, there was more information available to encourage strategic voting. Unlike the local character of parliamentary plurality elections, this was a national election. Even though the eventual winner and many other prominent candidates officially ran as independents, the top five candidates (Yeltsin, Zyuganov, Lebed, Yavlinsky, and Zhirinovsky) were well known. Voters could reasonably distinguish ideological tendencies on the basis of previous public service and electoral campaigns. With this knowledge, voters could establish a rank ordering of preferences among the top candidates more easily than in plurality races for parliament, which were contested by much less well-known local elites, many of whom based their campaigns on their economic or professional success, service to the community, and other non-political attributes. A flood of opinion polls also provided almost daily coverage of the relative public support for the competing presidential candidates. This supplied much-needed information on who was and was not in the running that was missing in parliamentary elections in the SMD tier. There are a number of possible counter-explanations for the discrepancy between the number of candidates competing in the presidential election and in parliamentary plurality elections, but each has major flaws that lend greater support to my view.

Perhaps the PR tier of the parliamentary election contaminated the plurality half by infusing it with marginal parties that emerged to contest the PR race and simply put up candidates in the SMDs as well. This may explain the existence of more parties in parliamentary SMD elections, but it does not clarify why voters did not defect from marginal candidates and constrain the number of contenders through strategic voting. It also does not correspond with other post-communist experience. Pure SMD parliamentary elections held in Ukraine did not constrain the number of candidates at the district level, nor did two-round majoritarian elections held in 1990 control the number of candidates to the Russian Congress of People's Deputies.[22] Moreover, there was not a proliferation of candidates in the SMD tier of mixed systems in consolidated democracies, and thus a contamination effect would have to be deemed particular to the Russian case.

A second alternative explanation for the greater consolidation of the presidential election is the power of personality. Boris Yeltsin participated in the presidential election and eventually managed to unite behind his campaign most significant reformist and centrist groups. Given this situation, his absence in the two preceding parliamentary campaigns may be the reason for the lack of consolidation in the reformist camp. Such an explanation also has serious weaknesses; greater consolidation occurred across Russia's political spectrum during the presidential election and could be argued to be more successful for the Communists than for the reformists—given that Zyuganov stood as the lone candidate of the left-wing opposition, while Yeltsin had competition for the reformist vote from Grigory Yavlinsky. Moreover, Yeltsin's backers, even reformist politicians such as Yegor Gaidar, viewed him as the lesser of two evils, suggesting a high degree of strategic rather than genuine support.

Neither of these competing explanations is persuasive, leaving the characteristics of the presidential election itself as the most likely reasons for increased party consolidation. Only a presidential race combined the necessary importance, information, and attention of a nationwide election with the constraining effect of an SMD electoral system. In the context of a weakly institutionalized party system that cannot provide the necessary cues for strategic voting, these aspects of a presidential election made a crucial difference in the constraining effect.

The Effects of Consolidation on Electoral Success

The consolidation of the vote choice in the 1996 election had profound consequences for the electoral outcome. Strategic voting in the first round eliminated many parties that had run in the parliamentary elections six months prior, benefiting Yeltsin and the reformist forces more than the Communist or nationalist camps. This can be demonstrated through a detailed comparison of the 1995 parliamentary and the 1996 presidential votes. The consequences of strategic voting in the 1996 Russian presidential can be illustrated best in a reconfiguration of the presidential vote in the 1995 parliamentary SMDs. Table 6.2 shows the results of the first and second round of 1996 presidential elections and the seat distributions these results would have produced under a hypothetical election in the 225 districts of the plurality tier of Russia's parliamentary electoral system.

The similarities in the mechanical effect of the hypothetical plurality election and the actual presidential vote are striking. Like the presidential vote, votes for also-ran candidates (Lebed, Yavlinsky, and Zhirinovsky) would have been

**Table 6.2: Reconfiguration of 1996 Presidential Vote
in 1995 Parliamentary SMD**

Candidate	Percent of vote (round 1)	Percent (number) of seats by plurality rules[a] (N = 225)	Percent of vote (round 2)	Percent (number) of seats by plurality rules (N = 225)
Yeltsin	35.28	53.33 (120)	53.82	66.22 (149)
Zyuganov	32.03	46.22 (104)	40.31	33.78 (76)
Lebed	14.52	0.00 (1)	n/a	n/a
Yavlinsky	7.34	0.00 (0)	n/a	n/a
Zhirinovsky	5.70	0.00 (0)	n/a	n/a

a From a reconfiguration of 1996 presidential results according to 1995 electoral districts in
Michael McFaul and Nikolai Petrov, eds.), *Political Almanac of Russia 1989–1997* (Moscow:
Carnegie Endowment for International Peace, 1998).

wasted, resulting in virtually no representation, and votes for the most significant candidates, particularly the winner, would have been inflated. Consequently, even on the basis of first-round results, a plurality election would have
manufactured a majority victory for a "Yeltsin party," increasing its share of
seats over votes by 18 percent. Hypothetically, if plurality parliamentary elections had consolidated the vote choice to the degree presidential elections did,
the mechanical effect of the plurality election would have manufactured a reformist victory in the SMD tier of the 1995 parliamentary election. Of course,
this did not occur in 1993 or 1995 because parties themselves were undermined
by independent candidates and the vote choice was not consolidated in the SMD
tier. These institutional effects have practical consequences on electoral outcomes; a lack of consolidation of the party system in parliamentary elections
has contributed to the emergence of antireform majorities in the legislature, and
consolidation of the vote choice was a major factor reelecting a reformist to the
presidency in 1996.

The impact of strategic voting on the outcome of the 1996 presidential election can also be seen by comparing partisan orientations of voters in 1995 and
1996. I argue that consolidation, rather than voter conversion, played the primary role in propelling Yeltsin to a first-place finish in the first round and to
reelection in the second round. In other words, in the first round, for the most
part reformists and centrists supported Yeltsin (or, to a lesser extent, Yavlinsky),
socialist voters backed Zyuganov, and nationalists went for Lebed or Zhirinovsky. This assertion is supported by statistical correlations between the 1995 vote
and the first round of the 1996 vote, as shown in Table 6.3.

The starkest difference among candidates was between Yeltsin and Zyuganov.
Every party or ideological camp was related to these two candidates in opposite
directions, with the sole exception of "other nationalist parties" which had no
statistically significant relationship with either Yeltsin or Zyuganov. The sup-

Table 6.3: Correlation Coefficients, 1995 PR Vote and 1996 Vote for Major Presidential Candidates in First Round

1995 vote	Yeltsin	Zyuganov	Lebed	Yavlinsky	Zhirinovsky
KPRF	-.7207 **	.8287 **	.0768	-.4789 **	.1440 *
LDPR	-.5561 **	.3183 **	.2732 **	-.2390 **	.8430 **
NDR	.5756 **	-.3432 **	-.3867 **	.1173	-.5786 **
YAB	.5567 **	-.6680 **	.2100 **	.6430 **	-.4382 **
KRO	.1318 *	-.3349 **	.5652 **	.2543 **	-.2181 **
Other Reform	.7328 **	-.6862 **	-.0246	.3530 **	-.4036 **
Center	.3264 **	-.5481 **	.2595 **	.3206 **	.2514 **
Other Left	-.4157 **	.5309 **	-.2411 **	-.4194 **	.2390 **
Other Nationalist	-.0432	-.0878	.4151 **	.1336 *	-.1406 *
Other	.5010 **	-.7286**	.2229 **	.4435 **	.1123

Note: KPRF = Communist Party of Russian Federation, LDPR = Liberal Democratic Party of Russia, NDR = Our Home is Russia, YAB = Yabloko, KRO = Congress of Russian Communities, Other Reform = Democratic Russia's Choice, Forward, Russia!, Common Cause, Pamfilova-Gurov-Lysenko bloc, Transformation of the Fatherland; Center: Women of Russia, Worker's Self-Government bloc, Union of Labor, Ivan Rybkin bloc; Other Left: Agrarian Party of Russia, Power to the People, Communist-Working Russia-For the Soviet Union; Other Nationalist: Derzhava, Stanislav Govorukhin bloc, National-Republican Party, My Fatherland. Other: KEDR, Beer Lovers' Party, NUR Moslem Movement, Electoral Bloc including Defense of Children, Electoral Bloc including Defense of Veterans.

* p = .05, ** p = .01

port for other major candidates was a bit more ambiguous but did possess some identifiable patterns. As expected, Yavlinsky's support base looked quite similar to Yeltsin's, whereas the Zhirinovsky vote was closer to Zyuganov. The vote for Lebed appeared most varied, being positively correlated at the .01 or .05 level with every ideological grouping but the left and Yeltsin's core reformist vote (Our Home is Russia and other such parties).

This kind of analysis is supported by survey research comparing the 1995 and 1996 vote, which shows that Yeltsin gained a majority of the vote given to centrist parties such as Women of Russia and even the more nationalist Congress of Russian Communities. Evelyn Davidheiser has found similar correlations between the 1995 vote and the first round of presidential elections, with the partial exception that the 1995 LDPR vote was found to be split almost evenly among Yeltsin, Zyuganov, and Zhirinovsky.[23] Using discriminant factor analysis, Rose and Tikhomirov found that four of the five major candidates had relatively well defined bases of support, with Yeltsin and Zyuganov appealing to diametrically opposed constituencies. Only Alexander Lebed possessed a "fuzzy" support base.[24]

While statistical correlation and survey evidence helps to establish a clear link between the 1995 reformist/centrist vote and Yeltsin and the left-wing vote and Zyuganov, it does not adequately show the disproportionate benefit consolidation of the vote choice provided to Yeltsin in the first round. Here multivariate analysis of the relationship between the 1995 and 1996 vote adds some clarity. Multiple regression is a useful statistical tool, because it tests the relative strength of different factors on a common outcome, controlling for the effects of all the others. Thus, one can determine how influential the 1995 vote for a particular party or group of parties was for the 1996 vote for Yeltsin or Zyuganov, while holding the influence of other parties' voters constant. The Beta score for each variable shows the proportion of the variance explained by that variable independent of all others. The R^2 score measures the amount of variance explained by all of the variables in the model. Thus, multiple regression demonstrates the relative impact of swing voters, who chose strategically, that is, who did not have their 1995 preferences represented by a viable candidate in the 1996 presidential election and opted to support the major candidate who was closest to their ideological position. Table 6.4 presents the results of multiple regression of the 1995 vote on the Yeltsin and Zyuganov vote in the first round.

The KPRF accounted for much more of the variance of the first round vote for Zyuganov than Our Home is Russia (NDR) did for Yeltsin's first round vote. Bivariate regression between only the 1995 KPRF vote and the first-round Zyuganov vote and the 1995 Our Home is Russia vote and the Yeltsin vote demonstrates this. These models (not shown in the table) produced R^2 scores of .68

Table 6.4: Multiple Regression of 1995 Vote on First-Round Vote for Yeltsin and Zyuganov

Yeltsin				Zyuganov			
Variable	B		Beta	Variable	B		Beta
Constant	.0171	(.0145)	—	Constant	-.0700	(.0151)	—
NDR	.9963	(.0582)	.4974 **	KPRF	1.065	(.0383)	.7408 **
YAB	.3493	(.0949)	.1267 **	LDPR	.2650	(.0652)	.1097 **
Other Reform	1.140	(.0860)	.4710 **	Other Left	.8281	(.0602)	.3986 **
Centrist	.5515	(.1273)	.1557 **	Other			
Other	1.719	(.4769)	.1422 **	Nationalist	.3798	(.0898)	.1177 **
	MR = .9135				MR = .9240		
	R^2 = .8346				R^2 = .8537		
	Adj. R^2 = .8307				Adj. R^2 = .8510		
	SE = .0535				SE = .0522		

Note: Other Reform: Democratic Russia's Choice, Forward, Russia!, Common Cause, Pamfilova-Gurov-Lysenko bloc, Transformation of the Fatherland; Center: Women of Russia, Worker's Self-Government bloc, Union of Labor, Ivan Rybkin bloc; Other Left: Agrarian Party of Russia, Power to the People, Communist-Working Russia-For the Soviet Union; Other Nationalist: Congress of Russian Communities, Derzhava, Stanislav Govorukhin bloc, National-Republican Party, My Fatherland; Other = KEDR, Beer Lovers' Party, NUR Moslem Movement, Electoral Bloc including Defense of Children, Electoral Bloc including Defense of Veterans.

**p = .001

and .33. In other words, the 1995 KPRF vote could account for almost 70 percent of the variance in the Zyuganov vote, whereas the 1995 Our Home is Russia vote could account for only one-third of the variance in the Yeltsin vote. The same could be said of the core left-wing (including the Agrarian Party, Communists-Working Russia, and Power to the People) vote's share of the Zyuganov vote vis-à-vis the core reformist vote influence on the Yeltsin vote in the first round. Multiple regression of all left-wing parties on the Zyuganov vote (not shown in the table) showed that socialist parties alone could account for 83 percent of the variance of the Zyuganov vote in the first round ($R^2 = .83$). This was improved only marginally with the addition of nationalist parties in the full model, shown in Table 6.4, which accounted for 85 percent of the variance ($R^2 = .8537$), suggesting that nationalist voters made up a small part of Zyuganov's first-round vote total.

Unlike in Zyuganov's situation, the 1995 vote of one single party did not make up a majority of Yeltsin's first-round support. A multiple regression of all 1995 reformist parties on Yeltsin's first round vote, (not shown here) explains 76 percent of the variance ($R^2 = .76$). This is a marked improvement over the influence of Our Home is Russia alone, which suggests that Yeltsin benefited greatly from the support of voters who backed marginal reform parties that failed to overcome the 5-percent barrier in 1995. The Beta score for other reform parties (.4710) supports this assertion, showing that other reform parties had about as much weight on the Yeltsin vote as did Our Home is Russia. Finally, the 1995 vote for centrist and other unclassified parties (which correlated most closely with centrist parties) also was positively correlated with the Yeltsin vote and deemed statistically significant, suggesting that Yeltsin also benefited from centrist voters.

All in all, Table 6.4 depicts a situation in which Yeltsin profited much more from voter consolidation than did Zyuganov. This consolidation propelled Yeltsin to a first place finish in the first round; Zyuganov drew most of his support from KPRF voters and did not gain very much from swing voters from the nationalist or centrist camps. Yeltsin drew less than half of his support from Our Home is Russia, in 1995 but gained significantly from swing voters from minor reformist, centrist, and unclassified parties. These findings are even more significant when one considers that Yeltsin had direct competition for the reformist vote from Grigory Yavlinsky, whereas Zyuganov was the sole candidate for the left-wing opposition.

The second round of voting narrowed the field even further, to the two top vote-getters from the first round. Much of the attention paid to this second round has revolved around Yeltsin's deal with Alexander Lebed, who ran a distant third in the first round balloting but hypothetically held the balance between Yeltsin and Zyuganov, if he could deliver his 11 million votes to one side or the other. The deal between Yeltsin and Lebed resulted in Lebed's second-round endorsement of Yeltsin in exchange for the appointment of the former general to presidential advisor on national security and secretary of the Security Council. Yeltsin was thought to have sown up the second round, with Lebed's support, as long as voter participation was sufficiently high.[25] However, both statistical regression and survey research suggest that Yeltsin's majority victory in the second round was assured more by the further consolidation of the reformist vote—in particular support from voters who voted for the reformist opposition candidate Grigory Yavlinsky in the first round—than by any swing vote from traditionally nationalist candidates. Thus, even in this round, Yeltsin's presidential victory was fueled for the most part by reformist and centrist voters, who scattered their votes across a multitude of parties in the 1995 election. The greatest aid nationalist voters gave was abstaining from voting and thus not influencing the vote either way.[26] Table 6.5 shows OLS multiple regression analysis of the 1995 parliamentary vote and the second round of the 1996 election.

The most surprising thing about the relationship between the 1995 vote and the second round of the 1996 presidential election is how similar it is to that between the 1995 vote and the first round. Although the run-off produced a forced choice between the status quo and Communist opposition in the second round, the regression models for both Yeltsin and Zyuganov changed very little. The 1995 nationalist vote as represented by the LDPR, Congress of Russian Communities, and smaller nationalist parties (such as the National Republican Party of Russia) remained unrelated (not statistically significant at the .05 level)

Table 6.5: Multiple Regression of 1995 Vote on the Second-Round Vote for Yeltsin and Zyuganov

Yeltsin				Zyuganov			
Variable	B		Beta	Variable	B		Beta
Constant	.1366	(.0121)	—	Constant	-.0807	(.0127)	—
NDR	1.0732	(.0485)	.4890 **	KPRF	1.014	(.0322)	.6638 **
YAB	.7175	(.0790)	.2374 **	LDPR	.9062	(.0549)	.3530 **
Other Reform	1.036	(.0716)	.3904 **	Other Left	.8447	(.0507)	.3826 **
Centrist	.7075	(.1060)	.1823 **	Other			
Other	2.4788	(.3972)	.1872 **	Nationalist	.7216	(.0756)	.2103 **
	$MR = .9510$				$MR = .9530$		
	$R^2 = .9044$				$R^2 = .9082$		
	Adj. $R^2 = .9022$				Adj. $R^2 = .9065$		
	$SE = .0446$				$SE = .0440$		

Note: Other Reform: Democratic Russia's Choice, Forward, Russia!, Common Cause, Pamfilova-Gurov-Lysenko bloc, Transformation of the Fatherland; Center: Women of Russia, Worker's Self-Government bloc, Union of Labor, Ivan Rybkin bloc; Other Left: Agrarian Party of Russia, Power to the People, Communist-Working Russia-For the Soviet Union; Other Nationalist: Congress of Russian Communities, Derzhava, Stanislav Govorukhin bloc, National-Republican Party, My Fatherland; Other: KEDR, Beer Lovers' Party, NUR Moslem Movement, Electoral Bloc including Defense of Children, Electoral Bloc including Defense of Veterans.

*p = .01, **p = .001

to the Yeltsin vote. The same groups of electoral blocs (reformists, centrists, and other unclassified parties) remained the only ones positively correlated and statistically significant with the Yeltsin vote, and they could now account for 90 percent of the variance. The major change in the model from the first round to the second was the contribution of voters for Yabloko in 1995. The dramatically increased B and Beta scores both support the hypothesis that a significant vote swing from Yavlinsky supporters accounted for a large part of the increase of the Yeltsin vote. The difference in the Beta score for Yabloko from the first to the second round suggests that 1995 Yabloko voters had almost twice as strong an influence on the Yeltsin vote in the second as in the first.

Similar continuity in the relationship between the 1995 vote and the two rounds of presidential balloting existed for Zyuganov. Multiple regression of the 1995 vote on the second-round Zyuganov vote looked very similar to the same analysis on the first round, indicating that Zyuganov did not attract many new supporters from among centrists nor a wave of increased support from nationalists. Survey research generally supports this analysis; Rose and Tikhomirov show that the largest contingent of voters who supported the nationalist LDPR in 1995 did not vote at all in the second round of the presidential election (46 percent). The remainder split their support between Yeltsin and Zyuganov, with 24 and 25 percent supporting each. Lebed's endorsement surely helped Yeltsin. A majority of those who supported the Congress of Russian Communities, Lebed's bloc in 1995, ended up voting for Yeltsin in the second round (52 percent), but a significant proportion also did not vote or voted against all candidates (28 percent). Clearly, the nationalist vote did not contribute to either candidate in a decisive way. But in not swinging to Zyuganov in fulfillment of the mythologized "red-brown coalition," nationalist voters in the second round helped to deny Zyuganov a come-from-behind victory.

Presidential Elections in Other Postcommunist States

Is the Russian presidential election unique in its consolidating effects? Or have presidential elections in other postcommunist states also tended to constrain the number of candidates? Table 6.6 shows the effective number of candidates in eleven postcommunist presidential elections. All figures are taken from first-round voting in two-round majoritarian elections.

The data suggest that presidential elections have produced a relatively small number of candidates in postcommunist states. Most of the cases had an effective number of presidential candidates that was reasonably close to what the literature suggests. The $M + 1$ rule would predict three effective presidential candidates in the first round of two-round majoritarian elections and two effective candidates in plurality elections. With the exceptions of Poland and Roma-

Table 6.6: The Effective Numbers of Candidates
in Eleven Postcommunist Presidential Elections

Country/ Election	Electoral formula	Effective number of presidential candidates
Poland/1995	Majoritarian	4.00
Slovenia/1997	Plurality	2.78
Romania/1996	Majoritarian	4.31
Bulgaria/1996	Majoritarian	3.15
Croatia/1997	Plurality	2.21
Macedonia/1994	Plurality	1.51
Lithuania/1997	Majoritarian	3.27
Ukraine/1994	Majoritarian	3.72
Moldova/1996	Majoritarian	3.94
Armenia/1998	Majoritarian	3.64
Georgia/1995	Plurality	1.67

Source: Elections around the World website, www.agora.stm.it/elections/
election.htm

nia, each case was within one effective candidate of this expectation. The average number of effective candidates for the eleven cases was 3.11, which is quite low, considering the extent of party fractionalization in postcommunist parliamentary elections.

Ukraine and Lithuania provide the most compelling evidence for an additional constraining effect of presidential elections. Like Russia, these countries employ SMD elections for at least part of their legislative seats.[27] In both cases the two-round majoritarian systems constrained the number of candidates in the presidential elections to a much greater degree than they did in parliament elections. Ukraine had an average of 5.44 candidates per district in its 1994 parliamentary election, compared to only 3.72 candidates in the first round of its 1994 presidential election. In Lithuania, there was an average of about six significant candidates per district in its SMD tier in 1996 but only three significant presidential candidates in 1997. These findings mirror the experience in Russia and suggest that in postcommunist states presidential elections constrain the number of candidates to a greater extent than parliamentary elections, despite similar district magnitudes.

Implications for the Timing of Elections

These findings suggest that the timing of elections may have a great impact on Russian politics. Scholars have shown that greater proximity between presidential and parliamentary elections have produced a lower degree of party fractionalization in the legislature and a greater likelihood that the president will have majority or near-majority support there. When presidential and parliamentary elections are held at the same time, the constraining effect of the more important presidential election is expected to influence the legislative election, reducing legislative multipartism. Moreover, presidential coattails increase the chances that the president will have a large legislative contingent supportive of the president.[28]

Concurrent elections could be especially important in Russia, since presidential elections are the only ones that appear capable of constraining party fractionalization. If concurrent elections could spread the consolidating effect of presidential elections to parliamentary elections, party fractionalization could be significantly lowered. Moreover, if voters would vote a straight ticket in concurrent elections the debilitating executive-legislative conflict that has plagued Russian politics since the collapse of the Soviet Union could be mitigated. Given that conflicts between the executive and legislature have escalated to armed conflicts that threatened the viability of the democratic regime, any improvement in this vital institutional relationship would enhance the prospects of democratic consolidation.

The current sequence of elections—with parliamentary elections held six months before presidential elections—creates relatively close proximity between the two votes but a sequence that produces greater independence. As a counter-honeymoon election, such a progression requires that voters' prospective presidential choice will influence their current legislative vote. For presidential elections to influence parliamentary voting under such a sequence, the presidential campaign must be highly developed by the time the parliamentary election is held.[29] Given the highly volatile nature of Russian politics, this is not likely, when one considers that only three months prior to the 1996 presidential election Boris Yeltsin's poll numbers ranked him behind not only Communist Party leader Gennady Zyuganov but also Zhirinovsky and Lebed.[30]

But it is far from certain whether Russian voters would cast straight tickets in concurrent elections, as do voters in countries with more institutionalized party systems. There was a high degree of split-ticket voting in both the 1993 and the 1995 parliamentary elections, in part as a result of the high number of independent candidates competing in the plurality tier.[31] A continued tide of nonpartisan candidates may hinder the constraining influence of presidential elections and the effect of presidential coattails in the SMD parliamentary elections. Much also depends on the behavior of party elites, especially presidential candidates. Boris Yeltsin, for example, impeded the development of political parties in Russia by refusing to affiliate with any of the fledgling political parties or to build a party of his own. Connection between presidential and parliamentary elections, held concurrently or nonconcurrently, will depend greatly on whether prominent presidential candidates affiliate with parties capable of winning parliamentary seats or run populist campaigns as independents above party politics.

Conclusions

Unlike plurality elections to the Russian legislature, the two-round majoritarian election for the Russian presidency significantly constrained the number of candidates. Upon the completion of this manuscript, there has been only one presidential election in Russia so this finding is necessarily preliminary. Yet, comparative experience in other postcommunist states suggests that presidential elections constrain the number of significant candidates even in cases where single-member district elections for parliament do not. I have argued that in the absence of well-institutionalized parties, only presidential elections provide the necessary information and incentives for voters and politicians to engage in the strategic behavior that lowers the number of significant electoral competitors.

Presidentialism's consolidation of the vote has had dramatic consequences on electoral outcomes in Russia. I have argued that the key factor determining Yeltsin's surprising reelection in 1996 was the consolidation of reformist and centrist voters behind a single candidate; this case is demonstrated by the substantial continuity in voting patterns between the 1995 parliamentary election that produced an anti-reformist legislature and the 1996 reelection of a reformist president. The key difference between December 1995 and June–July 1996 was the level of consolidation of the vote choice by the electoral system; no great conversion toward either Boris Yeltsin or the cause of reform took place within the Russian electorate during that brief timeframe.[32] Moreover, although campaign strategy, domination of the media, and campaign spending were all factors that worked to the advantage of Boris Yeltsin, their influence was secondary and directly attributable to the consolidated electoral environment produced by the presidential election.

The dramatic differences produced by Russia's parliamentary and presidential elections raise basic questions about the quality of representation in Russia's emerging democracy. Much has been written about the forced choice between Yeltsin and Zyuganov and how the vote for Yeltsin was a negative majority, much more a rejection of the Communist past than an endorsement of Yeltsin or a reform agenda.[33] This is hardly a solid basis on which to lead a deeply troubled nation; however, one must realize that the parliamentary election was also an interpretation of popular will and as such produced its own misinterpretation of the desires of the electorate. While party fragmentation in both the PR and plurality halves of the 1995 election provided the Russian voter many more choices, 50 percent of the vote was left unrepresented in the State Duma. Moreover, the fragmented vote produced a legislature with a firm antireformist majority. Can this result be deemed an adequate representation of the electorate's will, when, forced to make a choice between a Communist candidate and the status quo six months later, a majority of Russian voters rejected the Communist Party?

7
Electoral Systems and Political Outcomes in Russia

Electoral systems do more than just influence the number of significant parties operating in a country or affect ascriptive representation; they are also the subject of struggle and manipulation by politicians, because they influence political outcomes. Parties win or lose, powerful special interests are more or less represented, and policy agendas are more or less likely to be advanced under certain types of electoral arrangements. This chapter will investigate the relationship between electoral systems and specific political outcomes in Russia.

Generally speaking, scholarship on electoral systems has concentrated on their systemic effects. These systems constrain the number of parties successfully operating in a polity, influence the proportion of women and minorities elected, or produce disciplined party organizations. These effects are assumed to be universal in nature, insofar as they are expected to apply to all actors in the system. No particular political party is deemed capable of escaping these effects as a result of its ideology, internal structure, or leaders.[1] Cross-national studies of electoral systems have necessarily concentrated on generalizable outcomes, such as the number of parties or level of disproportionality produced by a particular set of rules. The size of datasets for large cross-national projects is only part of the reason. Shares of votes and legislative seats are more easily operationalized and compared than policy output, the political character of the regime, or the fate of individual parties. However, by concentrating on the systemic effects of electoral systems, cross-national electoral studies have neglected their direct and indirect influence on specific political outcomes for any given country. It is the purpose of this chapter to specify the political implications of Russia's mixed electoral system not captured by the generalized concepts of the effective number of parties or disproportionality. In so doing, I will continue with the controlled comparison method of examining the similarities and differences found in the PR and plurality tiers of Russia's mixed electoral system.

Of course, depending on their status within the system and their geographical distribution of support, parties may be affected differently by electoral systems. A large party reaps the benefits of disproportionality by gaining greater representation in parliament from plurality elections, whereas a small party with an evenly distributed national vote is underrepresented or may be denied representation all together. Knowing this, parties will want to shape the electoral system to their own ends, which is essentially the crux of the endogeneity critique, which argues that party systems define electoral systems rather than the other way around. Such discrimination may also have policy implications. Two-party systems encouraged by plurality elections may preclude certain policy alternatives or even keep off the political agenda certain issues that would be championed by smaller parties that could achieve representation under different electoral arrangements. Coalitional politics produced by the multiparty governments typically associated with PR systems undoubtedly affect policy outcomes and government stability that differs from the majoritarian tendencies produced by SMD systems.

The arguments in this chapter concerning political effects of electoral systems in Russia vary somewhat from the political implications of electoral systems cited above. I do not find that geographic concentration of electoral support explains the success of small parties in the plurality tier; rather, I follow a more historical institutionalist approach, problematizing the issue of preference formation. I argue that PR or plurality electoral arrangements actually influenced the preferences of voters instead of simply providing incentives to defect from their exogenously held preferences if their preferred candidates or parties were deemed unlikely to win under the current electoral rules.

Proportional representation and plurality electoral arrangements affected vote choice in three crucial ways in Russia. First, through its election of deputies according to closed party lists, the PR tier bolstered the status of Russian parties as the dominant vehicle for the nomination and election of representatives; while the plurality tier undermined the status of parties allowing and even encouraging the proliferation of nonpartisan candidates, particularly in 1993 when the plurality tier was held under a nonpartisan ballot. Thus, the type of electoral system was an important influence over the role political parties would play in Russia. Second, PR and plurality electoral systems produced different electoral environments, which required different electoral resources for success. Consequently, the same political parties were more or less attractive to voters in the two tiers of the electoral system, depending on how well they mobilized resources necessary for success in that particular tier. Third, the different resources required for gaining office in PR and plurality elections produced legislators with very different ideological orientations. The PR elected a predominantly Moscow-centric elite that was more ideologically polarized, whereas the plurality elections sent to the State Duma a regionally based elite more centrist in its policy preferences.

Electoral Systems and the Emergence
of Russian Parties

In their classic book, *Transitions from Authoritarian Rule,* Guillermo O'Donnell and Philippe C. Schmitter argue that elections provoke parties.[2] The assumption underlying this hypothesis is that parties form the basis of modern democracy. Political parties are the vehicles most capable of, or at least best suited for, structuring the vote choice and contesting and wielding political power. Thus, when political power is subject to competitive election, parties naturally emerge to field candidates and form policy-making majorities or coalitions in the legislature.[3]

Similarly, rational-choice new institutionalism sees party formation as a natural extension of electoral competition and majority rule, arguing that political parties emerge because they help resolve problems of collective action and social choice in legislative and electoral arenas. In the legislature, the need to produce minimal winning majorities to realize policy goals creates incentives to form parties-in-government. While majority coalitions can form around individual issues without parties, a consistent voting equilibrium is unlikely. A party forms to produce a "structure-induced equilibrium," which allows partisan members to form long-term coalitions that reduce uncertainty and allow individual legislators to achieve their objectives more often.[4]

In elections, parties supply resources for overcoming collective action problems for voters and candidates alike. Parties help voters become sufficiently informed to choose between competing candidates by providing a great deal of information in a single party label, which conveys a lot about a candidate's general ideological profile and major policy positions. Once established among a sizable voting constituency, this brand-name effect can be a valuable resource for candidates, by providing instant credibility and reputation.[5] Winning a major party's nomination alone ensures a certain proportion of votes of that party's committed supporters. Moreover, parties provide economies of scale for individual candidates in their efforts to mobilize voter turnout. Whether a campaign is conducted by the party organization or by its individual candidates, getting out the vote for one candidate of a party often also helps other candidates of that party, especially when elections to more than one office take place simultaneously. Once at the polls, voters are likely to vote on all open offices, whether they have an interest in them or not, with partisan voters likely to cast straight tickets for candidates of their preferred parties.[6]

While not guaranteeing the existence of political parties, a rational-choice approach to party formation assumes a strong tendency toward party formation as long as competitive elections are the main avenues to political power and policy is determined by majority coalitions in elected legislatures.[7] Of course, certain conditions can prevent parties from forming. Other institutions may fill the roles of parties, or transaction costs of party formation may be so high that forming or joining political parties becomes impractical for individual candidates. But the ability of parties to overcome collective action problems faced by ambitious politicians makes party formation over the long term possible if not probable.

Western experience clearly supports such a role for parties in the modern democratic state, as do the democratization experiences of southern Europe and Latin America. In all of these cases, political parties quickly emerged to take center stage in electoral competition, albeit parties of varying levels of organizational strength and popular legitimacy.[8] The Russian case also supports the idea that elections are necessary for party formation, but it adds another caveat to the correlation between elections and party formation. The structure and context of elections, their rules, and the political environment in which they are conducted also play a significant role in the emergence of a multiparty system.

I noted one aspect of this caveat in chapter one; elections held under Soviet rule in 1989 and 1990 were not conducive to forming competitive political parties as the central organs structuring vote choice. Given the continued, although waning, dominance of the Communist Party of the Soviet Union and the late removal of Article 6 of the Soviet Constitution, which effectively forbade legal party activity outside the CPSU, partylike activity was relegated to an amorphous collection of umbrella movements, voter groups (sometimes surrounding single candidates), strike committees, and parliamentary factions.

The disintegration of the Soviet Union and the emergence of a sovereign Russian Federation did not greatly further the development of political parties; Yeltsin failed to call new elections immediately. The same fluid organizations continued to hold congresses, pass resolutions, and elect leadership bodies—with little effect on the dramatic political changes swirling around them. Without elections to supply an opportunity to capture state power and a reason to mobilize, newly formed parties existed in limbo for two years, waiting for a founding election.[9] Only with the dissolution of the Congress of People's Deputies and the calling of new elections in 1993 would electoral associations supporting candidates for office under specific labels emerge and take center stage in Russia, and only after the 1993 elections would the legislature in Russia organize itself around factions based first and foremost on the electoral blocs that successfully won representation in the PR tier of the election.[10] Although the weakness of the State Duma itself would mean that these nascent parties would play still only a marginal role in policy-making, this shift would greatly enhance the congruence between the electoral and legislative realms, with parties being the conduit uniting the two.

While the power of elections to provoke parties was present in Russia, the weakness of Russia's new parties was also strongly evident. As noted in chapter 2, the emergent political parties had weak internal mechanisms, poorly developed grassroots organizations, and barely existing social ties to the population. In 1993, most citizens knew the competing political parties and electoral blocs only by their leaders, if they knew them at all, with the possible exception of the Communist Party of the Russian Federation, which inherited the name recognition and organization of the CPSU. It was in this context that the electoral system had an effect on the status of political parties; the contrasting effects of the PR and plurality tiers on elite partisanship demonstrate that different electoral systems promoted or undermined the status of political parties as the central institution for structuring the vote choice in the election.

Viktor Sheinis, the main author of Russia's electoral law, put it most succinctly: "No proportional representation, no parties."[11] While the situation may not be quite as stark as that, comparison of the two tiers of Russia's mixed electoral system shows clearly that the PR tier made parties the central institution organizing the election by providing them with a monopoly over the nomination process. Just as the electoral system's creators had hoped, the PR system quickly established parties and electoral blocs as the central agents for structuring the electorate's vote choice. To get onto the ballot, elites were forced to form party lists, and voters had to choose between party blocs; nonpartisanship was not an option.

Conversely, the plurality elections undermined this central position of parties by allowing independent candidates on the ballot. In Russia's polarized political environment, nonpartisanship was a very attractive option because affiliation with either the proreform or the antireform ideological camps automatically alienated a large portion of voters. Moreover, the parochial nature of the SMD races worked against elite partisan affiliation because of the necessity for candidates to portray themselves as willing to fight against Moscow for the district. Given the Moscow-centric character of Russian parties, partisanship gave the impression that one was tied in with central authorities in Moscow and thus more likely to sell out the district's interests. Finally, the parties themselves have been so weak organizationally that they have little in the form of material or symbolic benefits to offer candidates. Consequently, the strongest contenders, particularly members of the regional executive branch, were likely to run on their own name recognition and personal appeal rather than risk the stigma of a partisan label.[12]

Put in the language of new institutionalism, party formation faced many more transaction costs in the plurality tier than in the PR tier of Russia's mixed electoral system. Ambitious elites seeking election in the PR tier were faced with more incentives to run under a partisan label (for example, exclusive ballot access to partisan organizations) than in plurality elections, which gave partisan and nonpartisan elites equal access to places on the ballot. By requiring party affiliation, the PR tier also enabled potential party-building elites to overcome obstacles that retarded partisan affiliation in the plurality tier. The issue of antiparty sentiment could be a meaningful deterrent to elite partisanship only if the option of nonpartisanship existed. As this existed only in the plurality tier, elites wishing to take advantage of the general mistrust of parties by avoiding partisan attachments could only do so in the SMDs. Attempts to field an electoral bloc of independents in 1995 drew very little support.[13]

Similarly, the issue of financial and organizational resources that parties can offer candidates is vastly different in PR and plurality elections. With the exception of the free television and radio airtime provided to all PR electoral blocs, parties did not have significantly greater resources at their disposal in the PR tier than in the plurality tier. However, the PR tier provided parties with the ultimate benefit: electable positions on the party list. A popular politician running in the PR tier had the choice of joining a major party likely to overcome the 5-percent barrier and negotiating a high place on its list in exchange for the prestige he or she lent it, or heading his or her own party list with the corresponding risks and burdens that entailed. Both options involved a certain amount of investment in an electoral organization; this was not the case in the plurality tier.

While the institutional design of proportional representation with closed party lists forced elites to adopt party labels, this did not necessarily mean there would be a greater connection between these nascent parties and voters. In fact, many studies have maintained that competition among PR electoral blocs has been based more on the personality of party leaders than any symbolic attachments to the blocs themselves or any differences in the policy programs advanced by them.[14] Arguably, if the nascent parties emerging from the PR tier were nothing more than the personal vehicles of their leaders, then the PR election really has done little more than to graft the candidate-centered nature of electoral politics found in Russia's SMDs onto a nationwide constituency under the guise of party labels. This seemed rather indiscreet in 1995, when electoral blocs headed by Ivan Rybkin and Stanislav Govorukhin simply adopted the names of their prominent leaders.

However, contrary to this depiction of Russian parties there is evidence that voters are developing partisan attachments independent of the popular standings of party leaders in Russia. Survey research has shown that Russian voters did not base their vote choices in the PR tier solely or even predominantly on the personality traits of leaders. Instead, there is emerging a structural basis for the PR vote in which identifiable social constituencies are consistently supporting parties they feel best support their interests. Arthur H. Miller, William M. Reisinger, and Vicki L. Hesli have found that many Russian voters have left behind much of their mistrust toward parties in general and, although still not rendering a positive evaluation of parties, have become increasingly neutral toward the idea of political parties as an institution. Moreover, there has been a dramatic increase in the proportion of Russians with partisan attachments. In 1992 only 20 percent of Russians identified one party that best represented their interests, but by 1997, 61 percent identified with a party in this way.[15] Other scholars have also found that social traits and political values are associated with support for certain parties, which suggests a social and ideological basis to vote choice that may develop into party identification over time as social cleavages solidify and parties hone their programs to appeal to specific groups.[16]

Is this increasing level of partisanship based primarily on personal traits of leaders? The empirical evidence suggests that it is not, at least not entirely. In 1995, when asked the basis on which they cast their votes in PR elections, Russian voters listed interest representation and policy programs above attraction to party leaders.[17] This varied among nascent Russian parties in the way one would expect; the Communist Party, with its longer history and greater organizational activity, attracted a greater share of its support from the representation of social interests than did all newer parties, while attraction to party leaders was more important for charismatic parties like Zhirinovsky's LDPR.[18]

The little empirical data on vote choice in SMDs suggests that partisan affiliation and policy programs were less important considerations for voters in the plurality tier. Colton found that voters in the 1993 SMD election based their decision on three major bases (each reported by 19 percent of respondents): each candidate's personal qualities, his or her attention to the needs of the region, and his or her policy program. Only three percent of respondents listed party affiliation as a basis for their plurality votes.[19]

Whether the growth of partisanship in the Russian electorate growing since 1993 suggested by these survey results was encouraged by, or perhaps even contingent on, a proportional representation electoral system cannot be satisfactorily determined here. More research using individual-level data on the degree of partisanship and policy-oriented voting in SMDs is needed. Yet, using survey research on PR voting showing increased party identification over time and the continued prevalence of independents in the SMD tier, one can make a plausible argument for the connection between PR and the development of political parties at both the elite and mass levels. It is unlikely that Russian elites would have managed to aggregate their efforts in national electoral blocs in the absence of PR and that Russian voters would have increasingly come to see these blocs as representative of social cleavages emerging in postcommunist Russian society. The little evidence that we have on vote choice in SMDs in Russia suggests that voters are more inclined to choose candidates on the basis of personal characteristics and regional issues, both of which are hardly conducive to the development of a national party system. The experience of regional elections only further supports this relationship between PR and party development. Independents have comprised a much greater share of legislative deputies in the regions, which rarely have PR elements in their electoral systems.[20]

Of course, these are initial elections in transitional regimes, which makes preliminary any argument regarding the relationship between electoral system and party development. However, our limited evidence allows some interesting initial assertions about the relationship between electoral systems and party formation in countries with weakly institutionalized party systems. First, the experience of Russia calls into question the automatic emergence of political parties as central actors in all democratic transitions once founding elections are called. In states with extremely weak party structures and little or no democratic experience, elections may not catapult parties to center stage without a push from the electoral system. Under such circumstances, the choice between PR and majoritarian elections may make the difference in whether a national party system forms. While post-Communism does not necessarily produce these circumstances, the former Soviet Union seems to be a breeding ground for such political contexts. Democratizing elites in the former Soviet Union hoping to encourage the development of political parties would do well to note the relationship between electoral systems and partisanship in Russia.

Finally, one must consider change over time; the status of parties and their control over access to elected office should increase as a country's parties develop. Nonpartisanship became less prevalent in 1995, in Russia's second parliamentary election, when the percentage of the vote going to nonpartisan candidates dropped from 48 percent to 36 percent and the percentage of winners who were independents dropped from 52 percent to 34 percent.[21] This downward trend may continue over time as parties become more established. Incumbents who ran as independents but joined parliamentary factions to have influence in the State Duma may have difficulties running for reelection as independents, especially if they joined the faction of a PR bloc. On the other hand, path-dependent development may freeze an element of nonpartisanship into Russia's party system long after the initial circumstances that produced the phenomenon have faded. These initial plurality elections, held under conditions of extremely weak parties, may have created a precedent for elite nonpartisanship, in which an independent label becomes a useful electoral tool that signals to voters an avoidance of the extreme polarization of Russia's political spectrum and greater attention to constituency service than to Moscow politics. As I will discuss in the epilogue, the rise of nonpartisan winners in 1999 to 1993 levels suggests the latter.

Moreover, rules governing the formation of parliamentary factions may also promote the continued salience of elite nonpartisanship in SMDs. Membership in a parliamentary faction is essential for legislators to have influence over the policy-making process. Each party that surpassed the 5-percent barrier in the PR tier is allowed to form a parliamentary faction. In addition, parliamentary rules allow deputies not affiliated with these parties to form their own factions— as long as they meet a threshold of thirty-five deputies. This was a compromise between large parties pushing for a higher threshold, to force independent deputies to affiliate with more established parties and independents that wanted a lower threshold, to allow greater opportunities for deputies to retain their independence from parties.[22]

Although this threshold places certain constraints on the ability of independents from the SMDs to form their own parliamentary factions, its result has been the formation of at least one faction with no tie to an electoral party in each of the first two parliamentary elections. In 1993, sixty-four deputies formed New Regional Policy, a parliamentary faction composed almost exclusively of independents.[23] In 1995, forty-two deputies joined Russia's Regions, the one parliamentary faction not tied to any PR electoral bloc.[24] The existence of such factions has supplied nonpartisan legislators with the same official standing as their partisan counterparts. In a parliament dominated by factions, this extends the viability of elite nonpartisanship from the electoral realm to the legislative. By allowing for the formation of parliamentary factions that have no tie to electoral party organizations, parliamentary rules permit ambitious politicians who avoided attachments to strong parties during the electoral campaign to continue avoiding party attachment in the legislature but retain influence over policy-making.

Electoral Systems and Party Success

It is not surprising that different electoral systems in Russia worked to the benefit or detriment of individual parties. One of the most important practical implications of the choice of system is the effect particular electoral arrangements have on individual parties. For example, in Great Britain the Liberal Party quickly lost much of its support when the Labour Party ascended as strategic voting pushed British voters to defect from the Liberals to avoid wasting their ballots on a third party sure to lose in the plurality system. The damage done to the Liberals was swift and decisive. With the ascendance of Labour in 1929, the Liberals' vote share dropped to a still- respectable 23 percent, but they received less than 10 percent of the seats, as a result of the disproportionality; by the next election, the Liberal Party could muster only 7 percent of the vote.[25]

The Russian case is interesting not for the fact that parties had different levels of success under PR and plurality rules, but for which parties most succeeded in each tier and for the reasons behind these different success rates. Two factors are usually deemed responsible for the impact electoral systems have on individual party success: the level of popular support and the geographic distribution of that support. Small parties with geographically dispersed support will be penalized by SMD elections and will benefit from PR elections with low electoral thresholds, and large parties will gain greater benefits under SMD elections, especially plurality elections.[26] This follows from the rational-choice framework of electoral-system studies and assumptions of strategic voting. The theory does not contend that an electoral system changes a voter's party preferences; rather, disproportionality produced by it affect incentives to stay with or defect from one's first preference. PR systems do not increase the number of voters who prefer smaller parties; they only allow strategically minded voters with such preferences to cast that vote with less fear of wasting it.

Russia's electoral experience, particularly in 1993, but also in 1995, suggests a very different dynamic; Russian voters split their votes between the PR and plurality tier of the election at a very high rate. Stephen White, Richard Rose, and Ian McAllister estimate that 70 percent of Russian voters cast split-ticket votes in 1993.[27] This would not necessarily run counter to the strategic voting hypothesis if the shift in the vote from the PR to the plurality tier ran from smaller parties with little chance of winning a plurality in a SMD to larger parties with better chances of winning. Indeed, such a shift from smaller to larger parties in Germany's mixed system is seen as evidence supporting the existence of strategic voting.[28]

However, in 1993, the party most hurt in the plurality tier was none other than Vladimir Zhirinovsky's LDPR, which won the most votes under PR. I argue that this suggests a different dynamic, one in which, in the absence of well-developed party identification in Russia, electoral systems influence individual parties' successes by demanding electoral resources that Russian parties possessed at very different levels unrelated to their geographic distribution of support.

Table 7.1 shows the number of seats from each electoral tier for parliamentary factions formed after the 1993 and 1995 elections. For each election most parties performed much better in one tier than the other. Of course, the large number of nonpartisan winners may skew the results by suggesting a failure of any one party in the plurality tier, when in reality all parties experienced a drop in support in the face of the general tendency toward nonpartisanship in the plurality races. However, closer examination of the fate of individual parties suggests that the differing fortunes of certain parties in the PR and plurality tiers also resulted from factors other than strategic voting or a general decline in the number partisan winners in the plurality races. Parties succeeded or failed in the two tiers of the mixed system based in large part on their ability to marshal the resources necessary for success in that particular tier. These resources turned out to be quite different for PR and plurality elections.

The ultranationalist LDPR, Zhirinovsky's party, provides the most dramatic example of how the electoral system has shaped the success of individual parties. Without the PR half of Russia's system, the LDPR would not exist as a significant player in Russian politics. In 1993, Zhirinovsky shocked the world with a first-place finish in the PR tier of Russia's first postcommunist competitive election. The LDPR gained 59 seats (26 percent of the 225 available) for its 23 percent of the PR vote. However, the same party managed only 5 (2 percent) of the 225 plurality seats contested in the same election. The same trend away from the LDPR in plurality races can be seen in the 1995 election; although the party lost more than half its support in the PR tier, it still made a respectable showing—garnering 11 percent of the PR vote, second only to the Communist Party. This provided the LDPR with fifty seats (22 percent of the PR total), resulting from the high level of disproportionality produced by the 5-percent

Table 7.1: PR and SMD Deputies Joining Parliamentary Factions in 1993 and 1995

Faction	Number of PR deputies	Number of SMD deputies[a]
1993		
Russia's Choice	40	35
Union of 12 December[b]	0	24
Yabloko	20	7
PRES	18	12
DPR	14	1
New Regional Policy[b]	0	68
Women of Russia	21	2
LDPR	59	5
KPRF	32	13
Agrarian Party	21	33
Russian Path[b]	0	15
1995		
Our Home is Russia	45	22
Yabloko	31	15
Russia's Regions[b]	0	40
Power to the People[b]	0	38
Agrarian Party[b]	0	35
LDPR	50	1
KPRF	99	50

Sources: Rossiiskaya gazeta, November 30, 1993, pp. 4–5; *Russia: Election Observation Report, December 12, 1993* (Washington, D.C.: International Republican Institute, 1994); Laura Belin and Robert W. Orttung, *The Russian Parliamentary Elections of 1995* (Armonk: M.E. Sharpe, 1997), 114–29.

a Includes independents and members of other parties that joined the faction after the election.
b Factions formed without PR members.

threshold in 1995. Meanwhile, the LDPR again performed dismally in the SMD races, managing to capture only one seat. If one takes the PR vote as the best indicator of party strength nationwide, the strategic voting hypothesis would predict a completely opposite trend. Russian voters should have been defecting away from minor parties and independents and toward the largest party (LDPR) out of concerns of wasting their vote.

The Agrarian Party of Russia (APR) presents the opposite case. In 1993, the Agrarian Party easily cleared the 5-percent barrier, finishing with 8 percent of

the PR vote and twenty-one seats. In the plurality tier candidates running officially under the Agrarian label won sixteen seats, giving the APR the second
highest total of plurality winners, following Russia's Choice. An additional sev-
enteen plurality winners, who ran independently or under a different party's label, would later join the Agrarian Party faction in the State Duma, making a
total of thirty-three Agrarian deputies elected in the plurality tier.[29] By the second parliamentary election in 1995, the APR's survival as a parliamentary party
was sustained only because of its prowess in single-member plurality races. The
Agrarian Party failed to pass the 5-percent threshold in the PR election but
gained twenty seats in the SMD races. With some additional independent deputies and "donor" deputies from its ally the Communist Party, the Agrarian Party
managed to form its own legislative faction after the 1995 election.

Why did the electoral systems have such divergent effects on individual political parties? The reasons seem to have less to do with geographic concentration of support than with the resources necessary to achieve success in each electoral tier. The PR contest is a national election; success requires either a well-
defined social constituency, such as the Communist Party still has among the
older generation, or a charismatic leader who can appeal to the large group of
undecided voters. Thus, the PR system has offered opportunities to political entrepreneurs such as Vladimir Zhirinovsky and Grigory Yavlinsky as well as parties with reliable social constituencies, like the Communists.

The pro-reform "party of power" (Russia's Choice in 1993 and Our Home is
Russia in 1995) has had a unique blend of assets and burdens in this environment. Given its preponderance of economic and political resources, the party of
power had the resources to wage an aggressive media campaign that should give
it a great advantage over its competitors in the PR race. Moreover, the party
lists of Russia's Choice and Our Home is Russia were populated by the best-
known politicians in the country. Of course, with these benefits of state power
came a major burden: association with all the social and economic problems
plaguing the country in its difficult transition from communism. This association with economic collapse and social degradation dwarfed the advantages in
resources the party of power might have and drove a significant segment of the
population into irreconcilable opposition of one stripe or another to the ruling
party.

Elections in the plurality tier had a much more local character. As reported
above, survey research suggests that voters paid greater attention to candidates'
personal characteristics and abilities to address local needs in the plurality tier.
Voters rewarded candidates who combined long-standing regional ties, name
recognition, and a prominent occupational status. Members of the regional political and economic elite (for example, regional government officials, enterprise
directors, collective farm chairmen, and private entrepreneurs) had an advantage over political newcomers from the professional classes (academics, doctors, lawyers) and Moscow-based politicians.[30] Thus, without some grassroots

organization and a cadre of well-known local politicians, parties could not attain widespread success.

The differential success of parties in the two tiers of the mixed system can also be seen in the proportion of votes received by individual parties in each tier. Table 7.2 shows a comparison of the plurality and PR vote in districts where the party had an individual candidate running in the plurality tier (defined in the table as contested districts).[31] This comparison provides several clues to the relationship between success in the each of the two tiers.

Why did certain parties perform better in the plurality tier than others? One possible explanation, dismissed thus far, would be the geographic concentration of a party's support. One might expect some parties to appeal to social constituencies that were geographically concentrated, producing a plurality in a number of SMDs that would give these parties an advantage over other parties with more dispersed support. The Agrarian Party's support in rural districts and Russia's Choice and Yabloko's support in major cities may be examples of this factor. If such were the case, however, one would expect to find a dramatic increase in the PR vote share for parties in the SMD districts they contested; a rural party such as the Agrarians would likely run candidates in rural districts, where it had the most support, and, similarly, urban parties like Russia's Choice or Yabloko

Table 7.2: Comparison of Plurality and PR Vote for Selected Parties

Party and election year	Average percent of plurality vote in contested districts	Average percent of PR vote in contested districts	Average percent of PR vote in SMD winners' districts	Plurality/ PR vote ratios for contested districts
APR 1993	16.0	9.7	14.6	1.65:1
APR 1995	13.6	5.2	11.8	2.62:1
KPRF 1993	12.9	14.2	17.5	0.91:1
KPRF 1995	21.3	23.6	28.8	0.90:1
NDR 1995	12.4	10.0	17.4	1.24:1
VR 1993	15.2	18.5	24.8	0.82:1
DVR 1995	8.8	5.3	9.0	1.66:1
YAB 1993	8.9	10.4	9.0	0.86:1
YAB 1995	10.7	10.1	15.3	1.06:1
PP 1995	9.9	2.7	4.8	3.67:1
LDPR 1993	10.1	24.3	32.4	0.42:1
LDPR 1995	6.6	11.6	22.0	0.57:1

Note: APR—Agrarian Party of Russia, KPRF—Communist Party of the Russian Federation, NDR—Our Home is Russia, VR—Russia's Choice, DVR—Democratic Russia's Choice, YAB—Yabloko, PP—Power to the People, LDPR—Liberal Democratic Party of Russia.

would run candidates in urban districts. However, most parties did not receive significantly greater shares of the PR vote in districts in which they ran SMD candidates. In fact, the PR vote in contested districts tracks rather closely to the national PR vote, the largest discrepancy being three percentage points for Russia's Choice in 1993. Of course, this may simply signal an attempt of parties to run candidates in as many districts as possible with little regard to their chances of victory.

Perhaps a better test of geographic concentration favorably influencing SMD performance is the PR vote in districts where a given party's candidate won the SMD seat. Here there is a much greater increase in the share of the PR vote for the party of the victorious SMD candidate. The Agrarian Party nearly tripled its national average PR vote in districts won by its twenty successful SMD candidates in 1995. Democratic Russia's Choice won more than twice as many PR votes than its national average in districts it captured (mostly in Moscow), and Yabloko won 50 percent more PR votes in the SMD districts it won. The LDPR won twice as many PR votes in the one SMD district it captured in 1995. However, it may be that a party's PR vote rose on the coattails of one its more popular candidates running as a candidate in the SMD race. Regardless, this concurrent rise in the PR and plurality vote in winners' districts at least suggests that the two tiers of the election were not completely isolated from one another, despite the very disparate national-level results that each tier produced.

On the other hand, simultaneous success in the PR and plurality tiers does not tell the whole story. Part of the explanation for certain parties' success in plurality elections lay in the ability of the individual candidates in plurality districts to exceed their parties' PR tier performance. Some parties nominated "overachieving" candidates who attracted more voters than their parties received in the PR tier; some parties had candidates who just maintained their parties' PR support; and some parties consistently fielded "underachieving" candidates who could not match their parties' successes in the PR tier. The ratio between the average plurality vote and the average PR vote presented in Table 7.2 tries to capture this relationship.

The Power to the People bloc and the Agrarian Party nominated candidates that averaged two and three times their party's PR votes, respectively. At the other extreme, LDPR candidates could attract only about half of their party's PR vote. Most of the other parties, including Russia's Choice and the Communist Party, which captured the most plurality seats in 1993 and 1995, respectively, fell somewhere in between these two extremes, only managing to maintain their PR votes in the plurality tier.

Thus, it seems success in the plurality tier depended on a combination of a threshold of party support and the ability to nominate well-known local elites. Some major parties, like Russia's Choice in 1993 and the KPRF in 1995, managed to capture a significant number of SMD and PR seats because they attracted a critical mass of voters in a large number of districts despite having relatively dispersed support. Other parties, like the Agrarians and Power to the People, won most or all of their seats in the plurality tier by nominating over-achieving candidates, who captured significantly more votes than the party itself. Finally, some parties, most notably the LDPR, could win only PR seats because they could not translate their relatively high PR support into a plurality of votes in SMD races, as they fielded a slate of underachieving candidates.

What made for overachieving and underachieving candidates in the SMD contests? The answer lies, first and foremost, with social status. Winning candidates in this tier came primarily from the political elite at the national or regional level and secondarily from the economic elite. The intelligentsia, which performed rather well in the first competitive elections under Soviet rule, were much less successful with each iteration of the electoral process. There is a clear difference between the profile of the LDPR and other parties that found more success in the plurality tier.

In 1993 the LDPR had no winning candidate who came from the political elite at either the national or regional level. The party's five winning candidates in 1993 were little-known activists in the LDPR, workers, journalists, and the leader of the bloc, Zhirinovsky himself. Conversely, those parties that did well in the plurality tier managed to recruit candidates from the political power structure. Over 40 percent of the winners from the Agrarian Party had political positions at the national or regional level in 1993. In 1995, the impact of incumbency (members of the State Duma winning reelection) produced an even greater proportion of the Agrarian SMD contingent (73 percent) who held national and regional elected office. Power to the People, a new party in 1995 and thus not as large a beneficiary of incumbency, also displayed a predominance of political elites among its successful SMD candidates. Over 55 percent of this party's winning candidates were national or regional office-holders.[32]

Yet, this condition did not produce clear or expected outcomes for every party. In particular, reformist parties, namely those whose power was most closely tied to President Yeltsin, did not perform as well as expected—whereas the Communist Party performed better than expected, considering its restricted ability to attract regional political and economic elites after the collapse of the Soviet regime and Yeltsin's "de-communization" campaign.

One would expect the party of power to have the greatest advantage in the SMD tier, given its access to regional political elites. As one might expect, both Russia's Choice and Our Home is Russia had distinct advantages in recruiting national and regional governmental elites as candidates. Both parties had a significantly greater percentage of their elected candidates come from the political elite than the average for all deputies.[33] Neither party performed as well as expected in the SMDs; Our Home is Russia's performance in 1995 (ten SMD seats) was particularly poor. This suggests that despite the primacy of candidate characteristics in gaining election in the plurality tier, parties could not completely overcome other disadvantages (most notably association with failed government policy) by fielding prominent local elites.

Unlike Russia's Choice or Our Home is Russia, the KPRF has not had much access to members of regional executive bodies, who often were appointees of President Yeltsin prior to the two elections studied here. The party has consistently elected a greater share of its SMD deputies from the intelligentsia in both parliamentary elections than have other parties, surely resulting in part from the Communist Party's more solid and committed social constituency. Communist winners in the SMDs invariably come from the regions with strong Communist support, the so-called red belt. The other part of the explanation of Communist Party success is strong grassroots organization, a legacy of the Soviet period.

Success in the plurality tier was not solely dependent on the local prominence of the candidates nominated by a party. The failure of the pro-government parties to translate their advantages in recruiting local elite from regional executive branches into widespread electoral success attests to this. Rather, success was achieved through a combination of the degree of underlying popular support and the nomination of noteworthy candidates.

This has important ramifications for Russian politics. As the only party with a solid social base and well-organized grassroots organization, the Communist Party is poised to continue dominating parliamentary elections, especially if the vote continues to be fragmented among a wide range of parties. As long as the KPRF remains the only relatively developed political party in Russia, it should benefit greatly from a mixed electoral system that rewards nationwide public appeal in the PR tier and party organization in the plurality tier. Moreover, since the Communists' nationwide appeal stems from party identification among an established social constituency (most notably pensioners) rather than from the charismatic following of a particular leader, its strength will not be as fleeting as more personality based parties, such as the LDPR. Since these tiers are unlinked, the advantages granted by each tier are exaggerated, and those parties that can combine the resources necessary for success in each will be doubly rewarded.

The Electoral System and the Ideological Composition of the State Duma

The political implications of Russia's mixed electoral system have been felt well beyond election day. The varying electoral outcomes in the PR and SMD tiers had a direct effect on the ideological composition of the State Duma. In general, the PR tier has polarized the Duma between two ideological extremes divided over the issue of democratic and market reforms. The SMD tier has elected many more centrist deputies, especially among the independents who shunned partisan labels during the electoral campaign.

I will demonstrate these divergent ideological outcomes of the two tiers of the electoral system through a comparison of legislative voting of PR and SMD deputies. This examination uses an ideological rating device of Russian deputies developed by Alexander Sobyanin who along with Edward Gel'man and O. N. Kaiunov closely analyzed legislative voting patterns in Russia. Sobyanin and his colleagues ranked each deputy along a continuum from +100 (most supportive of reform) to −100 (most opposed to reform) on the basis of a select number of key legislative votes.[34] I have added a hundred points to all scores to produce a positive scale ranging from 0 to 200 and then aggregated deputies into three categories: conservatives (0–50), centrists (51–150), and reformists (151–200). The large centrist category was used to capture the extreme polarization of the State Duma, which has been comprised of two large ideological blocs concentrated at the extreme ends of the ideological spectrum and a smaller, more diverse conglomeration of moderate deputies in between.

Table 7.3 shows the distribution of PR and SMD deputies across the ideological spectrum. The PR tier produced greater ideological polarization among its deputies than the SMD tier. In 1993, 78 percent of PR deputies displayed strong conservative or reformist orientations in their voting, compared to only 59 percent of SMD deputies. In 1995, polarization greatly increased in the PR tier. Nearly all deputies elected from PR party lists (96 percent) displayed strong conservative or reformist orientations, which is not surprising, since none of the four parties that overcame the 5-percent barrier was centrist. The SMD tier was a different story; centrist deputies maintained their share of those seats from

Table 7.3: Ideological Orientation of Deputies from PR versus SMD Tiers

Election tier	Percent (number) of Conservative deputies	Percent (number) of Centrist deputies	Percent (number) of Reformist deputies	Average ideological score
1993 PR (N = 218)	49.1 (107)	22.5 (49)	28.4 (62)	75.2
1993 SMD (N = 222)	34.7 (77)	39.6 (88)	25.7 (57)	90.8
1995 PR (N = 225)	63.1 (142)	4.0 (9)	32.9 (74)	72.6
1995 SMD (N = 225)	50.2 (113)	36.9 (83)	12.9 (29)	70.4

Source: Michael McFaul and Nikolai Petrov, eds., *Political Almanac of Russia* (Moscow: Carnegie Endowment for International Peace, 1998), 550–86.

Note: Conservatives = ideological score of 0–50, centrists = ideological score of 51–150, Reformists = ideological score of 151–200.

1993 to 1995, despite a dramatic shift against reform, which resulted from the devastating economic dislocation experienced under Yeltsin's reform program.

These findings complicate the view that Russian politics during this period of transition has been polarized, dominated by ideological camps with diametrically opposed world views and missing a vital center of moderate political discourse and policy platforms.[35] Russian parliamentary elections have indeed been polarized; however, the PR tier has driven this. Given the failure of a large centrist party to emerge and endure, the PR tier's legal threshold presents an obstacle, nonexistent in the SMD tier, that denies representation to centrist forces. Considered in this light, one could argue that the SMD tier provides greater substantive representation of the public will—since survey research shows that a large section of the Russian public has rejected both radical reform and a return to the old Soviet system. When asked about the pace of economic reform, those who preferred a gradual transition far outnumbered both advocates for a rapid shift to the market and those against market reform.[36] The large contingent of moderate deputies coming out of the SMD tier seems to reflect these preferences better than the polarized politics of the PR tier.

What drives this difference in ideological orientation between PR and SMD deputies? One potential factor is the fragmentation found in the SMD tier. The SMD tier has allowed more parties to gain representation, which has helped centrist parties, which were often smaller than their counterparts on the right and left. Essentially, SMD elections allowed well-known members of small centrist parties to win seats that could not be obtained in the PR election because of the 5-percent barrier. However, this is not the most important factor behind the increased moderation of SMD deputies. Instead, a closer look at the SMD legislators suggests nonpartisanship lies at the heart of the increased centrist tendencies of SMD deputies.

Table 7.4 compares the ideological orientation of SMD deputies who ran as candidates of political parties and those who ran as independents. Partisan SMD deputies displayed the same tendencies toward polarization as their PR counterparts did. In both 1993 and 1995, a large majority of partisan SMD deputies voted an either strongly conservative or reformist line. In fact, in 1993 partisan SMD candidates were more ideologically polarized than their PR counterparts. However, for both elections a majority of independents behaved as moderates in the legislature; this suggests that partisan winners in the SMDs came from either the conservative or the reformist camp, not from the center. The greater moderation of SMD deputies was not shared by all deputies but manifested only among nonpartisan deputies who, being unaffiliated with the major parties of the left or right, had centrist leanings.

**Table 7.4: Ideological Orientation
of Independent versus Partisan SMD Deputies**

Election tier	Percent (number) of Conservative deputies	Percent (number) of Centrist deputies	Percent (number) of Reformist deputies	Average ideological score
1993 Partisan SMD Deputies (N = 86)	43.0 (37)	19.8 (17)	37.2 (32)	94.5
1993 Independent SMD Deputies (N = 136)	29.4 (40)	52.2 (71)	18.4 (25)	88.5
1995 Partisan SMD Deputies (N = 175)	57.1 (100)	27.5 (48)	15.4 (27)	65.6
1995 Independent SMD Deputies (N = 50)	26.0 (13)	70.0 (35)	4.0 (2)	87.1

Source: Michael McFaul and Nikolai Petrov, eds., *Political Almanac of Russia* (Moscow: Carnegie Endowment for International Peace, 1998), 550–86.

Note: Conservatives = ideological score of 0–50, Centrists = ideological score of 51–150, Reformists = ideological score of 151–200

Electoral Institutions and Party Development in Russia

This chapter has attempted to establish electoral arrangements as institutions with direct influence over political outcomes in Russia. It has shown through a comparison of the two tiers of Russia's mixed system that electoral systems have influenced not only the number of parties in Russia but also the very status of political parties as electoral agents, the success or failure of individual parties, and the ideological character of the legislature. These findings suggest that the electoral system needs to be well integrated into any analysis of the development of political parties and democratization in Russia and other postcommunist states.

This analysis fills a gap in the literature on Russian party development. Scholars have acknowledged electoral systems' important roles in party development without methodically studying the subject.[37] Instead, they have concentrated on the timing of elections and the legacies of Soviet regime in explaining the various characteristics of Russia's emerging party system.

McFaul has argued that the sequence of founding elections has been a major determinant of party formation in postcommunist states. He claims that founding elections held while Communist parties were still in power produced two polarized camps, one Communist and the other anti-Communist, that are very volatile and lack social bases. However, founding elections held while Communist parties are in steep decline or disintegrating increases the chances for more stable parties and a more consolidated democracy. Comparing Hungary, Czechoslovakia, Poland, and Russia, McFaul claims that Hungary and Czechoslovakia benefited from holding founding elections soon after the fall of the Communist governments and as a result have had more developed political parties and more stable party systems. Conversely, Poland and Russia have suffered from weak parties partly because they held their first free elections during Communist rule and then failed to hold founding elections quickly after their respective Communist parties left power.[38] Similarly, Hough has noted the importance of timing in the development of parties arguing that the snap election called in 1993 intentionally discouraged the development of strong competitive parties, particularly centrist parties, so as to give all possible advantage to the party of power at the time, Russia's Choice.[39]

Fish has emphasized the legacies of the Soviet structure as sources of Russia's weak party system. Building on the work of Panebianco, Fish contends that central features of Russia's weakly institutionalized system, such as Moscow-centric organizations, weak liberal parties, and a polarized political spectrum arise mainly from state-society relations and socio-economic relations.[40] Moscow-centricity is deemed a natural extension of the overly centralized state of the Soviet period and the succeeding post-Soviet Yeltsin regime. Greater organizational and popular strength of anti-reformist parties are attributed to the conditions surrounding the initial formation of these parties. The main liberal parties, particular Russia's Choice and Our Home is Russia, were "born in power" and consequently had fewer incentives to organize as effective institutions. Finally, the main source of ideological polarization lies in the social structure of postcommunist Russia, which does not contain a large social constituency with a socioeconomic profile likely to be committed to moderate social democratic ideals.[41]

Integration of institutions need not come at the expense of these other factors. The absence of elections after the collapse of Soviet power in 1991 undoubtedly inhibited the emergence of political parties by leaving nascent parties in a state of limbo, with little reason to exist. The rapid emergence of parties and electoral blocs in anticipation of early elections in 1993 demonstrates the necessary link between founding elections and party development. Moreover, the weaknesses of Russia's nascent parties—a poor organizational base, weak social constituencies, fragmentation, and ideological polarization—are inseparable from societal conditions, which range from a pervasive anti-party sentiment among the elite and masses to weak and fluid socioeconomic interests thrown into chaos by poorly defined property rights and dramatic economic and social change.

Russia's mixed electoral system was introduced after the mold of weak, poorly defined parties had been set and thus cannot be seen as an original cause of these characteristics. As a result, the influence of electoral systems in the

Russian context lay in the interplay between the system itself, weak political parties, and the more general social context. Electoral systems matter because different rules help or hinder parties to overcome onerous environmental constraints to their development by providing incentives and disincentives to elite and mass partisan attachments.

Clearly, PR and plurality electoral systems provided very different sets of enticements for partisanship generally and the development and success of individual parties. Russian parties were likely to be organizationally weak and lack strong social ties under any electoral system. But their ability to control access to elected office, despite these weaknesses, lay principally with the type of electoral system introduced. Similarly, while the legacy of the Soviet regime may have pushed parties to be Moscow-centric, an arrangement of SMD elections spread across the country will provide a strong counterbalance pushing for decentralization and the rise of a regionally based elite. Finally, while the social structure of Russia may undermine the emergence of strong social democratic parties, the dramatically higher numbers of centrist deputies coming out of the SMD tier shows that electoral rules are an important intervening variable that also affects the ideological character of the legislature.

Russian party development is a product of a complex interplay among a matrix of institutional, social, and elite-driven factors. The purpose of this book has been to firmly establish electoral institutions as central to this process. Taken to their logical extreme, hypotheses concerning the timing and sequence of elections posit that parties automatically emerge to take center stage once elections are called. The Russian experience shows that countries with extremely weak parties need additional conditions, namely PR elections, to provoke parties. Moreover, socially induced weaknesses among Russian parties have been at least partially circumvented or exacerbated by the type of electoral system employed.

At the same time, institutional explanations can also be overdrawn; cross-national studies of electoral systems suggest that elites can engineer their preferred combination of minority representation and government stability through the manipulation of such systems. But the Russian experience shows that society can intervene in this causal relationship and complicate the effects of electoral systems, undermining the idea that successful democratization can be achieved simply by getting the institutions right.

8

The Mixed System
and Party Development
in Russia

This book began with the assertion that electoral systems significantly affected Russian politics, but not in ways predicted by the voluminous literature on electoral systems. I carried out a controlled comparison of the PR and plurality tiers of Russia's mixed electoral system, to examine the way political outcomes varied under different electoral arrangements, controlling for all other explanatory factors by holding them constant. This contention has been borne out in a number of ways.

First, contrary to the most famous dictum of the electoral-studies literature, at neither the national nor the district level did plurality elections limit the number of parties to two. Instead, parties proliferated in the plurality tier, or more correctly, the average number of candidates, many of them independents, exploded to quantities that matched those of the most fragmented systems found in PR systems in consolidated democracies. While the PR tier produced even more parties in the electoral realm in 1995, its 5 percent legal threshold was a far more powerful constraint on the number of parliamentary factions emerging out of this tier than was the effective threshold of the plurality tier.

Comparative analysis of other postcommunist states and new democracies suggested that some elements of Russia's experience were common and others unique. Postcommunist states in general seemed to experience both greater party fragmentation than did other nations of the world and also a corresponding lack of strategic behavior by elites and voters in initial elections. However, those postcommunist states with more developed party systems experienced greater mechanical effects in SMD elections and showed greater adaptation to electoral system incentives over time. Only in Ukraine did SMD elections fail to have a powerful mechanical effect, allowing extreme fragmentation in the legislature.

Second, contrary to Western experience, PR elections were not more conducive to women's representation than plurality elections in Russia. In fact, upon the failure of the Women of Russia bloc to overcome the 5 percent legal threshold in the 1995 election, this relationship was reversed—plurality elections produced significantly higher numbers of women in parliament than did PR. The experiences of other postcommunist states confirm the ambiguous relationship between electoral systems and women's representation in these states. Mixed systems in Lithuania and Ukraine, for example, showed no statistically significant effect of the PR tier on women's representation. Only in Hungary did PR seem to provide women with additional electoral advantages. On the other hand, four mixed systems in consolidated democracies each showed positive and statistically significant relationships between PR and women's representation. Again, Russia was an anomaly, the only case to show a negative relationship between the two.

Third, the relationship between electoral systems and the election of non-Russian minorities presented a number of interesting findings. Contrary to initial expectations, both the plurality and the PR tiers provided non-Russians with representation proportional to their share of the population. Russians did not enjoy an advantage in either tier, despite their numerical superiority. As expected, the plurality tier favored those non-Russian groups that have ethnically defined federal units (republics or autonomous okrugs). Republican status proved a powerful factor promoting non-Russian representation independent of the distribution of ethnic groups. Non-Russians could win districts with Russian majority populations if they were located in non-Russian regions. Most of the non-Russians gaining election in the PR tier were assimilated groups, particularly Ukrainians.

This examination of ethnic heterogeneity and representation in Russia uncovered another counterintuitive finding; contrary to comparative experience, ethnic heterogeneity in Russia diminished, rather than increased, the number of competitors at the district level (both PR blocs and plurality candidates). Conventional wisdom and empirical scholarship suggest that greater ethnic heterogeneity, used as a proxy for social diversity, will produce a higher number of parties; yet, in the chaotic context of Russia's transition, more ethnically diverse regions are also those most under the control of a regional power structure that can dampen competition. Moreover, in the midst of unsettling social change, ethnic identity may provide a bond uniting large groups of people that is missing in more ethnically homogenous Russian regions.

Fourth, Russia's 1996 two-round majoritarian presidential election did constrain the effective number of candidates, even in the first round. This was a significant break from parliamentary electoral experience, in which a more powerful electoral system could not limit the number of candidates at the district level. I argued that the nature of the presidential election—a high-stakes national election to the most powerful office in the land—provided the incentives and information necessary for strategic voting to occur, factors that were missing in more parochial plurality elections for seats in the legislature. This consolidation of the vote proved a primary reason behind President Yeltsin's surprising re-election, which came just six months after antireformist parties won a majority of seats in the 1995 parliamentary elections.

An examination of other postcommunist states with popularly elected presidents showed a similarly powerful constraining effect, suggesting that the timing of presidential and parliamentary elections may be a crucial factor in party fragmentation in postcommunist states. Concurrent presidential and parliamentary elections, which are not common in postcommunist states, could be a powerful instrument for limiting the number of parties in the legislature if the presidential election had a coattail effect on the parliamentary vote. But this effect may require a more developed party system, which makes questionable a significant constraining effect of concurrent elections in Russia.

Finally, electoral systems were shown to influence practical political outcomes in Russia. PR and plurality elections had very different effects on the status of political parties, the success of individual parties, and the ideological composition of the legislature. PR elections bolstered the status of political parties by forcing elites to form parties to get onto the ballot and in turn forcing voters to choose between party labels rather than individuals, whereas plurality elections undermined parties as the principal institution of electoral competition by allowing independents to compete on an equal footing with partisan candidates. Individual parties also fared better or worse in the two tiers, depending on their ability to marshal the very different resources that were necessary to achieve success in PR and SMD elections. Parties led by charismatic individuals, like the LDPR, could win the PR tier in 1993 but be virtually shut out of seats in the plurality tier. Conversely, parties denied representation in the PR tier like the Agrarian party could use their network of grassroots organizations and powerful, well-connected local candidates to maintain a position in the legislature through the plurality tier. Finally, the two tiers each elected legislative contingents with very different ideological profiles. A majority of PR deputies had extreme ideological orientations from both ends of the political spectrum, producing the oft-cited polarization endemic to Russian politics. But SMD deputies were much more moderate, particularly the large class of independents who staked out a centrist position between the two extremes. Throughout this study, it was consistently shown that institutions matter but their effects are molded by the social context in which they operate.

The Mixed Electoral System—
An Ideal Arrangement for Russia

Given these findings, what is the most appropriate electoral system for Russia and other postcommunist states undergoing democratic transitions? Giovanni Sartori has argued against mixed systems in new democracies, strongly denouncing them as "a mismarriage, a very unsound and counterproductive arrangement."[1] I disagree. Russia's mixed system is the most appropriate electoral arrangement for its weak party system and should be seriously considered by any state in a similar condition.

Sartori's critical assessment is based on the assumption that the PR tier allows party proliferation, whereas the SMD tier restricts the number of candidates to two, producing competing and contradictory incentives for party consolidation. As this book has shown, such is not the case for Russia or other post-Soviet states. Russia's mixed system does produce contradictory outcomes; however, these contradictions check the most detrimental effects PR and plurality elections have on Russia's weak party system, producing a complementary set of incentives that provide the greatest chance for long-term party development.

Both PR and plurality electoral systems offer advantages and disadvantages for Russian politics. PR has the chief advantage of establishing parties as the central institution structuring the vote. Without PR, there could emerge a large contingent of unaffiliated independents who retard the development of a stable party system, as found in Russia's plurality elections or Ukraine's 1994 majoritarian election. While PR parties in Russia are not the picture of organizational strength and cohesion, they are far more stable and meaningful than the parliamentary factions formed by independent deputies in the Duma, which do not carry over their labels or organizations to the electoral campaign and thus provide no concrete connection between the electoral and legislative spheres. Some element of PR that requires party affiliation to get on the ballot is essential for the emergence of parties in states with little or no democratic experience.

PR elections that institute a significant legal threshold also provide the greatest potential constraint on the number of parties in weakly institutionalized party systems like Russia's. Although Russia's 5 percent barrier has not yet produced significant levels of strategic behavior in its first two elections, it has produced a high level of disproportionality, which has served to limit the number of parties entering parliament and has denied representation to supporters and members of marginal parties, a penalty that was not felt by small parties in the plurality tier, because many of them managed to elect their leaders in SMD races. The disproportionality produced at the national level by the PR tier is more likely to push marginal parties out of business than that in the more permissive plurality tier.

There is an interesting caveat regarding the relationship between disproportionality and the number of parties produced by the PR tier. The high level of disproportionality produced by the legal threshold in 1995 may drive smaller parties to consolidate into larger coalitions and push voters to strategically defect to larger parties. I do not expect to see forty-three parties on the PR party-list ballot in future elections; however, this consolidation in the electoral arena will probably increase the number of parties in the legislature. Paradoxically, a less crowded field would most likely have produced substantially more PR parties in the State Duma than the four that won representation in 1995.

The major disadvantages of PR are its failure to promote the nationalization of parties in the regions, its emphasis on charismatic leadership (the Zhirinovsky phenomenon), and its tendency to promote ideological extremism and polarization. These side-effects produce a polarized party system that lacks strong roots in society and leans toward demagoguery and political extremism that threaten democratic consolidation.

The strengths and weaknesses of plurality elections counteract the central characteristics of PR, creating complementary cross-pressures that promote well-balanced party development. The strength of plurality elections lies in the incentives for the nationalization of party structures through building grassroots organizations and national networks of well-known local elites. Plurality elections parochialize the competition for seats to the Duma, enhancing the role of regional elites and counteracting the dominance of Moscow elites on PR lists. Parties must build a local presence around the country to win a large number of seats in the SMD tier. The main limitation of plurality elections is that in a weak party system they undermine the status of parties by allowing the proliferation of independents.

By combining these two very different electoral arrangements in a single system, Russia's has forced party leaders, candidates, and voters to engage in a more complete process of party formation that includes national-level peak organizations and regional grassroots mobilization. Such a system checks the excesses of pure PR and plurality arrangements, moderating the ideological polarization and Moscow-centricity of PR while establishing the basis of a party system lacking in the endemic nonpartisanship of Russian plurality elections. If democracy survives in Russia and competitive elections continue to be held under this system, the PR and SMD tiers may cross-fertilize over time. Over the long term, a process of attrition should produce Russian parties with characteristics that make them successful in both tiers, strengthening the role of political parties in representation and national integration. Leaders of PR blocs have already been forced to turn their attention to developing grassroots organizations and recruiting quality local representatives if they ever hope to be competitive in the election for the other half of the seats to the Duma. Likewise, powerful regional elites have been tempted to establish their own PR blocs or join established ones in order to translate their regional clout into success in the PR half of the election.

There is already evidence that such a process of convergence between the two tiers is under way: PR parties like Yabloko have devoted considerable time and resources to developing their grassroots organizations, while the emergence of Fatherland-All Russia as a bloc of regional elites demonstrates that they intend to try their hand at PR party politics in the next parliamentary election. Moreover, there has already been a considerable increase in partisanship from the first parliamentary election to the second. Conversely, the number of nonpartisan candidates and the level of support for independents declined from 1993 to 1995: in 1993, 46 percent of candidates officially ran as independents, compared with 40 percent in 1995. Voter support for independent candidates fell more dramatically;in 1993, independents received 48 percent of the vote, compared with only 36 percent in 1995. Similarly, independents won fewer seats in 1995 (34 percent) than they had in 1993, in which over half (52 percent) of the winning candidates had no official partisan affiliation.

Finally, there is also some indication of an increase in voting consistency between the two tiers. Table 8.1 shows the correlation between the PR vote (disaggregated to SMDs) and the plurality vote for major parties in the 1993 and 1995 elections. Since parties did not run candidates in every district (party penetration was particularly scant in 1993), bivariate correlations were conducted only for those districts in which a given party had a candidate running. There was a clear and significant rise in the correlation of the PR and plurality vote at the district level from 1993 to 1995 for all parties examined.

An institutional reason for this rise in the correlation in 1995 needs to be acknowledged. In 1993, the plurality elections had been contested on nonpartisan ballots, which did not provide the party affiliation of candidates, and thus voters may not have had enough information to cast straight-ticket votes even if they had wanted to. In 1995, party affiliation was included on the ballot, promoting partisan voters' abilities to identify their preferred parties' candidates on the ballot and cast straight ticket votes. This institutional change probably had at least as much influence over the increased congruity of the vote between the two tiers as did any change in the status of political parties in Russia. The electoral system is just one of a myriad of factors that will help determine the future character of Russia's nascent party system. But the combination of incentives produced by the current mixed system provides Russian parties with the best possible institutional environment.

Table 8.1: Correlation Coefficients for PR and Plurality Vote for Selected Parties

Party	Correlation between PR and plurality vote in 1993 (contested districts)		Correlation between PR and plurality vote in 1995 (contested districts)	
Russia's Choice	.3942**	(N = 106)	n/a	
KPRF	.2955	(N = 53)	.5842**	(N = 124)
LDPR	.4006*	(N = 58)	.7676**	(N = 176)
Yabloko	-.1273	(N = 83)	.6355**	(N = 64)
APR	.5749 **	(N = 69)	.7499**	(N = 85)
NDR	n/a		.5148**	(N = 102)

*p = .01   **p = .001

Possible Changes
to Russia's Mixed System

The above argument highlighting the positive effects of Russia's mixed electoral system does not imply that Russia's particular version is best adapted to its
needs or those of other new democracies. As chapter 1 shows, there are many
ways to combine PR and SMD elements in a mixed system, and perhaps variations other than Russia's parallel system would provide even more benefits for
party development. I will address the potential advantages and disadvantages of
four possible changes to Russia's current electoral arrangements.

A Linked System

Russia could adopt a linked system that prioritizes the PR tier in the final distribution of seats to the State Duma. In consolidated democracies like Germany
and New Zealand, linked systems are used to promote greater proportionality
between seats and votes. But that would not necessarily be the outcome in Russia, given the disparity of success for parties in the two tiers and the proliferation of nonpartisan candidates in the SMD tier. Perhaps linking the two tiers of
Russia's mixed system would curb these problems, producing greater correspondence in the vote under PR and plurality tiers. It is difficult, however, to imagine the ways a technical rule change affecting the final distribution of seats could
significantly affect the strategic decisions of voters. Moreover, the results of the
first two elections suggest that a linked system of compensatory seats would
benefit nationalist and leftist parties, given the relative success of the Communist Party and Zhirinovsky's LDPR in the PR tier.

Most important, such a system would be ill advised for Russia, as it weakens
the incentives produced by the SMD tier for the nationalization of political parties. While the PR tier has promoted the development of parties by establishing
them as the only avenue to get on the ballot, this tier does not encourage regional party building. In fact, PR has been blamed for the tendency toward
overcentralization of Russian parties around a small band of Moscow politicians.
On the other hand, the SMD tier has encouraged the development of grassroots
organization and the recruitment of local notables by parties, because these are
vital factors for success in that half of the election. If the system were linked,
the PR tier would gain ascendance over the SMD tier, weakening the incentive
for parties to concentrate on party-building at the grassroots level. If parties were
forced to subtract the seats won in SMDs from their PR totals, they would naturally concentrate on the PR race.

Regional PR lists

Another potential change to the Russian mixed system would be the replacement of its single, nationwide PR district with a number of smaller, regional ones. This innovation would constrain the number of parties in the PR tier not just with the 5 percent legal barrier but also by lowering the district magnitude in the PR tier. Besides the potential consolidating effect on the party system, regional PR lists could also combat the Moscow-centric orientation of parties, forcing parties to cultivate regional leaders to populate a regionalized list. In fact, Russia did implement a related change in its 1995 electoral law to promote greater regional representation in the PR tier. Every party was required to have a national list of twelve politicians and then divide the rest of the list according to regional designations of their choice and distribute seats past the initial twelve according to their regional distribution of the vote. This reform was part of a compromise between President Yeltsin, who wanted a greater share of SMD seats, and the State Duma, which was determined to maintain the even split between PR and SMD seats. District magnitude in the PR tier changed not because the number of seats awarded to parties in this tier still was based on the national PR vote. Rather, the change is usually seen as having produced more cosmetic than substantive changes in regional representation.

Regional PR lists are also not a good idea for Russia, mainly because of their possible detrimental effects on the nationalization of the country's nascent parties, which are beset by difficulties in becoming established in all regions of this vast country. Regional party-like formations headed by regional executives with little or no ties to national party organizations often dominate regional politics. For example, Edward Rossel and his Transformation of the Fatherland electoral bloc dominated the Sverdlovsk region in the 1995 parliamentary elections, winning the most votes in the region in the PR tier and one SMD seat. However, the bloc performed so poorly in all other regions that it fell far short of the 5 percent legal threshold. Over time the nationwide district should compel regional party formations such as Rossel's Transformation of the Fatherland to consolidate into national electoral blocs, improving national integration, but regional lists could encourage such regional parties.

Two-Round Majoritarian SMD Elections

One innovation I recommend is the introduction of two-round majoritarian elections in the SMD tier of Russia's mixed system, which do promise to prolong legislative elections and make them more costly—two significant concerns in a polity as unstable and cash-strapped as Russia. Moreover, by raising the district magnitude in the first round of elections to two (the number of candidates entering the run-off) such elections may produce even greater candidate proliferation in the SMD tier. However, the potential benefits of run-off elections for party building may outweigh these costs. Majority elections would mean that SMD legislators would enter office with a majority of votes (albeit a manufactured majority) rather than the small plurality most now enjoy, possibly adding a measure of popular legitimacy to these representatives. More important, a run-off between the two top finishers could be an institutional mechanism to produce the type of coordination at the elite and mass levels that currently has not been found in plurality elections in Russia. While the plurality arrangement has not produced the two-party system many expected, a second round run-off would force a two-candidate race that could help promote the development of two large electoral blocs in Russia—through the necessity of second-round negotiations between like-minded parties struggling to ensure the election of ideological allies and thwart that of despised enemies.

Concurrent Presidential Elections

Finally, it must be remembered that Russia has a popularly elected president with strong constitutional powers and that this popular election will naturally have a very significant effect on the development of the party system. If presidential elections were held concurrently with legislative elections, their consolidating effects might carry over into the legislative arena; however, the weakness of Russia's parties might not provide enough linkage between the two races to provide this contagion effect. Moreover, there is the risk of a contagion effect running the other way. The proliferation of parties produced in legislative elections could promote a higher number of candidacies in a concurrently held presidential election.[2] Parties that have already expended the resources to field a party list and SMD candidates in the legislative elections would not face many additional costs in fielding a presidential candidate. Granted, minor parties would still face the prospects of almost certain defeat; however, in the context of concurrent presidential and legislative elections, a presidential campaign might provide other benefits for parties. The media attention alone (especially if the state provides free airtime to presidential candidates) could prompt parties to put up a candidate. Since a weakly institutionalized party system might undermine the consolidating effects of presidential elections on the legislative party system and the reverse contamination of legislative elections on the presidential race could actually promote an increase of presidential candidates in the first round, the continuation of nonconcurrent presidential and legislative elections seems the safest course for Russia, in the short term at least.

The Impact of Party Institutionalization

Throughout this book, I have argued that a lack of party institutionalization has been the primary factor responsible for the unique effects of electoral systems in Russia and that weak parties have not provided the strong voting cues and information on the viability of candidates necessary for strategic behavior. I have offered only anecdotal evidence to support this claim: Postcommunist states with more developed party systems appeared to follow the more traditional pattern of electoral system effects. Countries like Ukraine, with party systems as weak as Russia's, displayed the same distinct characteristics of parties failing to even control access to elected office. The influx of independents produced similar party proliferation in the legislature, an effect that did not occur in states in which parties dominated the nomination process. In Lithuania and Hungary, SMD elections did not curtail the number of competitors during the election but did produce a significant mechanical effect that substantially reduced the number of parties entering parliament from the SMD tier.

This hypothesis can be more methodically tested through a comparison of party institutionalization in Russian electoral districts. In this study I have operationalized party institutionalization as the level of party control over access to office, that is, the number of partisan candidates versus nonpartisan candidates and their respective levels of electoral support. Russia's 225 SMDs offer a wide range of levels of party control over nominations. Some districts were exclusively nonpartisan or were overrun by independents or leaders of microparties (which, as personal vehicles of single leaders, were functional equivalents to independents). Other districts had relatively equal numbers of partisan and nonpartisan candidates or even were dominated by members of major parties.[3] An examination of the effect of party institutionalization on the effective number of parties in Russia, statistically controlling for other factors found to influence the number of parties, will bring more systematic evidence to bear on this question. If party institutionalization were a significant intervening variable influencing party fractionalization, one would expect a negative correlation: a rise in party institutionalization should produce a drop in the effective number of candidates at the district level.

To examine this relationship, a multiple regression analysis was conducted, one similar to the model used in chapter 4 to study the relationship between ethnic heterogeneity, electoral systems, and the number of candidates and parties at the district level. The dependent variable was the effective number of contestants competing in SMDs. This variable was operationalized as the effective number of parties per SMD in the PR tier and the effective number of candidates per district for the SMD tier.[4] The two tiers were pooled together, yielding 444 cases.[5]

The independent variable of greatest concern here, party institutionalization, was operationalized as the percentage of the plurality vote cast for members of major parties, defined as those parties which won five or more seats to the State Duma. This definition of party institutionalization assumes that the formation of major national parties will be a significant intervening factor constraining the number of candidates in the plurality tier and parties in PR elections. It is not enough for nominations simply to become more partisan if that partisanship is overrun by a plethora of microparties formed around a single individual and capable only of electing its leader in an SMD race if it is lucky.

It might be argued that this operationalization of party institutionalization produces a tautological relationship between the number of candidates and parties. By definition, the number of parties will go down in districts where a greater percentage of the vote goes to the few largest parties. But, this danger, while it needs to be seriously addressed, is not fatal, because of the unique nature of the emerging Russian party system. First, by my definition, there are eight major parties which allows for the possibility of extensive fragmentation of the vote in highly institutionalized districts.[6] Second, many independents were highly competitive, with good name recognition, high social status, and previous political experience—not the political outsiders that independents often are in consolidated democracies. In fact, they were among the most popular candidates in district races and thus just as capable as members of major parties to constrain the number of parties through accumulation of a large number of votes. Indeed, as a category, independents were the most successful class in the SMD tier; roughly a third of the 1995 plurality vote went to each of my three categories: major party candidates, independents, and marginal party candidates.

I introduced three other control variables—the electoral system variable and two social heterogeneity variables (percent of urban dwellers and percent of Russians in the district)—that were found to be statistically significant factors influencing the effective number of PR parties and plurality candidates at the district level. Table 8.2 shows the results of the regression analyses in two mod-

Table 8.2: Determinants of the Effective Number of Candidates/PR Parties per District, 1995

Independent Variables	Coefficient estimates (standard error)	
	Model 1	Model 2
ESYSTEM	—	1.92 (.21)***
PARTYINS	-3.21 (.70)***	-2.74 (.59)***
URBAN	—	0.04 (.006)***
RUSSIAN	—	0.04 (.006)***
Constant	9.40 (.28)***	2.19 (.58)***
Adjusted R^2 =	.04	.36
N =	444	444

*** $p < .001$

els. Model 1 shows the bivariate relationship between party institutionalization and the effective number of contestants; and Model 2 gives a fully specified model, including electoral system, social heterogeneity, and party institutionalization.

The regression results support my hypothesis that party institutionalization has been a significant factor influencing the number of parties and candidates competing in Russian elections. In both the bivariate and multiple-regression analyses the coefficient was negative, as expected, and statistically significant. As party institutionalization increased in Russia's single member districts, the effective number of parties and candidates at the district level decreased, even after controlling for the effects of the electoral system and social heterogeneity. The relatively low R^2 of the bivariate model suggests that party institutionalization is not the only or even the most important factor influencing party fractionalization, but it does have a significant impact independent of institutional and social factors.

Russia, New Institutionalism, and the Study of Comparative Politics

This study of electoral system effects in Russia has a number of implications for the new institutionalism approach in political science and the study of comparative politics. The short time period and transitional character of Russia's regime make any conclusions preliminary and tentative. Further examination of the interaction between institutions and social context in postcommunist states is needed to flesh out the commonalities and differences within this geographic region and between postcommunist states and consolidated democracies and other democratizing states.

Ideally, the effects of institutions in a transitional regime would be examined over a period of decades rather than of years; then it would be easier to distinguish long-term trends from ephemeral ones. However, the dramatic events surrounding the collapse of Communism and the pressing challenges of introducing democracy and capitalist markets require examination of the effects of rules and norms during the turbulent transition period, if for no other reason than that this is the period in which a new democratic regime is most at risk and institutions have the most opportunities to affect political outcomes. Ironically, we know very much about the effects of institutions in stable environments, in which institutions are least likely to determine the basic character of the regime, but much less about institutional effects in unstable environments, in which institutions may be a determining factor in the continuation or breakdown of democratic processes.

Russia and the New Institutionalism

It is crucial to note what this analysis does and does not imply about the effect of electoral systems and institutions more generally in a transitional regime like Russia. It reinforces the central dictum of new institutionalism—institutions matter. Electoral systems had a number of very important effects that shaped the character of the transitional regime currently in place and promises to influence the future trajectory of democratization in Russia. At the same time, this study calls attention to the interaction between institutions and the social context in which they operate. Electoral systems produced unique outcomes that ran counter to international experience because they were operating in a social context, unlike most of the countries that were the empirical bases for the theoretical assumptions in the literature.

The new institutionalism is a broad and varied approach that has had a significant impact on very different subfields in political science, ranging from legislative studies to comparative political economy to international relations. Peter A. Hall and Rosemary C. R. Taylor have identified four different schools of thought operating under the amorphous heading of new institutionalism.[7] The central difference between these schools concern the nature of preference formation. As Kathleen Thelen and Sven Steinmo argue, "Thus one, perhaps *the,* core difference between rational choice institutionalism and historical institutionalism lies in the question of preference formation, whether treated as exogenous (rational choice) or endogenous (historical institutionalism)."[8]

Rational-choice institutionalists view individual action as purposive and strategic; individuals are utility maximizers who examine their options and choose the one that provides the most benefit. From this perspective, institutions affect behavior by affecting both the costs and benefits of particular actions and the level of certainty about the behavior of other actors. The preferences of actors are exogenous to the model and thus not affected by institutions.[9] At the other end of the spectrum, historical and sociological institutionalism do not view individual behavior as singularly goal-oriented and purposive. Individuals are more likely "satisficers" than utility maximizers: as satisficers, much of daily activity is determined by established routines and patterns governed more by habit and cultural validation than rational calculation. From this perspective, institutions affect much more than strategic calculations of the costs and benefits of available options—they provide the codes or scripts upon which much action is based and actually can define interests, shape preferences, and construct identities that determine outcomes.[10]

The literature on the role institutional design plays in democratic consolidation has not addressed the more theoretical questions regarding the nature of institutional effects on individual behavior. Rather, such scholarship has been more empirical, using cross-national comparisons to highlight the correlation between certain institutional arrangements and political outcomes, most consequentially, the survival of democratic regimes.[11] These arguments encompass both strategic behavior associated with the rational choice paradigm and questions of preference formation, which is the realm of historical institutionalists.

The study of electoral systems can be more clearly placed within the rational choice school; the central dynamic underlying their constraining effects on the number of parties is strategic voting, a concept possessing rational choice assumptions. Voters are assumed to have ordered preferences for political parties, which are exogenous, and to maximize the influence of their vote, that is, vote for a candidate with a reasonable chance of winning. Candidates and parties are assumed to be utility maximizers as well, driven by the desire to maximize votes and seats in parliament. The electoral system does not affect voter preferences, only the strategic context in which these preferences are played out.

For the most part, this book follows the trend in the literature toward rational choice explanations for electoral system effects in Russia. When examining strategic voting (and lack thereof) in Russia, I see Russian voters and elites as rational actors. I assumed candidates and parties are primarily concerned with maximizing their share of votes or seats and voters want to maximize their influence. The failure of electoral systems to their expected constraining effects was not attributed to some lack of rational behavior; rather, I explained outcomes by a combination of factors that can fit into a rational choice understanding of voters and candidates. I saw the failure of elites to consolidate into larger electoral blocs as a product of incentives promoting such behavior found in Russia's electoral system and the lack of information needed to behave strategically. For example, some elites formed seemingly irrational PR parties because this provided them free media exposure that aided their campaigns in a SMD race. In addition, many candidates and parties threw their hats in the ring because the level of information on the distribution of electoral support made it impossible to determine who was and was not a viable candidate. Therefore, one does not have to abandon the assumption of rationality to explain the party proliferation that exists in Russia's mixed electoral system. The social context changed the incentive structure and denied actors the necessary information to behave strategically; their alternative behaviors were driven by these different incentives, resources, and information flows.

However, I also found institutions to have some influence over preferences of voters and candidates; for example, Russian and non-Russian voters alike seemed more inclined to support a non-Russian candidate in districts located in non-Russian regions. Moreover, in SMD elections Russian voters seemed more interested in personality and local issues than in the issues of economic reform or nationalism that separated constituencies in the PR race. These differences in preferences produced very different outcomes in the two tiers; the PR race was a partisan battle between polarized ideological camps divided over economic reform, and the plurality election was more parochial, less ideological, and produced more centrist deputies.

Extending the broader implications of this study to other policy areas, one could argue that the Russian experience with electoral systems reinforces the idea that Russia is unique. This finding might instruct other intellectual debates concerning Russia's turbulent transition from communism. For example, scholars are waging a heated debate over the applicability of neo-liberal strategies of economic reform to Russia and other postcommunist states. Proponents of shock therapy contend that certain economic principles apply in all contexts and, if properly implemented, can produce a functional market economy in Russia. Critics of this approach assert that cultural and historical conditions in Russia make that country unique and in need of a different approach toward market reform, one that takes into consideration the legacy of seventy years of Communist rule as well as the country's longer history of state centralization. They state that radical economic reform, including the introduction of mass privatization and macroeconomic stabilization, produced unintended consequences that have led to economic catastrophe in Russia, all resulting from a failure to consider Russian conditions.[12] Of course, this study cannot address fully these issues; but it can suggest that Russia is distinctive in some ways and that comparative experience with the effects of rules, institutions, or policies (whether governing elections or economic behavior) may be a poor indication of how those same rules, institutions, or policies will work in Russia.

Russia and the Study of Comparative Politics

Although I have argued that Russia is unique in some important respects, I do not contend that this should in any way preclude comparative study. Rather, this book has followed in the footsteps of a growing number of studies that adopt a comparative approach to the study of post-Soviet Russia and the former Soviet Union.[13] In examining the effects of electoral systems on Russian democratization, I used concepts, hypotheses, measures, and methods common to the comparative politics literature, implicitly accepting the premise that is fruitful to compare Russia's experiences with those of other countries, particularly third-wave democracies in Latin America, Southern Europe, and Eastern Europe. While this may be common practice in much of comparative politics, it remains a controversial enterprise in the study of postcommunist states of the former Soviet Union and Eastern Europe. Just as the experience of autarchic state socialism cut off the Soviet Union and its satellites from the rest of the world, this experience also insulated their study from much of the rest of political science scholarship. Integration of the study of postcommunist states into mainstream comparative politics has met a justified skepticism regarding the appropriateness of extending concepts and methods developed in the study of other regions to what remains in many ways a very unique context. Yet this doubt should not be used to renew the separation of the study of Russia from general comparative politics.

In a most stinging critique of transitology and comparative political analysis, Stephen Cohen argues that these approaches have promoted the ruin of the Russian economy and state through the adoption of misguided and inappropriate reforms.[14] By indicting comparative political analysis in the failure of shock therapy, Cohen wrongly assumes that comparative analyses of Russia have found, or, worse yet, presumed, that theories developed from the experience of other states will hold true in Russia. This was definitely not the case here, nor is it the case for numerous other studies of Russia that have adopted concepts and models from comparative politics.[15]

Skeptics of direct comparison of postcommunist states with other democratizing nations argue that post-Communism differs qualitatively from democratization in other regions—for a number of reasons, including the simultaneous challenge of transforming state socialism to a market economy, greater ethnic diversity and conflict, weaker civil societies, and a more inhospitable international environment. In postcommunist states, these differences have produced diverse actors, processes, and trajectories of transitions from authoritarianism—all of which make comparisons with democratization in Southern Europe and Latin America "unhelpful at best and misleading at worst."[16] Advocates of incorporating postcommunist states as the latest cases of third-wave democratization argue that these differences are overstated; they claim that other democratizing states have faced radical economic restructuring, ethnic conflict, and weak civil societies during their transitions. Moreover, comparing democratic transitions in different contexts need not overemphasize similarities at the cost of meaningful differences, as it is precisely these differences that move forward the study of democratization and comparative politics.[17]

This debate has brought to light many important considerations regarding the applicability of concepts from the democratization literature to the postcommunist context; however, it has also been plagued by grand generalizations and observations regarding the causes and effects of critical factors in the democratization process under post-Communism that need to be established through careful empirical study.[18] This book has assumed that more is gained than lost in applying concepts and testing hypotheses from established bodies of scholarship to the postcommunist context. Clearly, some postcommunist states possess certain characteristics that make them very different from consolidated democracies and other democratizing nations—indeed, this is the central finding of this book. However, I argue that rather than hinder the utility of cross-national comparison, such differences enhance it. It is only through comparative analysis of postcommunist states, using the same concepts and criteria used to study other regions, that one can discern what is distinctive about postcommunist democratic transitions. Moreover, only in placing a single case or region into comparative perspective can one contribute to a broader understanding of complex political processes, such as democratization, that has generalizable implications for other cases.

The study of electoral systems and their effects is the ideal vehicle for comparison of unique cases such as Russia's. The data (votes and seats) are basic and fundamental to democratic governance and thus easily and usefully compared across different contexts.[19] The hypotheses regarding electoral system effects on parties and representation use rational-choice theory, which has claims of universal generalizability among a wide variety of cases—as long as a few fundamental assumptions are met. The empirical evidence from cross-national studies has shown impressive regularity in electoral system effects, making exceptions that run counter to comparative experience theoretically important. Thus a symbiosis between theory and case exists in which the literature provides well-grounded hypotheses that have shed light on the Russian experience, while the exceptional characteristics of Russia have contributed to theories of electoral systems and strategic voting under conditions in which fundamental assumptions are not fulfilled. This study has, I hope, shown that comparative analysis of electoral systems provides useful insights on Russian politics even as Russian experience helps us rethink assumptions and theories of electoral systems and institutional engineering.

9
Epilogue

The manuscript for this book was completed in April 1999, well before the campaign for the December 1999 election to the State Duma was in full swing. Much has happened since then; that election produced a new Duma that looks significantly different from the one that preceded it. More important, the resignation of President Boris Yeltsin at the end of 1999 elevated Prime Minister Vladimir Putin to the position of acting president and made him the clear frontrunner in the early presidential election to be held in March 2000. While the full implications of the 1999 parliamentary election will be apparent only over the months and years ahead, this election does provide an opportunity to test, if only in a preliminary way, whether electoral systems continued to have the effects found in the first two Russian elections. Would Russian elites and voters react more like their counterparts around the world, or would they continue to behave in ways that ran counter to theoretical expectations and international trends?

The 1999 election witnessed a combination of change and continuity. Unity, a new party of power, launched at the last minute by the Kremlin, emerged as the major surprise of this election, nearly matching the vote share of the Communist Party. A rejuvenated reformist party, Union of Right Forces, also performed better than expected, raising the hopes for a major sea change in the composition of the Duma and the formation of a majority coalition committed to reform. Also, these latest elections witnessed a new phenomenon—a rival party of power in Fatherland–All Russia, which was formed by powerful regional executives in direct defiance of the Kremlin.

Despite these changes, there was an impressive continuity to the party system in 1999. Three parties that had won representation in both previous elections, the Communist Party, LDPR, and Yabloko, again managed to overcome the 5-percent barrier in the PR tier in 1999. If one sees Unity as the latest manifestation of the party of power, rather than as a new party, and equates the Union of Right Forces with Democratic Russia's Choice, upon which it was based, then five of the six parties that gained election in the PR race had roots in previ-

Table 9.1: 1999 Parliamentary Election Results

Party	Political orientation	Number of PR seats	Number of SMD seats
Union of Right Forces	Reformist	24	5
Yabloko	Reformist	16	4
Unity	Centrist	64	9
Fatherland–All Russia	Centrist	36	31
Communist Party	Leftist	67	47
Zhirinovsky bloc	Nationalist	17	0
Independents/Others	n/a	0	113

Source: Michael McFaul, "Russia's 1999 Parliamentary Election," p. 9.

ous elections. Table 9.1 shows the results for major parties, grouped in the four ideological types used throughout the book: reformist, centrist, leftist, and nationalist.

Another major development in the 1999 election was a significant shift toward the center of the political spectrum by major parties. The two rival parties of power, Unity and Fatherland–All Russia, provided voters with centrist messages of stability, promising neither new radical market reforms nor a retreat from the market processes already achieved. Unity claimed to have no ideology and based its appeal on association with executive power and the popular prime minister Vladimir Putin. The Communist Party's political platform was also significantly more moderate in its criticism of the market than it had been previously.[1] The ideological polarization that marked elections in the PR tier during the Yeltsin era has seemed to subside; this was demonstrated powerfully by a strategic coalition struck between the two largest factions in the Duma, Unity and the Communists, in which they split up most key committee assignments and elected a Communist, Gennady Seleznov, as speaker. This caused the first big scandal of the new Duma, when those factions left out of the agreement protested their exclusion from important committee leadership posts by staging a walkout. While the alliance between Unity and the Communists seemed to undermine hopes for a reformist governing coalition, it also marked a sharp break from the incessant confrontation of the Yeltsin era. It will take some time before it is clear who will make up the majority and opposition coalitions in the State Duma and how relations between this new Duma and a new Russian president will play out.

Although specific political implications of the 1999 election are still vague, one can make more certain judgements about electoral system effects. These are necessarily preliminary and incomplete, since there has been limited time to fully analyze the election results; however, some patterns are discernible. In general, the 1999 election followed the same outline as the previous two elections.

Table 9.2: Electoral System Effects in the 1999 Parliamentary Election

Election	Effective number of parliamentary parties (both tiers)	Effective number of parties in PR tier	Effective number of parties in SMD tier	Percentage of women elected in PR tier	Percentage of women elected in SMD tier
1993	$N_s = 8.16^a$	$N_v = 7.58$	$N_v = 5.48^b$	34	26
1995	$N_s = 5.71^a$	$N_v = 10.68$	$N_v = 6.61^b$	15	31
1999	$N_s = 7.63^a$	$N_v = 6.76$	$N_v = 5.57^b$	15	20

Sources: McFaul, "Russia's 1999 Parliamentary Election"; Central Electoral Commission website, http://www.fci.ru.

a Based on parliamentary factions.
b Based on the average effective number of candidates per district.

Both PR and plurality elections allowed for rather significant party proliferation, and once again, the cumulative effect of the two tiers created even greater party fractionalization in the State Duma, as candidates from the SMD tier (most of whom were independents) often formed their own parliamentary factions rather than join one of the PR blocs. Finally, although women's representation fell across the board in 1999, women continued to perform better in SMD elections than in the PR tier. Table 9.2 provides basic information regarding party and candidate proliferation and women's representation for all post-Soviet three elections to allow for easy comparison of the 1999 election to the previous two.

This is not to say that the 1999 election did not display any signs of change. There were signs of greater strategic behavior by elites and voters as the effective number of electoral contestants in both the PR and SMD tiers dropped. The most dramatic fall came in the PR tier, where the effective number of electoral parties dropped significantly from 10.58 in 1995 to 6.76 in 1999. What accounts for this sharp change? There are three possible causes: strategic behavior by elites (party consolidation), strategic voting, or both. There exists some evidence of party consolidation prior to the vote. The Union of Right Forces (SPS) represented a real attempt to avoid the splintering of the reformist vote that was so prevalent in 1995. But while this bloc did manage to combine a number of reformist blocs and leaders, it did not manage to create a single reformist party. As usual, Yabloko ran on its own, refusing association with fellow reformist leaders it deemed tainted by failed Yeltsin-era policies. Talks also broke down with last election's party of power, Our Home is Russia. There were a number of other manifestations of the old party proliferation; thus, although the twenty-six blocs on the PR ballot in 1999 was a significant drop from the previous forty-three groups there was still a large number of politicians willing to form parties with virtually no chance to win seats in the PR tier. This occurred despite a significant change in the electoral law designed to curb the use of the PR campaign to further the candidacies in SMD races: party leaders at the top of PR lists were not allowed to use free airtime if they were also running in SMD races.[2] While this law may indeed have restricted the number of minor PR blocs devoted to and often named after a single leader, it obviously did not constrain the nomination of many other parties with virtually no chance to gain election.

The big difference between 1995 and 1999 lay in the behavior of voters, not elites. While still faced with a myriad of choices, voters appeared to choose much more strategically. They refrained from voting for small parties and gravitated toward parties with genuine chances to overcome the 5-percent barrier and gain representation. The very small proportion of the vote cast for minor parties demonstrates this; although close to 50 percent of the PR vote was cast for parties failing to overcome the 5-percent barrier in 1995, less than 20 percent of the vote went to such parties in 1999. Moreover, there were six parties in 1995 that narrowly missed overcoming the legal threshold, gaining between 3 and 5 percent of the vote. In 1999 no losing party came within 2 percent of the threshold, and only four of the twenty losing parties gained 1 percent of the vote or more. This suggests that voters more easily identified parties with little chance for gaining representation and were more inclined to defect from their first preference to avoid wasting their vote; whether because of more information or greater pragmatism, the voters constrained the number of viable electoral parties in 1999 by refusing to cast their ballots for sure losers.

The greater instance of strategic voting did not mean fewer parties in parliament; quite the opposite occurred. As noted in chapter 8, there was an inverse relationship between disproportionality and the number of parliamentary parties. Since the vote was not dispersed across a wide array of parties, more significant groups managed to overcome the 5-percent barrier and enter parliament. Thus, in the PR tier, a greater concentration of votes produced less party consolidation in parliament.

There was also a drop in the effective number of candidates in the SMDs from 1995 to 1999. Where there had been close to seven significant candidates per district in 1995, there were less than six significant candidates per district in 1999—bringing the level of candidate proliferation back down to where it had been in 1993. Although this does represent a change, I would argue the continuity of party proliferation at the district level in the SMD tier is more striking. Prospects for further party consolidation are higher in the PR tier, which provides the information necessary for strategic behavior to a much greater extent than in SMD elections.

Electoral system effects on ascriptive representation also seemed to remain rather stable in 1999. I did carry out an initial analysis of these effects on women's representation, although I was not able to gather the data on ethnic background of newly elected deputies. Russian politics continued to show a disturbing decrease in the representation of women in 1999. Whereas 10 percent of deputies were women in 1995, women made up only 8 percent in 1999. Nevertheless, the unusual pattern of higher representation of women in SMD elections over PR elections persisted. Women comprised only 6.7 percent of PR deputies but 9.3 percent SMD deputies in 1999.[3] Once again, lower women's representation in the PR tier was fueled by parties from across the political spectrum that neglected to place women in electable positions on their party lists. The two largest parties, Unity and KPRF, managed to elect only three women from their PR lists, despite each winning more than sixty seats in the PR tier. Fatherland–All Russia turned out to be the party most favorable to women, electing five women out of thirty-seven PR deputies, or 14 percent, which was more than twice the national average. One difference in 1999 was that the number of women elected in the SMD tier dropped significantly, while the number of women elected in the PR tier remained the same. If this trend continues, the discrepancy between the two tiers may diminish.

The campaign for the March 2000 presidential race has again displayed the tendency for presidential elections in Russia to constrain electoral choices to a much greater extent than do parliamentary elections. The phenomenal rise of Vladimir Putin from obscurity to the position of unrivaled frontrunner in the presidential contest mirrors Yeltsin's rise in opinion polls during the 1996 campaign. Although the war in Chechnya has rightly been the focus of attention when explaining Putin's support, the consolidating nature of the presidential election has also played a role. Strong challengers, such as Yuri Luzhkov and Yevgeny Primakov, opted out of the presidential race after the parliamentary election suggested they did not have the support to make a serious run at the presidency. The perception that the parliamentary election serves as a primary for the presidential election has grown; in 1996 it pushed voters to defect from a field of non-Communist candidates who had not distinguished themselves in the 1995 parliamentary election and to vote for Yeltsin. In 1999 relative failure in the parliamentary race apparently pushed leading presidential candidates to opt out of the race all together. Despite some signs of change, the dominant trend in 1999 was continuity of electoral system effects, suggesting that Russian elections will remain anomalous in the short term, until parties become more central and stable institutions.

Notes

Notes to Chapter 1

1. For analyses of the circumstances surrounding the formulation of rules for Russia's founding election, see Michael McFaul, "Institutional Design, Uncertainty, and Path Dependency during Transitions: Cases from Russia," *Constitutional Political Economy* 10, no. 1 (1999): 27–52; Thomas F. Remington and Steven S. Smith, "Political Goals, Institutional Context, and the Choice of an Electoral System: The Russian Parliamentary Election Law," *American Journal of Political Science* 40, no. 4 (1996): 1253–79; Michael Urban, "December 1993 as a Replication of Late-Soviet Electoral Practices," *Post-Soviet Affairs* 10, no. 2 (1994): 127–58; Jerry F. Hough, "Institutional Rules and Party Formation," in *Growing Pains: Russian Democracy and the Election of 1993,* ed. Timothy J. Colton and Jerry F. Hough (Washington, D.C.: Brookings Institution Press, 1998), 37–73.
2. Arend Lijphart, "Constitutional Choices for New Democracies," in *The Global Resurgence of Democracy,* ed. Larry Diamond and Marc F. Plattner (Baltimore: Johns Hopkins University Press, 1993), 165–66.
3. Gary W. Cox, *Making Votes Count* (Cambridge: Cambridge University Press, 1997), 221.
4. Ibid., and Sartori, "The Influence of Electoral Systems" Faulty Laws or Faulty Method?" in *Electoral Laws and Their Consequences,* ed., Bernard Grofman and Arend Lijphart (New York: Agathon Press, 1986), 43–68.
5. The term "non-Duvergerian equilibrium" is from Cox, *Making Votes Count.*
6. There are a number of other facets of Russia's electoral law that influence political behavior, including rules governing ballot structure, candidate registration and nomination, and the public financing of campaigns. I will address these elements throughout the book when they are thought to affect party behavior or representation.
7. Geoffrey K. Roberts, "The 'Second-Vote' Campaign Strategy of the West German Free Democratic Party," *European Journal of Political Research* 16 (1988): 317–37.
8. For a discussion of the influence of various PR electoral formulae, see Rein Taagepera and Matthew Soberg Shugart, *Seats and Votes: The Effects and Determinants of Electoral Systems* (New Haven, Conn.: Yale University Press, 1989); and Arend Lijphart, *Electoral Systems and Party Systems: A Study of Twenty-Seven Democracies, 1945–1990* (New Haven, Conn.: Yale University Press, 1994).

9.   Maurice Duverger, "Duverger's Law: Forty Years Later," in *Electoral Laws and Their Political Consequences,* ed. Bernard Grofman and Arend Lijphart (New York: Agathon Press, 1986), 70.

10. Cox, *Making Votes Count,* 123.

11. Lijphart, *Electoral Systems and Party Systems,* 25–30.

12. Numerous scholars have used the adoption of the 1993 constitution to mark this division in contemporary Russian political development. See Katherine Stoner-Weiss, *Local Heroes: The Political Economy of Russian Regional Government* (Princeton: Princeton University Press, 1997), 5–6; and Eugene Huskey, "Democracy and Institutional Design in Russia," *Demokratizatsiya: The Journal of Post-Soviet Democratization* 4 (1996): 460.

13. A substantial literature has developed on the development of party and preparty organizations in the Gorbachev era and the First Russian Republic. See, for example, M. Steven Fish, *Democracy from Scratch: Opposition and Regime in the New Russian Revolution* (Princeton: Princeton University Press, 1995); Michael Urban, with Vyacheslav Igrunov and Sergei Mitrokhin, *The Rebirth of Politics in Russia* (Cambridge: Cambridge University Press, 1997); Michael McFaul and Sergei Markov, *The Troubled Birth of Russian Democracy: Parties, Personalities, and Programs* (Stanford: Hoover Institution Press, 1993); Alexander Dallin, ed., *Political Parties in Russia* (Berkeley: University of California, Berkeley International and Area Studies, 1993); Vladimir Brovkin, "Revolution from Below: Informal Political Associations in Russia 1988–1989," *Soviet Studies* 42, no. 2 (1990): 233–258.

14. Timothy J. Colton, "The Politics of Democratization: The Moscow Election of 1990," *Soviet Economy* 6, no. 4 (1990): 285–344.

15. Fish leaves unanswered the question of whether the 1990 election was a founding election of the postcommunist Russian state. I argue that the 1993 election is more appropriately conceived of as such, given the absence of the Communist Party of the Soviet Union and the existence of an independent Russian state. See Fish, *Democracy from Scratch,* 73.

16. See, for example, M. Steven Fish, "The Advent of Multipartism in Russia, 1993–1995," *Post-Soviet Affairs* 11, no. 4 (1995): 340; and John T. Ishiyama, "The Russian Proto-parties and the National Republics: Integrative Organizations in a Disintegrating World?" *Communist and Postcommunist Studies* 29, no. 4 (1996): 395–411.

17. See Scott Mainwaring, "Party Systems in the Third Wave," *Journal of Democracy* 9, no. 3 (1998): 67–81.

18. Leon Epstein, *Political Parties in Western Democracies* (New York: Praeger, 1967), 8.

19. Thomas F. Remington and Steven S. Smith, "The Development of Parliamentary Parties in Russia," *Legislative Studies Quarterly* 20, no. 4 (1995): 457–89; and Joel Ostrow, "Institutional Design and Legislative Conflict: The Russian Supreme Soviet—A Well-Oiled Machine, Out of Control," *Communist and Postcommunist Studies* 29, no. 4 (1996): 413–33.

20. Fish makes the distinction clear between those organizations contesting elections in 1990 and the nascent parties emerging during the elections in 1993. He calls the 1993 electoral blocs new parliamentary parties, while claiming those organizations of the Gorbachev era "were not genuine political parties, but rather movement organizations." Fish, *Democracy from Scratch,* 233.

21. Sarah Oates argues that Our Home is Russia presented a mixed policy message regarding the economy. But she places the party on the pro-market side of the political spectrum near Yabloko, which is consistently viewed as pro-market. Oates, "Party Platforms: Towards a Definition of the Russian Political Spectrum," in *Party Politics in Postcommunist Russia,* ed. John Lowenhardt (London: Frank Cass, 1998), 86–92.

22. Mikhail Dmitriev, "Party Economic Programs and Implications," in *Primer on Russia's 1999 Duma Elections,* ed. Michael McFaul, Nikolai Petrov, and Andrei Ryabov (Washington, D.C.: Carnegie Endowment for International Peace, 1999), 37–40.

23. Evelyn Davidheiser, "Right and Left in the Hard Opposition," in *Growing Pains: Russian Democracy and the Election of 1993,* ed. Timothy J. Colton and Jerry F. Hough (Washington, D.C.: Brookings Institution Press, 1998), 180–88.

24. Oates, "Party Platforms," 82–86.

25. Laura Belin and Robert Orttung, *The Russian Parliamentary Elections of 1995* (Armonk, N.Y.: M. E. Sharpe, 1997), 32–33.

26. Michael McFaul, *Russia Between Elections: What the December 1995 Results Really Mean* (Washington, D.C.: Carnegie Endowment for International Peace, 1996), 16.

27. Daniel Treisman, "Fighting Inflation in a Transitional Regime: Russia's Anomalous Stabilization," *World Politics* 50, no. 2 (1998): 235–65.

28. McFaul, *Russia Between Elections,* 26.

Notes to Chapter 2

1. Putnam, *Making Democracy Work.* For a study of institutional performance in postcommunist Russia using a similar approach, see Stoner-Weiss, *Local Heroes.*

2. Lijphart, *Electoral Systems and Party Systems,* 39–46.

3. Matthew Shugart, "Building the Institutional Framework: Electoral Systems, Party Systems and Presidents," in Ian Budge et al., *The Politics of the New Europe* (New York: Longman, 1998), 234.

4. Lijphart, *Electoral Systems and Party Systems,* 78.

5. Putnam, *Making Democracy Work;* Lijphart, *Electoral Systems and Party Systems.*

6. Lijphart, *Electoral Systems and Party Systems,* 78.

7. Steven Fisher, "The Wasted Vote Thesis," *Comparative Politics* 5 (1974): 293–99; Eckhard Jesse, "Split-voting in the Federal Republic of Germany: An Analysis of the Federal Elections from 1953 to 1987," *Electoral Studies* 7 (1988): 109–24; Kathleen Bawn, "The Logic of Institutional Preferences: German Electoral as a Social Choice Outcome," *American Journal of Political Science* 37 (1993): 965–89; Gary Cox, *Making Votes Count,* 82–83.

8. Erik S. Herron and Misa Nishikawa, "Reassessing Duverger's Law: The Mixed System and Its Impact on Political Parties," Paper presented at the Midwest Political Science Association Meeting, Chicago, Apr.15–17, 1999.

9. David Brady and Jongryn Mo, "Electoral Systems and Institutional Choice: A Case Study of the 1988 Korean Elections," *Comparative Political Studies* 24, no. 4 (1992): 405–30.

10. Gerald M. Easter, "Preference for Presidentialism: Postcommunist Regime Change in Russian and the NIS," *World Politics* 49 (Jan. 1997): 184–211; and Timothy Frye,

"A Politics of Institutional Choice: Postcommunist Presidencies," *Comparative Political Studies* 30, no. 5 (October 1997): 523–52.

11. Cox, *Making Votes Count*, 17.
12. Uncertainty also affects institutional choice as actors hedge their bets with institutions that include of mixture of different incentives. See Brady and Mo, "Electoral Systems and Institutional Choice"; Easter "Preference for Presidentialism"; and Frye, "A Politics of Institutional Choice."
13. Michael McFaul, "Institutional Design."
14. See Belin and Orttung, *Russian Parliamentary Elections;* and Boris Strashun and Viktor Sheinis, "Politicheskaya Situatsiya v Rossii i Novyi Izbiral'nyi Zakon," *Polis* 3 (1993): 65–69.
15. Belin and Orttung, *Russian Parliamentary Elections,* 29.
16. Fish, "The Advent of Multipartism in Russia," 340–83.
17. Michael McFaul, "Russia's 1999 Parliamentary Elections: Party Consolidation and Fragmentation," *Demokratizatsiya: The Journal of Post-Soviet Democratization* 8, no. 1 (2000): 5–23.
18. Scott Mainwaring, *Rethinking Party Systems in the Third Wave of Democratization: The Case of Brazil* (Stanford, Calif.: Stanford University Press, 1999), 39.
19. Ibid., 25.
20. Ibid., 25–26.
21. The following section is based on a scheme provided in ibid., 26–39.
22. Ibid., 29. The index of volatility is based on the absolute difference in the percentage of the vote captured by a party in subsequent elections divided by two.
23. Jack Bielasiak, "Elections and the Institutionalization of Party Systems in Postcommunist States," Paper presented at the annual meeting of the American Political Science Association, Atlanta, GA, September 2–5, 1999. Bielasiak's calculations of electoral volatility for Russia were somewhat lower than Mainwaring's, but the pattern was the same.
24. Stephen White, Richard Rose, and Ian McAllister, *How Russia Votes* (New York: Chatham House, 1997), 135.
25. Timothy Colton, *Transitional Citizens: Voters and Elections in Post-Soviet Russia* (Cambridge: Harvard University Press, 2000), 150.
26. See ibid., 151; and White, Rose, and McAllister, *How Russia Votes,* 145–47.
27. White, Rose, and McAllister, *How Russia Votes,* 46.
28. Mainwaring, *Rethinking Party Systems,* 36.
29. Mainwaring notes that nonpartisan and anti-party candidates have performed well in some Latin American countries such as Brazil and Peru. These countries also have a high degree of personalism in their political system (33–35).
30. Robert G. Moser, "Electoral Systems and the Number of Parties in Postcommunist States," *World Politics* 51, no. 3 (April 1999): 359–84

Notes to Chapter 3

1. This admittedly simplified list of electoral system effects has been shown in numerous works some of the most major of which include: Maurice Duverger, *Political Parties: Their Organization and Activity in the Modern State* (New York: Wiley, 1963); Douglas W. Rae, *The Political Consequences of Electoral Laws,* 2d ed. (New Haven, Conn.: Yale University Press, 1971); Arend Lijphart, *Democracies: Patterns*

of Majoritarian and Consensus Government in Twenty-One Countries (New Haven, Conn.: Yale University Press, 1984); Taagepera and Shugart, *Seats and Votes;* Lijphart, *Electoral Systems and Party Systems;* Cox, *Making Votes Count.*

2. There is another type of representation based on ascriptive qualities (gender, race) that may come into conflict with the realization of increasing levels of proportionality. See Richard E. Matland, " The Two Faces of Representation: Implications for the Design of Electoral Systems," unpublished manuscript. Women's and minorities' representation will be examined in the next two chapters.

3. Arend Lijphart, *Electoral Systems and Party Systems,* 151–52.

4. Not included in this classification are the single transferable vote (STV) and the single non-transferable vote (SNTV) systems, which allow votes for individual candidates in multimember districts. Lijphart considers both systems as part of the broad class of PR systems. See ibid., 40–42. Cox finds that both systems follow his generalized Duverger' s law, the *M*+1 rule in which the upper limit on the number of candidates tends to be one greater than the district magnitude. See Cox, *Making Votes Count,* 139–44.

5. See Rae, *Political Consequences of Electoral Laws,* 114–25; Taagepera and Shugart, *Seats and Votes,* 112–25.

6. Taagepera and Shugart, *Seats and Votes,* 112–14.

7. Lijphart has developed the idea of the effective threshold that can capture the effects of both district magnitude and legal thresholds in a single measure of the minimal vote percentage necessary for election. Lijphart, *Electoral Systems and Party Systems,* 25–30.

8. Marku Laakso and Rein Taagepera, " Effective Number of Parties: A Measure with Application to West Europe," *Comparative Political Studies* 12, no. 1 (1979): 3–27.

9. The effective number of parties index is calculated by squaring the proportion of the vote or seat shares of each party, adding these together, then dividing 1 by this total:

$$N_v = 1/\Sigma(v_i^2) \text{ or } N_s = 1/\Sigma(s_i^2)$$

The least-squared index of disproportionality is calculated by squaring the vote-seat share differences and adding them together; this total is divided by 2; and then the square root of this value is taken:

$$LSq = SqRt \text{ of } 1/2*\Sigma(v_i - s_i)^2$$

For discussion of these two measures see Lijphart (*Electoral Systems and Party Systems,* 67–72) and Taagepera and Shugart (*Seats and Votes,* 77–81, 104–5).

10. Duverger, 1963, 113, as cited in Maurice Duverger, "Duverger's Law," 70.

11. Duverger, "Duverger's Law" 69.

12. Taagepera and Shugart, *Seats and Votes;* Lijphart, *Electoral Systems and Party Systems.*

13. Sartori, "The Influence of Electoral Systems," 54–55; Cox, *Making Votes Count,* 181–202.

14. Peter Ordeshook and Olga Shvetsova, "Ethnic Heterogeneity, District Magnitude, and the Number of Parties," *American Journal of Political Science* 38 (1994): 100–123; Cox, *Making Votes Count,* 203–21.

15. Cox, *Making Votes Count,* 79.
16. Ibid., 182–93.
17. See Sartori, "The Influence of Electoral Systems," 55–56.
18. Lijphart, *Electoral Systems and Party Systems,* 35–36.
19. The law stated that no more than 15 percent of a bloc's signatures could come from any one region of the federation. This was meant to hinder the establishment of ethnic- or region-based electoral blocs and apparently worked well in 1993 (*Rossiiskie vesti,* October 12, 1993). For a discussion of the impact of this aspect of the electoral law on party development in non–Russian regions, see Robert G. Moser, "The Impact of Electoral Systems in Russia," *Post-Soviet Affairs* 13, no. 3 (1995): 383–87.
20. White, Rose, and McAllister referred to Russian parties as irrational actors. See their work, *How Russia Votes,* 199–204.
21. McFaul, *Russia Between Elections,* 17.
22. George Tsebelis, *Nested Games: Rational Choice in Comparative Politics* (Berkeley: University of California Press, 1990).
23. McFaul cites the example of the Republican Party (Pamfilova–Gurov–Vladimir Lysenko bloc), which claimed its surveys showed that the bloc enjoyed 6 percent support. The bloc ended up with less than 2 percent of the vote. See McFaul, *Russia Between Elections,* 17 and endnote #58, p. 46.
24. These dynamics are analogous to those of parties found in other democratizing states. Richard Gunther found that party elites in Spain sometimes failed to follow the incentives toward consolidation provided by the electoral system because they gave other goals, such as ideological purity or leadership positions within the party greater priority than they did maximizing the number of seats in the legislature. Gunther, "Electoral Laws, Party Systems, and Elites: The Case of Spain," *American Political Science Review* 83, no. 3 (1989): 853–54.
25. Russia's 6.40 effective parliamentary parties was higher than any that of other electoral system studied in Lijphart's large cross-national study. The level of disproportionality was higher than Germany' s electoral systems, which had similar effective thresholds, but lower than several other systems. Lijphart, *Electoral Systems and Party Systems,* 160–62.
26. India's least-squares index of disproportionality was 20.77 percent for the period 1952–1957 and 16.76 for 1962–1984. Ibid., 161.
27. A second methodological issue for the Russian case is the "against all" vote, in which voters are given the option to vote against all candidates. When calculating the effective number of electoral candidates, I included the against all vote and treated it vote the same way I did votes for individual candidates. This approximates the fragmentation of the Russian vote better than a calculation based exclusively on votes for candidates. In previous work I calculated the effective number of candidates without the against all vote and came up with a higher level of fragmentation in both elections but the same general trend. See Moser, "Electoral Systems."
28. Cox, *Making Votes Count,* 76–80.
29. In the case of the 1992 Lithuanian elections, district-level data was not available for the SMD tier; therefore, only the PR tier of the 1992 Lithuanian election was included in the study.
30. Ukraine has changed its majoritarian electoral system to a mixed system that is nearly identical to Russia's. It held its first election under its new mixed system in

1998. District-level data were not available at the time of writing and so this election was not included in the analysis.

31. Lijphart, *Electoral Systems and Party Systems,* 96, 160–61.

32. Cox, *Making Votes Count,* 309–11.

33. Lijphart, *Electoral Systems and Party Systems,* 96.

34. Taagepera and Shugart, *Seats and Votes,* 123; Lijphart, *Electoral Systems and Party Systems,* 97; Cox, *Making Votes Count,* 173–78.

35. Hubert Tworzecki, *Parties and Politics in Post-1989 Poland* (Boulder, Colo.: Westview, 1996), 194.

36. This is particularly true in Russia where surveys regularly report 40 percent of respondents answering " don't know" to questions regarding their candidate preferences for the next election, more than twice the percentage supporting the most popular political party. Rose, White and McAllister, *How Russia Votes,* 141.

37. Herbert Kitschelt, " Formation of Party Cleavages in Postcommunist Democracies," *Party Politics* 1 (1995): 457; Geoffrey Evans and Stephen Whitefield, "Identifying the Bases of Party Competition in Eastern Europe," *British Journal of Political Science* 23 (1993): 540–43.

38. Of course, majoritarian elections are more ambiguous in this sense; they provide more incentives for party proliferation in the first round. However, for majoritarian cases the expectation of reductive influence remains $M + 1$, with M signifying the number of candidates that can advance to the second round. Cox, *Making Votes Count,* 123.

39. Computed from data in Kenneth Benoit, "Votes and Seats: The Hungarian Electoral Law and the 1994 Parliamentary Elections," in Gabor Toka, ed., *The 1990 Election to the Hungarian National Assembly: Analyses, Documents and Data.* (Berlin: Edition Sigma, 1999). Dataset online. Available: http://data.fas.harvard. edu/staff/ken_benoit.

40. The effective number of parliamentary parties is based on estimates of partisan affiliation in the Ukrainian parliament for 338 of 450 deputies successfully elected after the first run-off election in April 1994 found in Marco Bojcun, "The Ukrainian Parliamentary Elections in March-April 19994," *Europe-Asia Studies* 47, no. 2 (1995): 239. Only 338 of the 450 district elections were declared valid after the first run-off, because the other districts failed to have both 50 percent participation and 50 percent support for the winning candidate. Until 1996, the rest of the seats were filled in special make-up elections. Given the fluid and unstable nature of partisan affiliation in Ukraine, this figure should be considered only an estimate of party fractionalization. In the Russian case, the effective number of parliamentary parties is based on membership in parliamentary factions, which renders a more accurate reflection of party fractionalization in the legislature.

41. Only a small minority of the candidates (11 percent) were officially nominated by parties rather than by groups of voters or worker collectives. This overestimates the number of independents because many candidates with a partisan affiliation chose to be nominated by nonpartisan methods. I used party membership rather than party nomination as the more accurate measure of partisanship among candidates. This figure is based on data from the International Foundation for Election Systems (IFES) website (http://.ifes.ipra.kiev.ua), which listed both the mode of nomination for a candidate (party, voter group, workers' collective) and the party affiliation of the candidate. The latter was used to define partisanship.

42. Jesse, "Split-voting in the Federal Republic of Germany," 112.

43. Calculations of effective number of parties were based on data in Samuel H. Barnes, et. al., "The German Electoral Party System and the 1961 Federal Election," American Political Science Review 56, no.4 (1961): 906.
44. Lijphart, *Electoral Systems and Party Systems,* 161.
45. Calculations for the 1996 and 1998 Indian parliamentary elections were based on seat distributions provided by the India Votes 1998 website, http://www. indiavotes. com.
46. Pradeep Chhibber and Ken W. Kollman, "Party Aggregation and the Number of Parties in India and the United States," *American Political Science Review* 92, no.2 (1998): 332.
47. Sartori, "The Influence of Electoral Systems," 55–56.
48. In the linked systems of New Zealand and Italy, separate disproportionality levels could not be calculated for the PR tiers, but since this tier determined the final distribution of seats in the legislature, the disproportionality of the whole system generally reflects the disproportionality of the PR tier, albeit more so for New Zealand than for Italy—since the former has nearly equal numbers of seats coming from both tiers.
49. The 1991 Polish parliamentary election was not included—no legal threshold was used.
50. James L. Newell and Martin J. Bull, "The April 1996 Italian General Election: The Left on Top or on Tap?" *Parliamentary Affairs* 49, no. 4 (1997): 616–47.

Notes to Chapter 4

1. Arend Lijphart, "Debate—Proportional Representation III: Double-Checking the Evidence," *Journal of Democracy* 2, no. 2 (1991): 42–48.
2. Wilma Rule, "Introduction: Equal Players or Back to the Kitchen?" in *Russian Women in Politics and Society,* ed. Wilma Rule and Norma C. Noonan. (Westport, Conn.: Greenwood Press, 1996), 2.
3. Wilma Rule, "Parliaments of, by, and for the People: Except for Women?" in *Electoral Systems in Comparative Perspective: Their Impact on Women and Minorities,* ed. Wilma Rule and Joseph Zimmerman (Westport, Conn.: Greenwood Press, 1994), 16–18.
4. Wilma Rule, "Electoral Systems, Contextual Factors and Women's Opportunity for Election to Parliament in Twenty-Three Democracies," *Western Political Quarterly* 40 (1987): 477–98.
5. Richard E. Matland and Donley T. Studlar, "The Contagion of Women Candidates in Single-Member District and Proportional Representation Electoral Systems: Canada and Norway," *Journal of Politics* 58, no. 3 (1996): 709–10.6. Rule, "Parliaments," p. 19.
7. Richard E. Matland, "Women's Legislative Representation in National Legislatures: A Comparison of Democracies in Developed and Developing Countries," *Legislative Studies Quarterly* 28, no. 1 (1998): 109–25.
8. Georgina Waylen, "Women and Democratization: Conceptualizing Gender Relations in Transition Politics," *World Politics* 46, no. 3 (1994): 327–55. This is not to say that women were not involved in the social movements that brought down the communist regimes in Eastern Europe; for a survey of women's roles therein, see

the country studies in Marilyn Rueschemeyer, ed., *Women in the Politics of Post-communist Eastern Europe* (Armonk, N.Y.: M. E. Sharpe, 1994).

9. Pippa Norris, "Conclusions: Comparing Legislative Recruitment," in *Gender and Party Politics,* ed. Joni Lovenduski and Pippa Norris (London: Sage, 1993), 309–30.

10. Karen Beckwith, "Comparative Research and Electoral Systems: Lessons from France and Italy," *Women and Politics* 12, no. 1 (1992): 1–34.

11. Richard Engstrom, "District Magnitude and the Election of Women to the Irish Dail," *Electoral Studies* 6 (1987): 123–32.

12. For studies showing a significant and positive relationship between district magnitude and women's representation, see Rule, "Electoral Systems, Contextual Factors"; and Engstrom, "District Magnitude." But other studies do not find such a strong connection. See Susan Welch and Donley T. Studlar, "Multi-Member Districts and the Representation of Women: Evidence from Britain and the United States," *Journal of Politics* 52 (1990): 391–412; and Donley T. Studlar and Susan Welch, "Does District Magnitude Matter? Women Candidates in Local London Elections," *Western Political Quarterly* 44 (1991): 457–66. Richard E. Matland argues that party magnitude—the number of seats a party has in a district—rather than district magnitude affects women's representation. See Matland, "Institutional Variables Affecting Female Representation in National Legislatures: The Case of Norway," *Journal of Politics* 55, no. 3 (1993): 737–55.

13. Norris, "Conclusions," 321–27.

14. Matland and Studlar, "The Contagion of Women Candidates," 709.

15. Ibid., 712–13.

16. Carol Nechemias, "Women's Participation: From Lenin to Gorbachev," in *Russian Women in Politics and Society,* ed. Wilma Rule (Westport, Conn.: Greenwood Press, 1996), 23–24.

17. Carol Nechemias, "Soviet Political Arrangements: The Representation of Women and Nationalities," in *Electoral Systems in Comparative Perspective: Their Impact on Women and Minorities,* ed.Wilma Rule and Joseph Zimmerman (Westport, Conn.: Greenwood Press, 1994): 94–95.

18. Nechemias, "Women's Participation," 26.

19. Nechemias notes a "send the women back home" syndrome among party leaders and the general public that demonstrated the popular conception that women did not belong in political service. Ibid., 27.

20. Nechemias, "Soviet Political Arrangements," 96. This preference for male candidates continued in 1993, when 64 percent of survey participants in Moscow, St. Petersburg, and Yaroslavl respondeded thusly. White, Rose, and McAllister, *How Russia Votes,* 118.

21. Nechemias, "Soviet Political Arrangements," 95–96.

22. This is based on my own calculations of women on the 1993 and 1995 lists for these parties. My numbers run contrary to the assertion of Wilma Rule who claims that Yabloko "greatly increased [its] nominations of women." Rule, "Introduction," 56.

23. Rule makes a similar observation. See ibid.

24. See Rule, "Parliaments," 18; Matthew S. Shugart, "Minorities Represented and Unrepresented," in *Electoral Systems in Comparative Perspective: Their Impact on Women and Minorities,* ed. Wilma Rule and Joseph Zimmerman (Westport, Conn.: Greenwood Press, 1994): 37–38.

25. Several methods were used to identify female deputies. For Russia and Ukraine, each female candidate could be easily identified, since patronymics have different endings in Russian and Ukrainian for males and females. In Japan, the names on the list of deputies were labeled "Mr" and "Ms". Designations of women by party and mandate in Hungary and Germany were taken from secondary sources. In Lithuania, Italy, and New Zealand, lists of candidates obtained from the internet were accompanied by photographs, which were used to identify female deputies. Finally, for the Latin American cases the least precise method was used; gender was attributed to candidates according to their first names, with the aid of native speakers of Spanish. The datasets constructed contained a number of dichotomous variables, identifying each candidate's gender, electoral mandate (the tier under which he or she was elected), and party affiliation (if any).

26. Phi is the most appropriate correlation statistic for dichotomous variables approximating correlation coefficient r. The chi-square statistic is used as the p-value for statistical significance.

27. Matland, "Women's Legislative Representation in National Legislatures."

28. This may also be the case for less developed countries in other regions, but the admittedly small sample of two cases examined here suggests it is not. Venezuela had equally low percentages of women elected in both PR and SMD tiers (about 7 and 5 percent) while Mexico had a respectable proportion of women elected in SMDs (10 percent) but more than double that amount in the PR tier.

29. For a discussion of party magnitude and its effect on women's representation in PR elections see Matland, "Institutional Variables Affecting Female Representation."

30. Rule, "Electoral Systems, Contextual Factors"; Pippa Norris, "Women's Legislative Participation in Western Europe," *Western European Politics* 8 (1985): 90–101.

31. Kathleen A. Montgomery and Angela Burnette, "Explaining the Puzzle of Women's Representation in the Hungarian National Assembly," Paper presented at the annual meeting of the Midwest Political Science Association, Chicago, April 23–26, 1998.

32. Hungary employs a three-tier electoral system, in which seats are distributed between SMD and territorial PR tiers and then compensatory seats are offered to parties that achieve more than 5 percent of the vote from a tertiary national PR tier.

33. Other logistic regression models were also run with only those parties that were shown to be statistically significant in the chi-square tests, but the larger models that included all parties performed better.

34. In the 1994 Hungarian election, the electoral system variable crossed the threshold of statistical significance at the $p < .1$ level ($p = .09$) and, when researchers controlled for the influence of political parties, remained positively correlated with the election of women. But the difference between the logistic regression and significance of the bivariate correlation in the chi-square test was marginal; moreover, the chi-square test for the logistic regression model was not statistically significant.

35. Silja Haas, Robert W. Orttung, and Ondrej Soukop, "A Demographic Who's Who of the Candidates From the Twelve Leading Parties," *Transition* 1, no. 22 (December 1995): 11.

36. Belin and Orttung, *Russian Parliamentary Elections,* 58.

37. Rein Taagepera, "Beating the Law of Minority Attrition," in *Electoral Systems in Comparative Perspective: Their Impact on Women and Minorities,* ed. Wilma Rule and Joseph Zimmerman (Westport, Conn.: Greenwood Press, 1994), 238.

38. Wilma Rule and Nadezhda Shvedova, "Women in Russia's First Multiparty Elec-

tion," in *Russian Women in Politics and Society,* ed. Wilma Rule and Norma C. Noonan (Westport, Conn.: Greenwood Press, 1996), 56.

39. Belin and Orttung, *Russian Parliamentary Elections,* 128.

40. Dawn E. Nowacki, "The Party Paradox: Electing Women Independents to Russian Regional Legislatures," Paper presented at the conference "Women's Political Representation in Eastern Europe: 10 Years After the Fall," University of Bergen, Bergen, Norway, May 28–29, 1999.

41. Taagepera, "Beating the Law of Minority Attrition," 243.

42. Using factor analysis, Rule showed that socioeconomic components—including non-Catholic population, women in the workforce, and unemployment—could explain 29 percent of the variance of women's recruitment to national legislatures in twenty-three Western democracies, whereas political structure components—including electoral system, district magnitude, and the strength of center and left political parties—accounted for almost 32 percent of the variance. Rule, "Electoral Systems, Contextual Factors," 490–91.

43. Logistic regression is the most appropriate method when the dependent variable is dichotomous.

44. A score of "5" denoted federal governmental service, which included members of the executive branch, deputies in the State Duma, and members of the Federation Council and the upper house of parliament. A score of "4" included all members of the regional political elite, which included regional executives (heads of administration, presidential representatives, republican presidents, members of oblast executive branches), regional legislative deputies, local executives, and local legislative deputies. A score of "3" included members of the economic elite: industrial managers, entrepreneurs, bankers, and collective farm chairpersons. A score of "2" denoted a broad category of professionals and political activists, including doctors, lawyers, engineers, academics, journalists, political advisors, legislative aides, and economists—as well as activists in political parties, social movements, trade unions, and religious organizations. A score of "1" marked the lowest occupational status, including workers, pensioners, students, and unemployed. For a slightly different index of political notability see Ishiyama, "The Russian Proto-parties," 402–3.

45. The primary source of candidate occupations was the official list of candidates which appeared in *Rossiiskaya gazeta,* September 6–October 17, 1995. Directories of past legislative bodies were also used to establish accurate occupational histories, particularly of those candidates listed as "unemployed." Many times, particularly in 1993, these individuals were members of disbanded legislatures. The highest occupational status was used for each candidate, even if that was not the candidate's official occupation when nominated. Thus, an incumbent from the State Duma or disbanded Congress of People's Deputies was coded as a "5," even if he or she ran as a member of a social movement or political party.

Notes to Chapter 5

1. George A. Persons, "Electing Minorities and Women to Congress," in *Electoral Systems in the United States: Their Impact on Women and Minorities,* ed. Wilma Rule and Joseph Zimmerman (Westport, Conn.: Greenwood Press, 1992), 20.

2. Bernard Grofman and Lisa Handley, "Preconditions for Black and Hispanic Con-

gressional Success," in *Electoral Systems in the United States: Their Impact on Women and Minorities,* ed. Wilma Rule and Joseph Zimmerman (Westport, Conn.: Greenwood Press, 1992): 38–39. This does not automatically mean that majority minority districts necessarily enhance substantive representation of minority interests. Charles Cameron, David Epstein, and Sharyn O'Halloran have argued that maximizing the number of representatives does not necessarily maximize the representation. For different sides of this debate, see Cameron, Epstein, and O'Halloran, "Do Majority-Minority Districts Maximize Substantive Black Representation in Congress?" *American Political Science Review* 90, no. 4 (1996): 794–823; David Lublin, "Racial Redistricting and African-American Representation: A Critique of 'Do Majority-Minority Districts Maximize Substantive Black Representation in Congress?'" *American Political Science Review* 93, no. 1 (1999): 183–86; and David Epstein and Sharyn O'Halloran, "A Social Science Approach to Race, Redistricting, and Representation," *American Political Science Review* 93, no. 1 (1999): 187–91. Because of limitations of data on roll-call votes in the Russian State Duma, this chapter will deal with only ascriptive representation of non-Russian minorities.

3. Taagepera, "Beating the Law of Minority Attrition," 237.

4. Chauncy Harris, "The New Russian Minorities: A Statistical Overview," *Post-Soviet Geography* 34, no. 1 (1993): 577.

5. Ibid., 570.

6. Ishiyama, "The Russian Proto-parties," 398.

7. Pauline Jones Luong, "Tatarstan: Elite Bargaining and Ethnic Separatism," in *Growing Pains: Russian Democracy and the Election of 1993,* ed. Timothy J. Colton and Jerry F. Hough (Washington, D.C.: Brookings Institution Press, 1998): 646–56.

8. In 1990 and 1991 the Russian Congress of Peoples' Deputies elevated the sixteen autonomous republics of the Russian Soviet Federated Socialist Republic (RSFSR) to constituent-republic status and raised four autonomous oblasts (Adigei, Gornii Altai, Karachevo-Cherkassia, and Khakhassia) to republic status. In 1992 the Chechen-Ingush Republic was split in two, making the twenty-one republics that currently exist. Ishiyama, "The Russian Proto-parties," 397.

9. Harris, "The New Russian Minorities," 571.

10. Philip G. Roeder, "Soviet Federalism and Ethnic Mobilization," *World Politics* 43 (1991): 196–232.

11. For evidence of greater intergovernmental transfers to republics, see Daniel Treisman, "The Politics of Intergovernmental Transfers in Post-Soviet Russia," *British Journal of Political Science* 26 (1996): 326–30.

12. For a discussion of the Urals Republic movement in Sverdlovsk oblast, see Robert G. Moser, "Sverdlovsk: Mixed Results in a Hotbed of Regional Autonomy," in *Growing Pains: Russian Democracy and the Election of 1993,* ed. Timothy Colton and Jerry Hough (Washington, D.C.: Brookings Institution Press, 1998), 397–430.

13. Harris, "The New Russian Minorities," 548.

14. These figures were calculated from Table 3 in ibid., 553.

15. Because of a lack of reliable data, Chechnya and Ingushetia were not included.

16. Ibid., 552–59.

17. Michael McFaul and Nikolai Petrov, eds. *Political Almanac of Russia* (Moscow: Carnegie Endowment for International Peace, 1998), 668–71.

18. The representation/population ratio is calculated by dividing an ethnic group's per-

centage of legislative representatives by its percentage of the population. A ratio of one indicates parity between an ethnic group's population and legislative representation. A ratio of under one indicates underrepresentation, and of over one indicates underrepresentation. Adapted from Wilma Rule and Pippa Norris, "Anglo and Minority Women's Underrepresentation: Is the Electoral System the Culprit?" in *Electoral Systems in the United States: Their Impact on Women and Minorities,* ed.Wilma Rule and Joseph Zimmerman (Westport, Conn.: Greenwood Press, 1992), 41–42.

19. Persons, "Electing Minorities and Women."
20. This assessment is based on the fact that over 50 percent of Ukrainians, Belorussians, and Jews have adopted Russian as their primary language, well over the national average for non-Russians. See Harris, "The New Russian Minorities," 572.
21. These groups are the Ukrainians, Belorussians, Germans, Armenians, and Jews.
22. Ibid., 572. Fifty-seven percent of Ukrainians are native Russian speakers, compared to 14 percent for Tatars.
23. Luong, "Tartarstan," 656.
24. Luong found that Tatars were three times more likely to support the right of self-determination and secession within the Russian Federation than Russians living in Tatarstan. Ibid., 646.
25. Henry Hale, "Bashkortostan: The Logic of Ethnic Machine Politics and Democratic Consolidation," in *Growing Pains: Russian Democracy and the Election of 1993,* ed. Timothy Colton and Jerry Hough (Washington, D.C.: Brookings Institution Press, 1998): 621–22.
26. Ibid.
27. Hale argues that ethnicity played a secondary role in voting patterns in SMDs, being outweighed by the influence of state power and socioeconomic interests, particularly agrarian ones. Candidates tended to avoid overtly ethnic appeals, and voters tended to vote according to other voting cues. The only SMD contest where ethnicity played a major role in Bashkortostan was in the one district where Russians made up a majority. In this district a Russian won with a campaign protesting against republican sovereignty aimed at disgruntled Russians. Ibid., 619–20.
28. The most systematic studies of this relationship are G. Bingham Powell, *Contemporary Democracies: Participation, Stability and Violence* (Cambridge: Harvard University Press, 1982); Ordeshook and Shvetsova, "Ethnic Heterogeneity"; Octavio Amorim Neto and Gary W. Cox, "Electoral Institutions, Cleavage Structures, and the Number of Parties," *American Journal of Political Science* 41 (1997): 149–74; Cox, *Making Votes Count,* 203–21; and Mark P. Jones, "Racial Heterogeneity and the Effective Number of Candidates in Majority Runoff Elections: Evidence from Louisiana," *Electoral Studies* 16, no. 3 (1997): 349–58.
29. For earlier assertions of this relationship between electoral structure and social structure not based on ethnic heterogeneity see Arend Lijphart, *Democracies: Patterns of Majoritarian and Consensus Government in Twenty-one Countries* (New Haven, Conn.: Yale University Press, 1984) and Taagepera and Shugart, *Seats and Votes.*
30. Cox, *Making Votes Count,* 215.
31. Ibid.; Ordeshook and Shvetsova, "Ethnic Heterogeneity," 111.
32. Cox, *Making Votes Count,* 206.
33. Mark P. Jones, "Racial Heterogeneity."
34. Since Jones does not control for urbanization and Cox does not control for ethnicity,

the question of which is the more appropriate measure of social heterogeneity at the district level is left open. Cox found a statistically significant effect of social heterogeneity on the number of parties at the district level when controlling for district magnitude. He also found that an interactive variable multiplying urbanization and district magnitude worked as well as but not better than an additive specification (each variable entered separately). I will here examine both ethnic heterogeneity and urbanization as measures of social heterogeneity. Jones, "Racial Heterogeneity"; Cox, *Making Votes Count,* 219–21.

35. The breakdown of the PR vote by SMD electoral districts was provided in *Rossiiskaya gazeta,* January 17, 1996: 1–16.
36. Both measures will be calculated according to the effective-number-of-parties formula commonly used in the literature. See chapter 2 for details.
37. Because of missing data in several districts, this does not include all 450 electoral districts.
38. This dichotomous variable was used, rather than district magnitude, because there was such a dramatic range in the district magnitude of the cases. As operationalized for this analysis, the total all of the cases from the PR tier would have a district magnitude of 225 and the the total of the cases from the SMD tier would have a district magnitude of one.
39. These two variables have been the two main proxies used for social heterogeneity in studies of the relationship between social context and the number of parties at the district level by Jones ("Racial Heterogeneity") and Cox (*Making Votes Count*).
40. The effective number of ethnic groups was calculated in the same way the effective number of parties or candidates was calculated. See chapter 2 for details.

Notes to Chapter 6

1. See, for example, Robert G. Moser, "Strong Presidency, Weakened President: Executive-Legislative Relations in Russia, 1991–1998," in *Russian Politics: Problems of Democratic Consolidation,* ed. Zoltan Barany, forthcoming; Paul Kubicek, "Delegative Democracy in Russia and Ukraine," *Communist and Postcommunist Studies* 27, No. 4 (1994): 423–41; Huskey, "Democracy and Institutional Design" 453–73; and Scott Parrish, "Presidential Decree Authority in Russia, 1991–1995," in *Executive Decree Authority,* ed. John M. Carey and Matthew Soberg Shugart, (Cambridge: Cambridge University Press, 1998): 62–103.
2. Rose and Tikhomirov, "Russia's Forced-Choice Presidential Election," 351.
3. Arend Lijphart, "Presidentialism and Majoritarian Democracy: Theoretical Observations," in *The Failure of Presidential Democracy: Comparative Perspectives,* ed. Juan Linz and Arturo Valenzuela, vol. 1 (Baltimore: Johns Hopkins University Press, 1994): 91–105.
4. Matthew Soberg Shugart and John M. Carey, *Presidents and Assemblies* (Cambridge: Cambridge University Press, 1992): 206–25.
5. Cox alludes to this effect in identifying presidentialism as a factor promoting the national coordination of political parties' nominations and success across electoral districts. Cox, *Making Votes Count,* 187–90.
6. The tendency toward a higher number of parties under majoritarian systems than plurality systems has been well documented. See Duverger, 1963; Lijphart, 1994; and Cox, *Making Votes Count.*

7. Mark P. Jones, *Electoral Laws and the Survival of Presidential Democracies* (Notre Dame: University of Notre Dame Press, 1995), 120.

8. Reconfiguration of presidential results in the 225 SMD electoral districts was found in Michael McFaul and Nikolai Petrov, ed., *Political Almanac of Russia, 1989-1997* (Moscow: Carnegie Endowment for International Peace, 1998): 472–478.

9. While such analysis runs the risk of the ecological fallacy, attributing individual-level phenomena to aggregate-level variations, it is common and appropriate in analyzing the relationship between electoral institutions and voting behavior. This is so for two reasons: First, one effect of electoral institutions on electoral results is mechanical, that is, contained in the translation of votes into seats and thus unrelated to individual vote choice per se. Second, the psychological effect of electoral systems on the act of voting is strategic in nature. While this is amenable to survey research, it is difficult to capture in survey questions and usually ignored in favor of questions aimed at illuminating the values and causes of the core vote choice. Consequently, strategic voting is usually implied from aggregate shifts in voting. Most of the literature on electoral systems is based on aggregate analyses of voting results rather than individual-level survey research. See, for example, Taagepera and Shugart, *Seats and Votes;* and Lijphart, *Electoral Systems and Party Systems.*

10. For a good overview of this debate, see Juan Linz and Arturo Valenzuela, eds., *The Failure of Presidential Democracy: Comparative Perspectives* (Baltimore: Johns Hopkins University Press, 1994); Shugart and Carey, *Presidents and Assemblies;* Giovanni Sartori, *Comparative Constitutional Engineering* (New York: New York University Press, 1994).

11. Juan Linz, "The Perils of Presidentialism," *Journal of Democracy* 1 (Winter 1990): 51–71; Juan Linz, "Presidential or Parliamentary Democracy: Does It Make a Difference?" in *The Failure of Presidential Democracy* (Baltimore: Johns Hopkins University Press, 1994), 3–87; Alfred Stepan and Cindy Skach, "Constitutional Frameworks and Democratic Consolidation: Parliamentarism versus Presidentialism," *World Politics* 46 (October 1993), 1–22.

12. Scott Mainwaring, "Presidentialism, Multiparty Systems, and Democracy: The Difficult Equation," *Comparative Political Studies* 26, no. 2 (1993): 198–230. See also Jones, *Electoral Laws.*

13. Shugart and Carey, *Presidents and Assemblies,* 207–58. An extensive treatment of the effects of electoral engineering in presidential systems can be found in Jones, *Electoral Laws,* 120.

14. Epstein, *Political Parties in Western Democracies,* 333–40. For a critique of this hypothesized relationship, see Sartori, *Comparative Constitutional Engineering,* 94–97.

15. Shugart and Carey, *Presidents and Assemblies,* 21.

16. Jones, *Electoral Laws,* 88–102.

17. For a discussion of the proliferation effect of majority presidential elections and alternative solutions see Shugart and Carey, *Presidents and Assemblies*: 213–18.

18. Rose and Tikhomirov claim that the 1996 election produced just such a negative majority for Yeltsin. Rose and Tikhomirov, "Russia's Forced-Choice Presidential Election," 373–74.

19. For a definition and discussion of the effective-number-of-parties measure and measures of disproportionality, see chapter 2.

20. Aman Tuleev withdrew from the race after successfully registering as a candidate.

21. Indeed, one set of Western observers deemed the choice between Yeltsin and

Zyuganov one between competing regimes. See Rose, White, and McAllistair, *How Russia Votes*.

22. There were a total of 6,705 candidates competing for 1,068 seats in the 1990 election for the Russian Congress of People's Deputies—an average of more than six candidates per district. Rose, White, and McAllister, *How Russia Votes*, 31.

23. Evelyn Davidheiser, "Russia's Transition to Social Democracy? Explaining Increased Support for Communism in Russia," Paper presented at the Conference on Economic and Political Liberalization, Duke University, February 28–March 2, 1997, 15.

24. Rose and Tikhomirov, "Russia's Forced-Choice Presidential Election," 361–67.

25. On campaign tactics by both Yeltsin and Zyuganov in the second round, see Michael McFaul, "Russia's 1996 Presidential Elections," *Post-Soviet Affairs* 12, no. 4 (1996): 342–43.

26. For individual-level data on vote choice between the first and second rounds and between the 1995 parliamentary elections and the second round of the presidential election, see Rose and Tikhomirov, "Russia's Forced-Choice Presidential Election," 368–73.

27. Lithuania uses a mixed electoral system in which half of its legislative seats are elected in two-round majoritarian elections and half are elected according to PR, with a single nationwide district. Ukraine used a pure two-round majoritarian system in its first postcommunist election and then changed to a mixed system very similar to Russia's. Other states—such as Armenia, Croatia, Georgia, Moldova, and Macedonia—also use mixed systems in their parliamentary elections. But district-level data were not available to compare the effective number of candidates in their parliamentary SMD contests to their presidential elections.

28. Cox, *Making Votes Count*, 209–19; Shugart and Carey, *Presidents and Assemblies*, 226–58; Jones, "Racial Heterogeneity and the Effective Number of Candidates in Majority Runoff Elections," 103–18. Shugart and Carey have argued that the interaction between presidential and legislative elections runs both ways; when held concurrently, the former have a dampening effect on the number of parties in the latter, which also slightly raise the number of presidential candidates.

29. Jones, *Electoral Laws*, 110.

30. According to an All-Russian Center for the Study of Public Opinion (VtsIOM) poll, Yeltsin had 8 percent support in January 1996—whereas Zyuganov had 20 percent, Lebed 10 percent, and Zhirinovsky 10 percent.

31. McAllister and White found that 48 percent of Russian voters planned to split their votes in the 1993 elections and 38 percent planned to cast split votes in 1995. Ian McAllister and Stephen White, "Split Ticket Voting in the 1993 and 1995 Russian Duma Elections," Paper presented at the annual meeting of the American Political Science Association, Boston, Mass., September 3–6, 1998.

32. McFaul makes a similar argument, but he cites reasons in addition to the presidential electoral system as major causes of the outcome of the 1996 election, including campaign strategy. Michael McFaul, "The 1996 Russian Presidential Election," *Post-Soviet Affairs* 12, no. 4 (1996): 344–45.

33. Rose and Tikhomirov, "Russia's Forced-Choice Presidential Election," 373–74.

Notes to Chapter 7

1. The geographical distribution of a party's vote may be argued to be a characteristic allowing certain parties to escape the constraining effect of plurality elections. Geographic distribution of the vote coincides well with the rational choice framework of electoral system studies and does not allow parties to defy the underlying logic of the wasted-vote thesis, that voters will defect from smaller parties unlikely to win seats to avoid wasting their votes. It merely allows certain geographically concentrated parties to replace one of the two major national parties in particular regions.

2. Guillermo O'Donnell and Philippe C. Schmitter, *Transitions from Authoritarian Rule: Tentative Conclusions About Uncertain Democracies* (Baltimore: Johns Hopkins University Press, 1986), 58.

3. For theories of party formation from a rational choice perspective see Joseph A. Schlesinger, *Political Parties and the Winning of Office* (Ann Arbor: University of Michigan Press, 1991); and John H. Aldrich, *Why Parties? The Origin and Transformation of Political Parties in America* (Ann Arbor: University of Michigan Press, 1995).

4. For a discussion of structure-induced equilibrium, see Kenneth A. Shepsle, "Institutional Equilibrium and Equilibrium Institutions," in *Political Science: The Science of Politics,* ed. Herbert F. Weisberg (New York: Agathon Press, 1986): 51–81.

5. Aldrich, *Why Parties?* 89.

6. Ibid., 48–50.

7. For a more extensive discussion of new institutionalist theories of party formation and the Russian case, see Robert G. Moser, "Independents and Party Formation."

8. For a discussion of party institutionalization in third-wave democratizing states, see Mainwaring, "Party Systems."

9. M. Steven Fish, *Democracy from Scratch,* 208.

10. This notion of party follows Leon Epstein, who defines a party as "any group, however loosely organized, seeking to elect governmental office-holders under a given label. Having a label (which may or may not be on the ballot) rather than an organization is the crucial defining element." Epstein, *Political Parties in Western Democracies,* 8.

11. *Rossiya,* 1993, No. 35, p. 3 as quoted in Stephen White, Matthew Wyman, and Sarah Oates, "Parties and Voters in the 1995 Duma Elections," *Europe-Asia Studies* 49, no. 5 (1997): 784.

12. A comparison of occupational backgrounds of candidates showed that members of regional executive branches were less likely to run under a partisan label. See Moser, "Independents and Party Formation," 147–65.

13. The Bloc of Independents contested the PR election in 1995 and received less than 1 percent of the PR vote. One of the bloc's leaders, Viktor Mashinsky, won election in an SMD.

14. Indeed, White, Rose, and McAllister have argued that other than the KPRF parties in the PR tier of Russia's elections were little more than fan clubs for their leaders. White, Rose, and McAllister, *How Russia Votes,* 209.

    For other assessments of the personality-based character of Russian parties see Peter Reddaway, "Instability and Fragmentation," *Journal of Democracy* 5, no. 2 (1994): 13–19; Peter Rutland, "Has Democracy Failed in Russia?" *The National Interest* 38 (1994): 3–12; Peter Ordeshook, "Institutions and Incentives," *Journal of Democracy* 6, no. 2 (1995): 46–60; and Richard Rose, "Mobilizing Demobilized Voters in Postcommunist Societies," *Party Politics* 1, no. 4 (1995): 549–63.

15. Arthur H. Miller, William M. Reisinger, and Vicki L. Hesli, "Leader Popularity and Party Development in Post-Soviet Russia," in *Elections and Voters in Postcommunist Russia,* ed. Matthew Wyman, Stephen White, and Sarah Oates (Cheltenham: Edward Elgar, 1998).

16. White, Rose, and McAllister, *How Russia Votes,* 141–47; Stephen Whitefield and Geoffrey Evans, "The Emerging Structure of Partisan Divisions in Russian Politics, 1993–1996," in *Elections and Voters in Postcommunist Russia,* ed. Matthew Wyman, Stephen White, and Sarah Oates (Cheltenham, UK: Edward Elgar, 1998).

17. Arthur H. Miller, William M. Reisinger, and Vicki L. Hesli, "Leadership Popularity and Party Development in Post-Soviet Russia," in *Elections and Voters in Postcommunist Russia,* ed. Matthew Wyman, Stephen White, and Sarah Oates (Cheltenham: Edward Elgar, 1998).

18. Miller, Reisinger, and Hesli, "Leadership Popularity and Party Development," 4.

19. Timothy J. Colton, "The Russian Voter in 1993: Some Patterns in the National Survey Data," Paper presented at the Russian Election Conference, Harvard University, Cambridge, April 1994.

20. Kathryn Stoner-Weiss, "The Limited Reach of Russia's Party System: Under-Institutionalization in Dual Transitions," unpublished manuscript.

21. However, this difference may not be as dramatic as it appears. Many of the winning candidates (12 percent) who had partisan affiliation in 1995 were leaders of marginal PR blocs that gained less than 2 percent of the PR vote. Most of these parties—with the possible exception of Power to the People, which managed to form a parliamentary faction based around its nine SMD deputies—have very few chances of developing into stable national parties. Over the long term, the leaders of these personality parties do not contribute much to the formation of stable parties and have more in common with nonpartisan candidates than with candidates belonging to a party with a viable chance of gaining representation in the PR tier.

22. Haspel argues that the vote concerning faction threshold also followed a left-right split, with large reformist parties like Russia's Choice supporting lower thresholds to undermine anti-Yeltsin forces from forming parliamentary majorities that could threaten Yeltsin's political agenda. Moshe Haspel, "Should Party in Parliament be Weak or Strong? The Rules Debate in the Russian State Duma," *Journal of Communist Studies and Transition Politics* 14, nos. 1, 2 (1998): 178–200.

23. *Pyataya Rossiiskaya Gosudarstvennaya Duma* (Moscow: Gosudarstvennaya Duma, 1994): 192–95.

24. *Federal'noe Sobranie: Sovet Federatsii I Gosudarstvennaya Duma spravochnik* (Moscow: Panorama, 1996): 183–85.

25. Taagepera and Shugart, *Seats and Votes,* 2.

26. These are the assumptions underlying Brady and Mo's analysis. Brady and Mo, "Electoral Systems and Institutional Choice," 404–29.

27. Rose, White, and McAllister, *How Russia Votes,* 139.

28. Steven Fisher, "The Wasted Vote Thesis"; Jesse, "Split-voting in the Federal Republic of Germany"; Kathleen Bawn, "The Logic of Institutional Preferences"; Cox, *Making Votes Count,* 82–83.

29. These numbers are based on election results reported in Timothy J. Colton, "Introduction: The 1993 Election and the New Russian Politics," in *Growing Pains: Russian Democracy and the 1993 Elections,* ed. Timothy J. Colton and Jerry F. Hough

(Washington, D.C.: Brookings Institution Press, 1998), 22; and parliamentary faction membership reported in *Pyataya Rossiiskaya Gosudarstvennaya Duma* (Moscow: State Duma, 1994): 176–78.

30. For occupational status of Duma deputies see Moser, "Independents and Party Formation."

31. Examining only contested districts is an important distinction for Russian parties, because no Russian party ran candidates in every district—as is common in countries with more institutionalized party systems.

32. All of these figures come from Robert G. Moser, "Independents and Party Formation."

33. Ibid.

34. All ideological scores were obtained from Michael McFaul and Nikolai Petrov, eds., *Political Almanac of Russia* (Moscow: Carnegie Endowment for International Peace, 1998), 550–86. For a detailed account of the methodology and use of Sobyanin scores, see Alexander Sobyanin, "Political Cleavages Among the Russian Deputies," in *Parliaments in Transition: The New Legislative Politics in the Former USSR and Eastern Europe*, ed.Thomas F. Remington, ed., (Boulder, Colo.: Westview Press, 1994), 181–215.

35. McFaul argues that polarized politics has marked Russia's first three postcommunist elections, increasing over time and culminating the contest between Yeltsin and Zyuganov in the second round of the 1996 presidential election. However, he argues that this election marks the end of Russia's polarized politics. Michael McFaul, *Russia's 1996 Presidential Election* (Stanford: Hoover Institution Press, 1997). 36. In response to the question "What do you think about the transition to a market economy in Russia?" 7 percent said they preferred a rapid transition, 44 percent favored a gradual transition, and 23 percent were against a market economy in 1995, which was moderately more conservative than 1993 responses to the same question, which saw 13 percent for rapid transition, 42 percent in favor of gradual, and 19 percent against a market economy. Jerry Hough, Evelyn Davidheiser, and Susan Goodrich Lehmann, *The 1996 Russian Presidential Election*, Brookings Occasional Paper, (Washington, D.C.: Brookings Institution Press, 1996), 40.

37. For example, Fish has promoted proportional representation as a key instrument in encouraging the formation of parties in Russia yet does not systematically integrate the role of electoral institutions in his analysis of the formation of parties and social movements in the Gorbachev period. Fish, *Democracy From Scratch*, 220–21.

38. Michael McFaul, *Post-Communist Politics: Democratic Prospects in Russia and Eastern Europe* (Washington, D.C.: The Center for Strategic and International Studies, 1993): xvi–xvii.

39. Jerry Hough, "Institutional Change and the 1993 Election Results," Paper presented at the reporting conference of the Russian Election Study, Harvard Russian Research Center, Cambridge, Mass., April 1994. On the point of engineering elections to favor those in power see also, Michael Urban, "December 1993."

40. For a general model of many of these ideas based on Western European experience, see Angelo Panebianco, *Political Parties: Organization and Power* (Cambridge: Cambridge University Press, 1988).

41. Fish, "The Advent of Multipartism," 353–77.

Notes to Chapter 8

1. Sartori, *Comparative Constitutional Engineering,* 74–75.
2. Although much of the literature concentrates on the consolidating effects of presidential elections on legislative parties, in their discussion of electoral cycles Shugart and Carey note the possibility of a two-way causal relationship between executive and legislative elections. Shugart and Carey, *Presidents and Assemblies,* 241–42.
3. I define a major party as one that won at least five seats to the State Duma in a single election.
4. As in chapter 4, the PR vote was disaggregated to the SMD level, producing an effective number of PR parties for each of the 225 SMDs, even though PR deputies were elected in one nationwide district.
5. Six districts had missing data and thus were not included in the study.
6. In 1995 parties winning five or more seats were: KPRF, LDPR, Our Home is Russia, Yabloko, the Agrarian Party, Democratic Russia's Choice, Power to the People, and the Congress of Russian Communities.
7. Peter A. Hall and Rosemary C. R. Taylor, "Political Science and the Four New Institutionalisms," Paper presented at the Annual Meeting of the American Political Science Association, New York, NY, September 1994.
8. Kathleen Thelen and Sven Steinmo, "Historical Institutionalism in Comparative Politics," in *Structuring Politics: Historical Institutionalism in Comparative Analysis,* ed. Sven Steinmo, Kathleen Thelen, and Frank Longstreth (Cambridge: Cambridge University Press, 1992), 9.
9. Hall and Taylor, "Political Science."
10. Ibid., 15; Thelen and Steinmo, "Historical Institutionalism in Comparative Politics," 7–10.
11. Juan J. Linz, "Presidential or Parliamentary Democracy"; Shugart and Carey, *Presidents and Assemblies;* Alfred Stepan and Cindy Skach, "Constitutional Frameworks and Democratic Consolidation," 1–22; Scott Mainwaring, "Presidentialism, Multipartism, and Democracy: The Difficult Combination," *Comparative Political Studies* 26 (1993): 198–228; Timothy J. Power and Mark J. Gasiorowski, "Institutional Design and Democratic Consolidation in the Third World," *Comparative Political Studies* 30 (1997): 123–55.
12. The latest shot in this increasingly hostile debate is Stephen Cohen, "Russian Studies Without Russia," *Post-Soviet Affairs* 15, no. 1 (1999): 1–37. See also Anders Aslund, *How Russia Became a Market Economy* (Washington, D.C.: Brookings Institution Press, 1995); Joel Hellman, "Winners Take All: The Politics of Partial Reform in Postcommunist Transitions," *World Politics* 50 (1998): 203–34; Daniel S. Treisman, "Fighting Inflation"; and Clifford G. Gaddy and Barry W. Ickes, "Russia's Virtual Economy," *Foreign Affairs* 77, No. 5 (1998): 53–67.
13. Philip G. Roeder, *Red Sunset: The Failure of Soviet Politics* (Princeton: Princeton University Press, 1993; Stoner-Weiss, *Local Heroes;* Steven Solnick, *Stealing the State: Control and Collapse in Soviet Institutions* (Cambridge: Harvard University Press, 1998). For comparison of postcommunist states with other regions by scholars who are not area specialists, see Juan J. Linz and Alfred Stepan, *Problems of Democratic Transition and Consolidation: Southern Europe, South America and Postcommunist Europe* (Baltimore: Johns Hopkins University Press, 1996); Adam Przeworski, *Democracy and the Market: Political and Economic Reforms in Eastern Europe and Latin America* (Cambridge: Cambridge University Press, 1991);

and Arend Lijphart and Carlos H. Waisman, eds., *Institutional Design in New Democracies: Eastern Europe and Latin America* (Boulder, Colo.: Westview Press, 1996).

14. Cohen, "Russian Studies without Russia."
15. Katherine Stoner-Weiss's book on social capital and government performance in Russia is a good example of this. See Stoner-Weiss, *Local Heroes*.
16. Valerie Bunce, "Comparing East and South," *Journal of Democracy* 6, no. 3 (1995): 87. See also Sarah Meiklejohn Terry, "Thinking About Postcommunist Transitions: How Different Are They?" *Slavic Review* 52, no. 2 (1993): 333–37.
17. Philippe C. Schmitter and Terry Lynn Karl, "The Conceptual Travels of Transitologists and Consolidologists: How Far to the East Should They Attempt to Go?" *Slavic Review* 53, no. 1 (1994): 173–85; and their "From an Iron Curtain to a Paper Curtain: Grounding Transitologists or Students of Postcommunism?" *Slavic Review* 54, no. 4 (1995): 965–78. For a systematic attempt to compare Southern European, South American, and East European democratic transitions, see Juan J. Linz and Alfred Stepan, *Problems of Democratic Transition and Consolidation*.
18. One example is Bunce's claim that "in postcommunism, political institutions seem to be more a consequence than a cause of political developments." This is a claim that the findings of this book would counter. Bunce, "Comparing East and South," 97.
19. Taagepera and Shugart, *Seats and Votes,* 5–6.

Notes to Chapter 9

1. Mikhail Dmitriev, "Party Economic Programs and Implications," 37–60.
2. Michael McFaul, "Russia's 1999 Parliamentary Elections," p. 9.
3. Nine SMD elections were declared invalid, so the percentage of women elected in the SMD tier is somewhat higher, because the pool is 216 rather than 225 deputies.

Index

Agrarian Party of Russia (APR), 17, 42, 62, 123–24, 126–27; platform of, 15, 29
analysis, cross-national, 22; of representation of ethnic minorities, 90–91; of representation of women, 57–58, 65–67, 69, 73–74
Anpilov, Viktor, 17
APR. *See* Agrarian Party of Russia
Article 6 (Russian Constitution), 11, 116
assimilation, Russian, 169nn20–22; link to electoral success, 86–87
Australia, 58

Baburin, Sergei, 17
Bashkirs, representation of, 88
Bawn, Kathleen, 22
Bloc of Independents (Russia), 173n13
Burnette, Angela, 69

centrists, 13, 16–17, 152. *See also* Civic Union for Stability, Justice, and Progress; Democratic Party of Russia; Ivan Rybkin bloc; Svyatislav Fedorov's Worker's Self-Government bloc; Women of Russia
Chechnya, 81
Chernomyrdin, Viktor, 13, 16
Christian Democratic Union/ Christian Social Union (CDU/CSU; Germany), 50
Civic Union for Stability, Justice, and Progress (Russia), 14
Cohen, Stephen, 149
Colton, Timothy, 30, 119
Common Cause (Russia), 15, 39
Communist Party of the Russian Federation

(KPRF), 17, 43, 96–97, 128, 151–52; platform of, 14–15; representation of women in, 62, 64–65, 155; support for, 29, 117, 119, 128
Communist Party of the Soviet Union (CPSU), 11, 59, 116–17
Communists–Working Russia–For the Soviet Union, 17
Congress of People's Deputies (CPD), 1, 25, 59–60
Congress of Russian Communities (KRO), 17
Congress Party (India), 50–51
contagion effect: in concurrent elections, 142, 155; in representation of women, 63–64
Cox, Gary, 3–4, 22, 24, 35–36, 90–91
CPD. *See* Congress of People's Deputies
crisis, constitutional, 25, 81
Croatia, electoral system of, 10
cross-contamination, 22–23, 53, 101–2
Czechoslovakia, founding elections in, 132

Davidheiser, Evelyn, 104
democracy, 4–5, 97, 116, 149–50; and electoral systems, 2–3, 19, 49–54, 140; and representation of women, 58, 60, 66–68, 166n28
Democratic Forum (MDF; Hungary), 69
Democratic Party of Russia (DPR), 14
Democratic Russia's Choice, 1, 13–15, 64, 124, 126–27, 132, 151
Derzhava bloc (Russia), 17
district magnitudes, 9–11, 33–35, 141; and representation of women, 58–59
Duverger, Maurice, 2, 9